YOUR GARDEN IN SPAIN

From planning to planting and maintenance

Clodagh and Dick Handscombe

SANTANA BOOKS

Designed by Chris Fajardo
Illustrations by the authors

Your Garden in Spain
is published by Ediciones Santana S.L.
Apartado 41, 29650 Mijas-Pueblo (Málaga) Spain
Telephone: (0034) 952 48 58 38 - Fax: (0034) 952 48 53 67
e-mail: info@santanabooks.com

Printed in Spain by Gráficas San Pancracio

Depósito Legal: MA-2.520-2009
ISBN: 978-84-89954-67-0

Where electronic addresses of useful organisations are
mentioned they were correct at the time the book went to press.
Their inclusion by the authors does not imply that the publishers
endorse their services or products. Likewise, where practical
solutions to problems are given there is no guarantee by the
publishers or authors that they will be appropriate or work in
every situation.

DEDICATION

To all experienced and inexperienced gardeners who wish to develop practical and realistic gardens that match their lifestyle in Spain. We hope that this compendium of ideas, advice and information helps you plan, plant up and maintain an attractive and productive garden wherever you have settled. Whatever you do design your garden for tomorrow – a garden to live in and enjoy for the rest of your lives.

ACKNOWLEDGEMENTS

This book would not have been so comprehensive but for the host of good friends and acquaintances –both Spanish and other nationalities living in Spain– who allowed us to visit their gardens and share their experiences from the Pyrenees down through Spain to the Canary Islands. There are many and for fear of leaving one out by mistake we thank all jointly for their support.

CONTENTS

INTRODUCTION

Your Garden in Spain and its sister books *Growing healthy fruit in Spain* and *Growing healthy vegetables in Spain* aim to help you develop, plant and maintain a garden that matches your intended lifestyle and budget, whether you are resident in Spain or an absentee owner. A garden at its best, full of the colourful, perfumed flowers, aromatic herbs and fresh wholesome fruit and vegetables for which Spain is renowned.

This will take some years to achieve as gardening in Spain is very different from that in northern Europe. Between us we have 40 years of gardening experience under Spanish conditions both on the coast and inland and we have travelled widely around the mainland and islands to see what thrives in a wide variety of situations. In our books we share with you what we have learned — much of it the hard way — about coping with the soils, regional climates, plants, pests and diseases to enable you to avoid our and others' mistakes.

More than four million expatriates now live in Spain, a resettlement even greater than that of the 16th and 17th centuries when families from other regions moved to the Mediterranean coast and islands after the ejection of the Moors. In 1605 the book *Agricultura y Jardines por Vivo* (Agriculture and Gardens for Life) was published to provide the new settlers with essential information about establishing gardens and growing crops. Our trilogy of books seeks to do the same for you.

Your Garden in Spain tells you all you need to know about developing and caring for a new garden or transforming an established one, whether it is a small terrace or a plot of several thousand square metres. The two sister books cover in depth the growing of fruit and vegetables. In all three books ecological/organic solutions to problems are offered, where appropriate, in order to create gardens safe for people and pets.

This book is a practical compendium of both basic knowledge and creative ideas. Do take it out into the garden and to garden centres. Part Four, in particular, was prepared to help you make sensible choices of plants, shrubs and trees — sensible both for your size of garden and the local microclimate.

We hope you soon achieve the garden of your dreams. A garden you want to be out in summer and winter so that it becomes one of the most-used "rooms" of your house.

— Clodagh and Dick, 2007

PART ONE

THE SPANISH GARDENING CHALLENGES

Spain is a wonderful country in which to garden whether starting from scratch or improving an existing garden but there are some challenges to be overcome particularly in respect of climate extremes, soils, plants, insects and diseases.

1.1 YOUR NEW GARDENING OPPORTUNITIES

For many of you, gardening in Spain will be very different to your previous gardening experiences. Luckily, many of the differences are positive and you will have every chance of creating a spectacular and practical garden, a garden that will satisfy your aspirations whether you are a keen gardener or a reluctant one.

You will have the opportunity to create a garden that is in flower and perfumed and yielding fruit and vegetables every day of the year, and a garden that is comfortable to work in for much of the year.

The favourable climate enables you to grow an amazingly wide range of temperate, sub-tropical and even tropical plants, provided the local microclimate of your garden is sufficiently warm and sheltered during the winter months. Naturally there are high and low extremes of temperature that can create occasional problems.

If retired and fit you will now have, at last, all the time in the world to enjoy designing and developing a garden in one of the best climates in the world. You will also have the chance to contribute to the re-greening of recently urbanized coastal and inland areas by using natural organic practices where mules, oxen, manures and compost have been largely replaced by tractors, rotovators and chemicals.

No wonder gardening is such a popular hobby for many in Spain, not only for expatriates but also for the increasing number of Spaniards moving from city apartments to suburban houses.

Against this background, the horticultural industry has transformed itself in the last 20 years and new gardeners should have little difficulty in finding the supplies and services they need, such as:

• New nurseries and garden centres staffed by knowledgeable assistants, many of them offering garden design, landscaping and maintenance services.
• An ever-expanding range of plants – with planes and pantechnicons bringing millions of plants monthly into Spain from all over the world.
• More organic material for enriching soils, such as improved peat substitutes, manure-based organic compost/fertilizers, composted garden waste and seaweed from municipal Eco parks, and horse manure from the growing number of riding stables.
• More and more trained, professional gardeners and jobbing gardeners to help with some of the creative and heavier landscaping and maintenance tasks.

The opportunities are there for all and the Spanish soil awaits your creativity and hard labour. Success can be yours if you have the imagination, physical fitness, time and determination to overcome the several problems (discussed in the next section) that most gardeners face during their early years in Spain.

Most importantly, do grasp the opportunity to design a garden that matches your planned lifestyle and ensures that you are able to enjoy the wonderful climate that prompted you to come to Spain in the first place.

The list below summarises those things that could help you realise your dream, so bear it in mind as you read through the chapters that follow. An ideal Spanish garden should:

1. Suit your lifestyle, whether you are a resident or absentee owner and retired or working.

2. Be a garden to live in, the main room of the house for much of the year, enabling an outdoor lifestyle.

3. Provide areas of cool summer shade and warm, sheltered, winter sun.

4. Allow space for al fresco cooking and eating.

5. Make good use of site and surroundings.

6. Match your interest or disinterest in gardening.

7. Provide space for working on hobbies.

8. Require minimum maintenance and watering once it matures.

9. Give year-round colour, perfume and interest.

10. Have appropriate plantings for its microclimate and soils.

11. Produce flowers, herbs, fruit and vegetables 365 days a year.

12. Include open spaces and cosy restful corners.

13. Give shelter from cold and hot winds and frost and snow in colder situations.

14. Have good internal and external views.

15. Ensure privacy and security.

1.2 TYPICAL PROBLEMS AND RISKS

Many expatriates buy properties in Spain with dreams of their own "Garden of Eden" with views of the sea, virgin mountain-sides, sub tropical climbers, lush vegetable patches, colourful orange orchards and picturesque olive groves. But these dreams are not always realised, either in the short or long-term, because there are a number of problems and risks newcomers have to face, whether they are resident or absentee gardeners.

Below is a list of some typical problems and risks to help you make the right decisions and be more realistic in the plans for your garden. For convenience, they are presented as a checklist with suggestions for practical preventive or corrective actions.

TYPICAL PROBLEMS AND RISKS

TYPICAL CURRENT PROBLEMS OR FUTURE RISKS	TICK WHICH YOU HAVE OR COULD HAVE	TYPICAL PREVENTIVE/ CORRECTIVE ACTIONS
Poor quality soil.		Immediately improve your soil. See Section 6.1.
Shallow soil over bedrock.		Buy soil and build raised beds. See Section 2.5 and 6.1.
Steep, terraced or rocky plot.		Incorporate terraces and rockeries in garden design. See Chapters 3.1, 5.9 and 5.10.
Shortages and cost of water.		**a.** Plant least thirsty plants and install economic irrigation system. See Part four and section 6.5. **b.** Aim to collect/store rainwater. See section 2.17. **c.** Maximize areas of paths and terraces. See section 2.4.
Exposure to winds and gales.		**a.** Plant hedges and boundary trees. See sections 2.9. **b.** Ensure posts and ties are firm and do not strangle trees. See section 2.4.
Very high summer temperatures for persons and plants as illustrated in the following "Typical Temperature Patterns" table.		**a.** Retain existing or plant new trees for shade. See Chapter 2.9. **b.** Avoid dark coloured terraces. See Chapter 2.4.
Gardens exposed to winter frosts, even if only every five years. Occasional snow on Mediterranean beaches.		Don't plant frost tender plants unless knowingly experimenting and protecting in the winter. See Part Four and section 6.15.
Heavy spring and autumn rains turn clay gardens into aquagmire.		**a.** Cover plot as soon as possible with paths, terraces and areas of stone chippings. See sections 1.3, 1.5 and 2.4. **b.** Channel water to where flower beds will be. See section 2.17.
Loss of initial views from garden due to new construction.		Retain or plant high hedges and spreading trees. See section 2.10.

TYPICAL CURRENT PROBLEMS OR FUTURE RISKS	TICK WHICH YOU HAVE OR COULD HAVE	TYPICAL PREVENTIVE/ CORRECTIVE ACTIONS
Security problems in fast expanding areas.		Build high walls or fences (good for climbing plants), plant thick hedges and install strong gates. See Section 2.10.
No shade, all trees felled		Purchase and plant one or two mature trees before the first summer or plant younger trees for the future. See Section 2.9.
Shortage of time to prepare bare plot for lettings.		Take on a gardener fast. See sections 1.5 and 7.1.
Will only be an absentee gardener for the first few years.		**a.** Don't be over ambitious. See section 1.5. **b.** Keep the garden simple to minimise maintenance. c.Plant only drought resistant plants.
Swimming pool dominates the current garden.		Redesign the swimming pool area as a secluded mini garden. See section 3.3.
Very hard sun baked soil.		**a.** Dampen before attempting to dig, move or plant. **b.** Add compost to lighten soil. **c.** Use Spanish mattocks instead of a spade and fork. See section 7.2.
New Spanish lifestyle doesn't allow much time for garden maintenance.		Design/redesign for minimum maintenance. See Section 2.18.
Geraniums decimated by geranium moth.		**a.** Plant more resistant trailing varieties. **b.** Spray preventatively weekly. See section 6.7.

TYPICAL PROBLEMS AND RISKS (continued)

TYPICAL CURRENT PROBLEMS OR FUTURE RISKS	TICK WHICH YOU HAVE OR COULD HAVE	TYPICAL PREVENTIVE/ CORRECTIVE ACTIONS
No gap left by builder between swimming pool terrace and boundary walls for plants.		Build raised beds around the boundary. See section 2.5.
Plot too large to ever cope with in retirement.		**a.** Maintain a central controllable garden and develop the rest as a wild garden. See section 3.10. **b.** Take on a gardener. See section 7.1.
Saline soil		**a.** Wash through with good water. **b.** Plant salt compatible plants. See section 5.12.
Over exertion in the Spanish sun.		**a.** Have a realistic garden development plan. See sections 1.3, 1.4, 1.5, 1.6, 1.7, 2.1 and 2.5. **b.** Work early in the summer before the sun comes up. **c.** Design the garden to match your lifestyle. See sections 2.1 and 2.18. **d.** Wear a sun hat.

Above all else, find out about your local microclimate, not just the average temperature and average rainfall but also the minimum and maximum. Most Spanish plants love the average climate, provided they are watered, but the extremes can often be hostile and surprising to newcomers.

During our nearly 20 years in Spain, our garden has experienced temperatures between 47 and -5°C, no rain for periods up to five months, non-stop pouring rain for six days, a maximum rainfall of 69cm in a day and 24cm in an hour, and on several occasions almost hurricane winds. But our love of Spain as a wonderful place for gardening is still strong, even if at times the conditions are rather challenging.

TYPICAL TEMPERATURES PATTERNS

AREA	DAY TIME TEMPERATURES				NIGHT TIME TEMPERATURES				CHANCE OF FROST INLAND
	W	S	S	A	W	S	S	A	
Costa del Sol	W	W/H	V/H	H/W	Cd	C	W/H	C	Low/medium
Costa Blanca	C/W	W	H/VH	W	Cd	C	W	Cd	Medium/high
Costa Brava	C	W	H/VH	W	Fr	C	CW	Cd	High
Madrid	C/Cd	C/W	H/VH	W/C	Cd/Fr	C/Cd/Fr	C/W/H	C	High
Balearics	C	C	W/H	W/C	Cd	Cd	CW	Cd	Medium/high
Canaries	W	W	W/H	W	C	C	C/W	C	Low/high*

* In the mountainous areas.

CODES:
VERY HIGH (over 35ºC) = **VH**: High (30 – 35ºC) = **H:** Warm (20 – 30ºC) = **W.** Cool (10 – 20ºC) =
C: Cold (0 – 10ºC) = **Cd:** Fr = below zero.

The above table illustrates temperatures you might expect to experience. Both the hottest and lowest temperatures need special attention when designing and planting your garden. Shelter from northerly and southerly winds and shade are very important in Spanish gardens if the more tender plants listed in Part Four are to be grown successfully.

1.3 ESTABLISHING A GARDEN FROM SCRATCH

You have now moved into your new Spanish home. Everything is unpacked and arranged. All the urgent DIY jobs are done and you have a clear day ahead to start on your new garden.
The first essential steps are the same, whether you have a small town- house patio, an acre or two of level or terraced land, an area of pine forest or a rocky perch on a mountainside.

As outlined in chapter 1.1, the opportunities for designing, developing and enjoying your new garden in Spain are many. At the same time, as outlined in chapter 1.2, there are start up and ongoing problems to be faced before finalising your garden design and starting the construction and landscaping work.

We therefore suggest the following initial programme of work. It might take six months if you are retired and resident or a year or two if you are an absentee gardener:

1. Review and finalise your lifestyle needs as well as those of your partner and resident family, if any. Also give some thought to the probable needs and expectations of visiting family members, visiting friends and possibly tenants, if you plan to let for part of the year. Recognise that if you want an open-air life, taking full advantage of the Spanish climate, the garden will be the place where you spend much of your time for most of the year. For us, the house is a place to sleep and a shelter from adverse weather. Section 2.1 and Part Three will help you with this important step.

2. With your lifestyle analysis in mind, start to decide on the features and facilities you would like incorporated into the garden, for instance summer shade, sunny sheltered winter corners, a pool or Jacuzzi, cooking facilities, terraces for eating and relaxing, facilities for children and exercise. If space allows, would you build a tennis court, table tennis terrace or petanc/boule piste? Would you like to grow organic vegetables or keep some hens? More ideas are listed in section 2.1 and Part three. You may end up with a long list, so set priorities for the space you have.

3. Sketch out a site plan on a large sheet of paper. Draw the boundaries, house, drive and pool (if already built) to scale. Don't draw in any more features at this stage. Make a few copies of the outline plan. Then complete the following steps 4, 5, 6 and 7 in parallel. If you have not yet finalised the siting of the house to be built, develop several tentative plans before making a final decision.

4. If you are a keen gardener, go over your plot systematically. Make notes of the following and think about whether they offer opportunities or constraints for a creative garden design:

  a. The direction of the prevailing winds.

  b. The existing natural features, such as mature or seedling trees, large rocks, terrace walls, hollows, slopes, clumps of herbs, bulbs and other natural plants that are worth preserving.

  c. Views to be protected and enhanced.

  d. Views to be blotted out if possible.

  e. The depth and quality of the soil. Dig holes at several points around the garden to test for variations. See section 6.1.

  f. The location of large surface or buried rocks. If you suspect they exist, knock a metal rod into the ground to locate them and their size. We failed to do this sufficiently. As a result, some early-planted trees remain stunted.

  g. Mark on your plan where weeds grow profusely and where nothing grows wild. The former may be a good place for flowerbeds and the latter areas best covered with paths and terraces.

  h. Naturally sheltered corners and the most exposed parts of the plot.

  i. Signs of erosion by storm water. You may want to retain or divert natural water flows.

  If you are a non-gardener and have already decided that you want nothing more than a minimalist garden, totally terraced, with high walls and no flower beds or trees, then just focus on a, c, d, and h.

5. Start to visualise a few possible garden layouts and sketch them out on a copy of the site plan. Check out their viability against your lifestyle analysis and site survey information. Have vision and be creative. Read through other sections of the book to stimulate further ideas and enhance the ones you have. Part Two, Three and Five include relevant sections.

6. The chapters in section Four give the details of 400 popular plants. Study them to gain an insight into the plants that are the easiest to grow and the most colourful and perfumed. Especially note the indications of drought and frost resistance, if your garden has a fast drying soil or is exposed to cold winter winds.

7. Wander around your neighbourhood, public gardens in local towns and nearby botanical gardens, if they exist. Make a note of the types of plants and trees that do particularly well and those that look as if they struggle. Note whether the plants are in full sun or shade and protected from winds. Also record the fact that certain plants that you expected to see are conspicuous by their absence. You will now have a feel for the types of plants that do well. Now visit local garden centres to see what they have available – the sizes of trees and typical prices. Find out if they grow and harden off their own plants or if they are mainly imported from hot houses in Holland, France or Italy, for instance. We give guidelines for buying plants in section 6.2.

8. You now have the information at your fingertips to make informed decisions, so review and integrate all your ideas into an initial garden design. We say "initial" because most of us make modifications as we progress. Before finalising the design:

- Review relevant sections in Part Two, Three, Four and Six.
- Ensure you plan sufficient shade and shelter from winds.
- Decide whether the garden is to be formal or informal.
- Consider the colour combinations that would give you greatest pleasure. Reflect on the ideas of Section 2.6, "Painting with Plants".

9. Now draw up a list of the main things that need to be done during the next year and decide whether the work is for you, a landscape gardener or a regular handyman gardener. We discuss this issue in depth in Section 7.1.

10. If you have not been preparing the site parallel with the above tasks, now is the time to start in earnest. Gather up all visible and shallowly buried stones, rocks and rubble and stack them in graded piles. They will all come in handy over the next few months, as indicated in this page.

11. While gathering rocks and rubble start to deal with any weeds. On a small plot, do this by hand using a Spanish tool, preferably a mattock, for less effort. Section 7.2 describes the tools to use on Spanish soils.

Start a compost heap in an out-of- the-way corner of the garden.

As an alternative to a compost heap, lay weeds as a thick layer on an area where you plan to have an

RECYCLING ROCKS, STONES AND RUBBLE

Large rocks:
Dry stonewalls
Rockeries
Pond surrounds
Enhance natural outcrops
Spray painted sculptures
Stand alone features
Weigh down umbrella

Medium sized rocks:
Edging of paths and beds
Cobbled paths/terraces
Building walls
Watering rings around trees
Topping boundary walls
Building a stone seat
Building a barbecue or oven

Small rocks or stones:
Natural surround for cacti
Mosaic designs in paths
Firming stakes and posts
Bottom drainage in pots
Weighting pond plant pots
Mulch over black plastic
Levelling pots and tables

Building rubble:
Terrace/path foundations
Soak aways/surface drains
Shed foundations
Bottom drainage of raised beds
Infill behind walls
Base for a rockery
Firming posts and stakes

important flowerbed or to grow vegetables. Add a layer of dampened horse, goat or sheep manure and then cover with an old carpet.

In several months the soil will have been improved with the help of earthworms and will be ready for planting.

If you have a large plot, arrange for the plot to be ploughed or rotovated, except where you plan to construct terraces and paths, which will require a firm base.

12. You can now start laying out the garden in earnest, preferably during the autumn and winter months:

> **a.** Plant hedges first, as they will take time to mature.
>
> **b.** Then plant any large trees that will provide vital summer shade.
>
> **c.** Proceed to lay out a network of paths and terraces, as discussed in Chapter 2.4.
>
> **d.** While laying the above, build in conduits for an electrical circuit for lights, and pumps for the pond and fountain, or consider solar alternatives.
>
> **e.** Plumb in a water system with taps at several convenient places around the garden.
>
> **f.** Follow with the construction of flowerbeds and special features in the most sensible sequence. Aim to complete the garden section by section, leaving areas that are not an eye-sore until last.
>
> Guidelines for the planting, supporting, watering and feeding of plants are given in Part 6. One important task is to improve the soil in the planting holes for trees and large shrubs and flower beds in general before doing any planting. This is discussed in detail in section 6.1.

13. Aim to have the garden sufficiently developed by the first or second summer, so that you can acclimatise yourself to summer temperatures and humidities, and start to enjoy an outdoor lifestyle.

Our top ten priorities would be as follows:

a. Plant a thick fast growing hedge.

b. Plant or retain trees for shade.

c. Buy a large umbrella or gazebo to use until the trees have grown.

d. Fill the semi-shade of the covered terrace or naya with colourful and cheerful plants to warm it up.

e. Fit awnings if the suns rays come into the naya or shine through unshuttered windows.

f. Make early sheltered areas comfortable. The more cool and tempting you make it, the more likely family members will realise that an afternoon in a Spanish garden does not have to be sweltering.

g. Purchase or build a temporary barbecue, and purchase a paella ring and pan, so that a variety of dishes can be cooked al fresco.

h. Install a drip irrigation system.

i. Install a mini water feature or fountain for the cooling sound of water.

j. Close-plant your first flowerbeds to give a mass of summer colour rather than the odd dot.

14. Get used to wearing a straw hat when working in the garden.

1.4 RECOVERING AND IMPROVING AN EXISTING GARDEN

When you buy a property, the existing garden might look wonderful but by the time you move in it might have become a jungle, especially if there has been no-one resident or no gardener for some months.

You should recover the existing garden as quickly as possible and prevent further deterioration, though it's advisable to live in the garden for a year before deciding on major changes, unless the garden is a real disaster.

Decide on changes not by reference to gardens you had in northern Europe but by thinking about the new open-air lifestyle you can enjoy in Spain, the new types of plants that are possible to grow here, and the need for summer shade, winter sun and shelter from gales.

If there is a lot to do, decide immediately whether to try to do it all yourself or employ a gardener, whether to do an initial clean up and some construction work, or to garden on a continuous basis.

If you continue to employ an existing gardener, evaluate his or her efforts over the first six months before deciding whether you need to make a change. Section 7.1 enlarges on the two points above.

The following is a list of issues that you need to consider when taking over an existing garden:

a. The sighting, style and surfaces of terraces.

b. The style and sense behind the network of paths and their safety, including steps.

c. The provision for summer shade and winter sun.

d. The extent of shelter from strong winds.

e. The cleanliness of plants near to the swimming pool.

f. The cleanliness and condition of the swimming pool and its surround.

g. The existence of quiet corners for a read or siesta.

h. The possibilities for outdoor cooking.

i. The quality of hedges.

j. The framing and blocking of the best views.

k. The effectiveness of the watering system.

l. The diversity, age, condition and health of plants and whether you will have year-round colour. You will need to be resident for a year to gain the full picture.

GUIDELINES FOR TAKING OVER AN EXISTING GARDEN

Type/Condition of garden taken over	Suggested first actions
A perfectly maintained garden that at first sight you don't want to change.	**a.** If it is now midsummer, check that there are no wilting plants. If there are, water them fast. **b.** If there is a watering system, check that all jets are working and clear if necessary. If there is no watering system, consider installing one as soon as possible. **c.** From day one keep on top of weekly deadheading, pruning, cutting the lawn and cleaning the pool. See sections 3.3 and 6.8. **d.** Ensure that you carry out a first winter cutback in January and February as described in section 6.9. **e.** If you do not have the time to do the above or you don't know where to start, employ a gardener. If a gardener exists keep him/her, at least for a time.
A well- maintained garden that is not really your cup of tea but the position and views are marvellous.	**a.** Live in it for a year and get the feel of it. **b.** See what flowers during each season. **c.** Review the garden along the line of section 1.7. Decide on the most attractive features, the horrors and the priorities for change. Some issues that you will need to consider are listed in the "Some Issues to Consider" table on the facing page. **d.** Observe other gardens to get some idea of what plants grow well locally.
A garden that was well maintained garden above but has been allowed to become untidy.	**a.** Don't let it get any worse. **b.** Do a little weeding and tidying up every day. **c.** If you have to, weed kill gravel drives and paths. **d.** If there is a lawn, mow it and trim the edges. **e.** Prune straggly shoots on climbing shrubs and trim other shrubs to shape. **f.** Keep on top of it for the next year before deciding on any major changes. **g.** During first year proceed as in c and d in second section above.
The garden is bleak and bare. The previous owner never made much effort.	Treat as a new site and read section 1.3.
The 25 year- old garden of a previously absentee gardener. What shrubs or trees exist are large, mature and possibly dominating.	**a.** Live in the garden for a few months and see what summer shade and winter sun you have before deciding whether any plants are really overcrowding the garden. **b.** Recognise that new replacement plants will take years to give the same shade and seasonal colour. Rather than cutting down mature trees, hire a tree surgeon to prune them professionally and check their health **c.** Decide whether the garden will be manageable. Will you be physically capable of pruning large plants such as prickly cacti, palms and yuccas, bougainvilleas and bignonias covering walls, pergolas and buildings and 20-metre-high trees? **d.** Review the garden along the lines of the "Some Issues to Consider" section on the facing page, and section1.7. **e.** Most importantly, decide where you need some extra colour. If the soil is root-bound from old trees and shrubs, it is often best to construct raised beds for planting smaller succulents, bulbs, perennials and shrubs. See section 2.5.

Type/Condition of garden taken over	Suggested first actions
What was a garden is now a wilderness. Plants haven't been pruned for years and are taken over by weeds, stunted or dead due to lack of water. Small plants are smothered by larger ones, and everything is entwined.	**a.** Have a good breakfast. Get out into the garden with large pruners and a garden saw. **b.** Start to go through the garden methodically, clearing the path around the house and then follow each path in turn. **c.** As you progress, concentrate on removing low, over-hanging branches, any dangerous spiky and pointed ends and excess branches of cacti, aloes and yuccas, so that you can start to clear areas safely. **d.** Aim to clear a terrace area or part of an overgrown lawn as soon as possible so that you can occasionally rest awhile in comfort. **e.** Clear off the cascading weeds from dry stonewalls. **f.** Start to clean up perennial and shrub beds one by one. Go through them carefully. Remove weeds, prune each plant as you discover it. Search underneath the larger plants for signs of lower growing plants or bulbs. The best time to clean up the flower- beds is from October to March or even May, as you can prepare the beds for new growth in the spring. If you clear the beds during the summer, the sudden change from deep shade to sun and the late heavy pruning will cause much stress to plants and some won't survive the shock. **g.** As each flowerbed is cleared, give it a good soaking and a liquid feed to encourage new growth. Check and restart the watering system if one exists. If not, install one. If you intend to be an absentee gardener, water sufficiently to keep plants alive. Any more may result in the return of the jungle. **h.** If you decide to employ someone to help – beware. He or she may come in and chop and clear and, if not an experienced gardener, may not recognize what is worth saving. **i.** Having rediscovered and cleared the heart of the garden, prune trees to shape and cut out rampant climbers. If cut hard, most will soon rebud and grow. **j.** If there are large unplanted areas of long grass and weeds, use a strimmer to speed progress. **k.** Finally, complete the clearing by trimming the outside hedges, possibly a tough job if they haven't been cut for years. **l.** Now sit back and watch the garden recover through a spring and summer. Decide whether the garden is really what you want and what you need to change in the short and longer term. Refer to "Some issues to consider" below, section 1.7 and Part Five.

SOME ISSUES TO CONSIDER

1. The possibility that plants such as bamboo, cacti and aloes have been allowed to grow into unsightly and overpowering clumps and whether they would be best split or cleared out and replanted.

2. The condition of the soil. Is it hard and baked? Is it the same 10cm and 20cm down? Is it root bound? If worried about some areas of plants, dig up one or two and check the extent and health of their root balls.

3. If (2) indicates a problem you can mulch the beds with 10-15cm of good compost and work into the soil each winter for two years, or dig out each flower bed in rotation and enrich the soil as you would in a new garden. See section 6.1. Recognise that you will probably loose a few plants doing this but you will also be able to consider totally different plantings.

4. The variety, state and health of fruit trees, bushes and plants.

5. Where could a vegetable patch be fitted in? If there is no area of good soil, could a raised bed or two be constructed?

6. The condition and effectiveness of the irrigation system.

7. The condition of the greenhouse and garden frame if existing.

8. The possible location of features such as a fountain, pond, rockery or vegetable garden.

9. The signs of wildlife in the garden.

Whatever you do, think hard before destroying a good existing garden, and if you do so, at least offer the plants you might otherwise destroy or bury to nearby neighbours. What you don't want may be a goldmine of new varieties to them.

1.5 SPECIAL CHALLENGES FACING ABSENTEE GARDENERS

The main challenge you face as an absentee gardener is the creation of a garden that can survive during long absences and is easy to rejuvenate to its full glory once you are back in Spain.

The first thing you must decide is whether you can maintain such a garden alone, working on it for very limited periods of the year, or whether you will need the help of a gardener.

The table below illustrates the different types of absentee owners as well as our suggestions for the type of gardens they should have, and whether or not they need the help of a gardener.

If you decide to hire a gardener to construct and maintain your garden, we suggest you next read the following sections:

• Section 2.1 and 2.2 to help you decide on the type of garden that would satisfy both yourself and tenants when letting.

• Section 7.1 to help you decide on the type of gardener you need.

• Sections 2.17 and 2.18 and 6.5, which include ideas for minimising the costs of watering and maintaining the garden.

To help you get to grips with what lies ahead, some important 'Do's and Don'ts are listed below. We suggest you review them and then read the following chapters:

• Sections 2.1 and 2.2 to help you decide on the type of garden for your planned lifestyle in Spain.

• Sections 2.17, 2.18, 6.8 and 6.9 which include ideas for keeping the maintenance and watering requirements of your future garden to a minimum.

• Section 2.3 for suggestions related to understanding and cleaning up your site. In many cases you will want to include time-consuming features in your design but will wisely delay working on them for a few years until you are retired. In the meantime, you can work on the garden framework, leaving spaces for those future features.

If you are resident for 25 weeks each year, you will have rather more time for gardening than when you were working, so do enjoy the challenge and exercise but be sure you find a reliable gardener who can keep your winter-by-winter progress intact during the summer months.

PROPOSED PATTERN OF PERSONAL VISITS	EXTENT OF LETTING PLANNED	TYPE OF LETTING U: Unsophisticated S: Sophisticated		YOUR PERSONAL INTEREST IN GARDENING		SUGGESTED TYPE OF GARDEN	YOUR NEED FOR A GARDENER
		U	S	High	Low		
4 weeks yearly, increasing by 2 weeks yearly for 4 years until full retirement in Spain	None			•		Develop at own pace zone by zone but keep simple until you have retired.	Low
				•	•	Have a basic garden laid out during year one	High
4 to 6 weeks in summer. Unlikely to retire to Spain	None				•	As above	High
4 weeks in summer, 2 at Christmas and Easter, possibly 2 in the autumn. Will probably retire to Spain	None					Develop at own pace zone by zone but keep simple until retired or you decide to sell.	Low
					•	Hire gardener to develop and maintain basic garden	High
6 to 8 weeks in spring and autumn. No intention of retiring to Spain.	As much as possible in summer.	•		•		Self-develop basic garden as quickly as possible.	Low/ Medium
			•	•	•	Have a good but low maintenance garden laid out as soon as possible and self-improve when in Spain, if a keen gardener. If not, get gardener to work under your supervision	High

PROPOSED PATTERN OF PERSONAL VISITS	EXTENT OF LETTING PLANNED	TYPE OF LETTING U: Unsophisticated S: Sophisticated		YOUR PERSONAL INTEREST IN GARDENING		SUGGESTED TYPE OF GARDEN	YOUR NEED FOR A GARDENER
		U	S	High	Low		
180 days a year from October to April.	Let throughout the summer.	•		•		Work hard during first winter to get all the site neat and good framework of garden established. Progress during each winter visit to achieve the sort of garden you would have if resident.	During autumn and winter low to medium, but high during summer.
					•	Hire a landscaping contractor to install instant garden.	High throughout the year to construct & maintain.
			•	•		As above	As above
					•	As above	As above
1 or 2 weeks only. Property bought as an investment.	As much as possible year-round.	•		•	•	Hire a contractor to establish a minimal garden as soon as possible.	High
			•	•	•	Hire a contractor to establish a more complete garden to support the rental you plan to charge.	High

GETTING STARTED

Prepare a plan that gives first priority to:

    a. Stabilising the soil around the house. It can get very muddy if it rains.

    b. Creating a temporary terrace in order to sit and eat out (stone chippings over black plastic is the most serviceable).

    c. Introducing some early colour from plants in pots at the front door and on the naya or terrace. See sections 4.1, 4.3, 4.12 and 4.17.

    d. Providing shade and shelter from the wind. Plant trees on thewindward side and where the main siesta terrace will be.

e. Making your garden secure and private. Build high walls/fences with tall gates and plant fast growing hedges. See section 2.10.

TEN ESSENTIAL DO'S

1. While you are an absentee gardener, work on the garden only 40-50 % of the time you spend on holiday visits, plus a week dedicated to developing the garden each spring and autumn. Remember that you bought your holiday home in Spain to enjoy the climate and lifestyle, not to work all day in a hot garden during July and August. Work in the early hours before the sun gets up (you won't see many Spaniards in the fields after lunch until the sun is well down).

2. Be realistic about what can be achieved each year when gardening on a part time basis. Decide on a phased development plan for a period of three or five years. Delay the more complex, time-consuming features until you retire. You will then have the time to enjoy the challenges.

3. First decide on those areas of the plot that can be left for the time being as they are not eyesores for instance, the areas of meadow grass that can be strimmed each spring, copses of trees that give shelter and have a good underlay of leaf mould, areas allocated longer term as a vegetable garden, orchard or swimming pool area.

4. Then focus your efforts on the other areas, starting with the areas immediately around the house or those that can be seen from doorways and windows.

5. Recognise that all the other sections in the book are relevant to you, but that you need to constrain your enthusiasm to have a complete garden for a few years or until you are resident.

6. As in all gardens, focus first on completing those things that make an outdoor life-style possible. A practical programme would be as follows.

• Lay a main path around the house, leaving a gap for plants. Cover the soil with stone chippings to avoid splash back.

• Decide where the most important terraces will be and lay them quickly with stone chippings laid over black plastic sheeting with a few drainage holes pierced with a fork – or use a proprietary woven plastic underlay. See section 2.4.

• Decide on the joining paths and likewise lay provisionally with stone chippings over black plastic. Later when you lay the primary paths with a solid surface you can use the chippings as the ballast for your concrete foundations. With (a) and (b) done, you can now move around and eat on pleasantly located terraces and avoid taking dust or mud into the house.

• Buy an umbrella, chairs, table and loungers and you can already enjoy the tidy areas of the garden.

• Construct a temporary barbecue, knowing that a better-designed version will come later, or invest now in a trolley barbecue or Mexican oven. Both are convenient ways of cooking and both can be moved around the garden as it develops, before you decide on their permanent location. Now you can enjoy al fresco eating between your labours.

• Start to dig a trench around the plot for planting a hedge during your first late-autumn, winter or spring visit. Put down a layer of well-rotted manure or bags of an organic compost/fertilizer along the bottom of the trench in preparation.

• Decide where you will plant trees and dig large planting holes in preparation. Use the holes as temporary compost heaps and fill with green kitchen waste. Cover with a layer of soil when full and leave for a year to rot down. Alternatively, buy bags of compost ready for planting. Plant at the same time as the hedge to give shade for next summer.

• Lay out a watering system with a battery-operated, timer switch in readiness to water the hedge and other plants during your absence. Batteries should last about a year.

• Now decide where the first flowerbeds will be, in addition to those around the house. Mark them out and improve the soil ready for your first plantings as outlined in section 6.1. Areas for later flowerbeds are best covered with plastic sheeting and chippings at this stage for neatness and to minimise the evaporation of moisture from the plot. Just rake away the chippings and roll back and cut the plastic to shape when you are ready to do the next bed. Edge the beds with small rocks to keep the chipping off the soil.

• Select drought-resistant, low-maintenance plants and plant as per hedges and trees to ensure that good root systems are developed to survive during the first hot, dry summer and early autumn. See Part Four.

• Recognise that an attractive, typically Spanish garden can be achieved using just palms, an olive tree, cacti, aloes, succulents, aromatic herbs, bougainvilleas, orange bignonia, plumbago, oleanders, lilies, agapanthus and lantanas. As an absentee gardener, buy young climbing plants with big root balls to give them the best chance of establishing themselves. Once you start to plant daisy-like margaritas, etc., your maintenance needs will start to go up, as they need regular deadheading and trimming to prevent them from becoming leggy.

7. Mulch around all plants with stones, compost or bark chippings laid over woven plastic to help keep roots cool and minimise evaporation and the weeds that grow during your absence.

8. For some instant colour, buy a few attractive containers that will fit in with your vision of the finished garden and plant them up with trailing geraniums and annuals. Treat the annuals as expendable and replace on the first day of each visit. Put the geraniums on a low volume drip on the irrigation system. See section 2.14.

9. Above all keep the garden simple while you are an absentee gardener to ensure that the maintenance required during the first week of each visit is low and the preparations for leaving at the end of each visit are minimal. Just remember before you leave to ensure that the watering system is working and set it on, say, five minutes a day. See section 2.18.

10. Year by year, review whether you are still happy to persevere without a gardener to help you with the construction of paths, terraces, rockeries etc., or do some maintenance work between your visits. Consider the progress you are making and the time and effort that you are putting into it. If you are still having fun, enjoying the exercise and seeing satisfying results, stick with your solo efforts.

10 ESSENTIAL DON'TS

1. Don't waste time on laying a lawn. It will be impossible to give it the early care and attention required as well as the regular cutting and weed control afterwards, unless you retain a gardener. Lawns are thirsty! They need regular watering.

2. Don't plant thirsty plants and expect them to be there when you come back. The tables in Part 4 indicate which plants are most drought- resistant and vice versa.

3. Don't lay loose crazy paving or slabs without concrete foundations to create instant paths. They won't stay level after a couple of storms and the gaps between will soon be home to weeds.

4. Don't start a vegetable plot until you have the time to do it properly, but once you have enriched the soil in all   flowerbed areas, you can mark out the area and start to improve the soil in anticipation of your retirement. See section 6.1.

5. Just because you see plants growing alongside motorways and on hillsides, don't assume that Spanish plants don't need watering. They do. Even drought-resistant plants need watering until they have established deep-tap roots.

6. Don't despair if a few plants die. It's part of the learning process. They may have done so even if you had been a resident gardener.

7. Don't forget that the more you plant the more maintenance work you create. Most shrubs and perennials need to be trimmed or cut back during the winter to secure good spring and summer colour, so don't plant very vigorous climbers that will create jungles in your absence. See section 6.9.

8. Don't plant plants that are too tender for your area. Avoid them if you know that frost is possible on even one night a year.

9. Don't forget to provide for summer shade and shelter from cool winter breezes for the non-gardening members of the family.

10. Don't assume that your garden will be as colourful as the garden of your neighbour, a fulltime resident and keen gardener who is in the garden every day.

The above guidelines should enable you to make a quick start and steady progress visit by visit. If they come as a shock, then reconsider your decision to go it alone and employ a good gardener to assist you or a landscape gardener to do it all. But don't forget that landscape gardens still require aftercare.

1.6 TYPICAL APARTMENT AND PENTHOUSE CHALLENGES

In theory there is no reason why most apartment and penthouse terraces should not be green and colourful, at least for part of the year, even producing a few organic peppers and tomatoes, strawberries,peaches and lemons. After all, the areas are small, the time required to design, construct and maintain a mini garden is rather less than a typical small villa, and water is readily at hand.

In addition, the horticultural industry is geared up to help. The manufacturers of pots and containers now offer a wide range suitable for apartment terraces. Some hang on terrace balustrades, on end and inner walls and from the ceiling like hanging baskets. Others are regular pots that stand on end sideboards or on the floor. Many now incorporate a self-watering reservoir to minimise the frequency of watering and water absorbing gels can be mixed into the potting compost to make things even easier.

Furniture designers and manufacturers are giving special attention to improving the style and durability of furniture, not only seats, chairs and sideboards for terraces, but also pergolas, trelliswork, planters etc., for penthouse roofs.

We were therefore somewhat saddened when we carried out a survey of some two hundred apartments in early July in a well established development on the Costa Blanca where the occupancies are approximately 40% permanent, 30% absentee owners who generally reside for the summer months, and 30 % holiday lets. Less than 10% had good displays of flowering or evergreen plants, less than 1% grew tomatoes or peppers, less than 10% had attractive displays of ornaments or artefacts, 15% had empty window boxes, troughs or pots, and 15% only displayed a clothes horse. Few looked like a 'home' in the sun, yet the best display could not be bettered. The situation with penthouses was very similar.

The opportunity is waiting for you. You could in one go:

- Improve the attractiveness of your outdoor living space.
- Improve the appearance of the total apartment block.
- Enhance the neighbourhood.
- Start an enjoyable small scale terrace garden or a spectacular penthouse roof garden from which to enjoy 360 degrees views.

Yes, there are a few problems such as the strong winds and salt spray on front line blocks, plus carrying all materials and plants up several floors but the furniture arrived safely!

Where there's a will there's a way. We have seen some wonderful terraces, not only on the seafront but inland, with geraniums surviving winter snows because the heat loss through terrace doors established a sufficiently cosy winter microclimate.

Sections 5.4 and 5.5 present practical ideas for transforming your terrace. A list of plants suitable for terraces facing east, south, west and north is included in Sections 5.4 and 5.5.

1.7 IMPROVING YOUR GARDEN ANNUALLY

Most gardeners are never totally satisfied with their gardens, for a number of reasons. As the various areas of the garden mature, they look different to when first planted out.

New ideas are inspired by travels, reading and visits to garden centres.

New gardeners are not fully aware of the outdoor lifestyle that the Spanish climate offers and the need for additional terraces, facilities and internal mini-gardens becomes apparent later on.

After a couple of years, we all realise that some plants do well in our individual micro-climates while others struggle or die. And the scenery can change. Unexpected new construction work can obstruct a favourite view or nearby woods can be felled.

Such internal and external changes inevitably inspire ideas for a series of improvements that year by year take us nearer to our visions of the ideal garden in Spain. Rather than initiate ad hoc changes, we suggest you carry out a thorough review of your garden once a year in order to decide which of the many possibilities will be most beneficial. The best time for a total audit is late summer or early autumn. Major changes can then be made during the cooler autumn and winter months.

Unless your garden is simply a small patio or an apartment terrace, we suggest you assess the pluses and minuses of your garden area by area.

Divide the garden up into manageable, self-contained chunks for instance, the front garden, the back garden, the side gardens, the pool area, the naya, upstairs terraces, the cooking and eating terraces, the orchard and vegetable gardens.

Reflect on each area in turn, preferably with your partner and other living-in family members. Involve your gardener, too, if you have one. Then ask yourself the following basic questions:

a. What have been the greatest successes in the garden, season by season, during the past year?

b. How can similar effects be achieved in other parts of the garden?

c. What have been the real disappointments and failures in the garden during the past year?

d. What changes should be made now?

Sometimes it helps to look at any photographs you might have taken of the garden area you are reviewing. It also helps to use a checklist of questions (such as the one below) to ensure that nothing is left unturned.

AUDIT OF ....
DATE ....

a. Have we been totally satisfied with the overall result achieved season by season (autumn, winter, spring and recent summer)?

b. Was the development and maintenance work involved worthwhile?

c. Did we have a continuous display of colour from last September until now?

d. Are we likely to have a colourful garden this autumn and for Christmas?

e. Has there been perfume in the air when we worked, strolled, rested or ate in the area?

f. Have there been sufficient contrasts or harmony between the various colours, textures, shapes and heights of the various varieties of plants and trees and the colours of paths, terraces, walls and garden furniture etc?

g. Have we made sensible use of planted or empty pots, ornaments and sculptures to enhance the area? Could we do more or have we over done it?

h. Do we have adequate shade and are the shady areas as colourful, restful and interesting as the sunny areas of the garden?

i. Do we have shelter for sitting out in the winter sun when cool breezes blow?

j. Are all the plants and trees healthy and in good condition?

k. Are all constructed features – terraces, paths, steps, walls, etc., – attractive, in good condition and safe?

l. If annuals were planted during the past year, were they worth the effort of dead-heading and the cost of watering? Should we replace them with perennial plantings?

m. What are the main focal points of the garden? Is this part of the garden one of them or is the garden too focussed on the swimming pool, for instance?

n. Do we attract a good assortment of wildlife such as butterflies, birds and lizards to the garden? When we wander round the garden, does each area/mini garden link with the next in an attractive or creative manner?

o. Do we have colourful, stimulating and entrancing views from overlooking windows and doorways, seats, etc?

p. Was the vegetable area productive? Should we extend it?

q. Did fruit trees crop well? Should we plant more or replace some with other trees or shrubs?

r. What were the watering needs? Were individual specimen plants and the overall effect worth the cost?

s. How many hours a week were spent on maintaining this area of the garden? Was it worthwhile or should we redesign the area to reduce the maintenance required? (Section 2.18 may give some relevant ideas).

t. Last but not least in importance, does this area enhance our enjoyment of the garden and support our planned lifestyle?

Having completed the audit area by area, ask yourself the following questions:

- What do we need to change?
- What do we need to add?
- What do we need to take out/away?
- Do we need different plantings or colour schemes?
- How can we best reduce the amount of maintenance work required now, or as we grow older?
- How can we reduce the cost of watering the garden?
- How can we make more parts of the garden eye-catching for next year?

Inevitably, you will come up with ideas for improving each area, but it might take too much effort and cost too much money to complete them all this autumn and winter. In this case, review the list, set priorities, decide when to make the changes and whether to do them yourself or seek outside help. Finally, start some of the changes now. It's amazing how the gardening year soon passes.

THE SPANISH GARDENING CHALLENGES

PART TWO

PLANNING YOUR SPANISH GARDEN

You will get most out of your garden in Spain if you design and develop it to match the lifestyle you came to Spain for, in particular taking advantage of the generally sunny climate that allows an outdoor life to be enjoyed throughout most of the year.

2.1 DESIGN THE GARDEN TO MATCH YOUR LIFESTYLE

Most expatriates buy property in Spain with a very different lifestyle in mind to the one they knew in their previous country. This new lifestyle has more to do with the open air – in a climate that on average is warm, dry and healthy. Good gardens are an extension of the house. Many families spend more time in the garden than in the house for most months of the year, retreating inside only to sleep and avoid the occasional storm.

Such changes in lifestyle are only successful if your garden is properly designed and constructed from day one. You should provide shade for hot summer days and sheltered sun for cooler winter days, and maintain a sensible balance between terraces, paths and flowerbeds, planted with plants that require the minimum of maintenance and the minimum of watering. You should also give careful consideration to outdoor cooking facilities and to planning a pool if you decide to have one. And in making decisions it is important to keep in mind whether you are gardeners or non-gardeners, resident or non-resident owners.

We regard an early analysis of your planned lifestyle, short and longer term, as the important first step in designing your garden. With an outdoor lifestyle, what your garden and surrounding vistas look like from within the garden is more important than what the garden looks like from within the house. The latter, of course, is also important, but less so than in northern and central Europe where the garden is normally seen more from inside the house, and most of the time in the garden was spent cutting the lawn and weeding – when it wasn't raining.

So how do you want to spend your time? What proportion of the typical day do you yourself, family members and visiting friends wish to spend in the garden in good weather? What facilities will be desirable? And so on. The questionnaire that follows is designed to help you clarify your preferred lifestyle, so that the garden you end up with, whether it's just a few square metres of apartment terrace or town house patio or one to ten thousand square metres of land, is both practical and a pleasure.

A GARDEN LIFESTYLE QUESTIONNAIRE

YOUR DEDICATION TO GARDENING

1. Am I a dedicated gardener interested in making gardening my number one or two hobby? Does my partner have similar interests so that the design, construction and maintenance of the garden will be a team effort?

2. For how many hours a week will other hobbies and commitments allow us to garden?

3. For how many years are we likely to be able to cope with doing everything ourselves?

4. Are we likely to take on a gardener in the short or longer term? If so, will we want to simplify the design to minimise the cost of the gardener?

EATING AND COOKING PLANS

1. How frequently would we want to eat out in the garden at breakfast, lunch and dinner (not forgetting tapas and sun downer) time?

2. Would we want to do the above on the naya, a terrace close to the house or on cosy, interesting, colourful and perfumed terraces spread around the garden?

3. How many people will be eating in the garden on a normal day, and how frequently are we likely to entertain guests? What is the maximum number we need to cater for when designing terraces and cooking facilities?

4. Do we want to cook in the open air, using a barbecue, Mexican oven or paella stand, for instance?

RESTING PLACES

1. Would we prefer to read, rest and take siestas in beautiful corners of the garden in both the winter and summer – or prefer the haven of the centrally heated and air-conditioned house?

2. Do we need a number of quiet corners or just one area to accommodate the entire family? Are we happier if everything happens on one big terrace around the pool?

3. Will we want to hang hammocks or sky chairs between or from trees?

ACTIVITY SPACE

1. What leisure activities – for instance, quiet card or board games, painting, table tennis or basketball, petanc/boule – do we need to provide for?

2. Do we want to grow fruit and/or organic vegetables?

3. How often will children be resident? Do we need to provide for a dedicated children's corner along the lines of section 3.6?

4. Do we plan to have a pool or jacuzzi? If so, how large?

5. What open-air activities are we likely to give up and take up as we grow older?

A GARDEN LIFESTYLE QUESTIONNAIRE (continued)

OPPORTUNITY FOR ONGOING GARDENING CREATIVITY

1. Do I, my partner or other family members want an instant garden or a garden that will give opportunities for creative construction projects for a number of years (such as constructing ponds and waterfalls, introducing fountains and rockeries, building up collections of plants on raised beds, or building an oven)?

2. Do we need a greenhouse, cold frame and potting table? Do we need an area for compost heaps in order to recycle kitchen and garden waste?

PROVISION FOR ANIMALS

1. Do we need to provide a kennel and run for a dog or dogs?
2. Are we likely to keep poultry, rabbits or any other animals?

GENERAL AMBIENCE

1. Do we need to make the garden safe for elderly, impaired or infirm persons?
2. Do we want to feel enclosed and totally private or open to the surrounding countryside?
3. Do we want to hear the dawn chorus, evening crickets and frogs, or the constant sound of water from fountains?
4. Do we want to maximise the possibilities for colour and perfume throughout the year?
5. Do we want a formal, tidy garden or a more romantic, rustic and natural garden?
6. To what extent do we want a gardener to be around when we are in residence?

The vision and needs of your future garden are developing. Meanwhile, to stimulate an outdoor lifestyle, construct something early on that draws you into the garden on a regular basis. It could be a terrace under a tree or, initially, a large umbrella, a seat in a sheltered corner to enjoy the winter sun, a temporary barbecue until you have time to decide on your final cooking facilities – or anything that helps you to start enjoying the freedom of the garden and to adapt to the Spanish climate.

2.2 WHAT TYPES STYLES OF GARDEN ARE POSSIBLE?

The next step is to clarify your vision of the type and style of garden that you wish to develop. It is important to do this before finalising the features that it is to include.

Fifteen general possibilities are described below. Review them and choose one that would match your life style, personality and ambitions. If you already have a clear idea of what you want, use the list to test whether there might be other options worth considering seriously. One option is a garden comprising a series of connected mini gardens, each having the same or contrasting styles:

1. THE URBAN GARDEN – Straight pathways, square or oblong terraces and pool or lawn, with plants only around the boundary and in pots. Perhaps a reminder of a garden left behind, or the easiest option.

2. THE NATURAL GARDEN – A plant oriented garden aiming to recreate or even improve on nature. At the extreme, a mini botanical garden including a large range of plants with the emphasis on blending colour, perfume and textures. Perhaps meandering paths between a series of mini gardens on either side of the house.

3. THE COURTYARD OR PATIO GARDEN – Aiming to create a magical and cool inner garden with the emphasis on an attractive terrace surface, plants cascading from pots on the walls, climbers going upwards and with flowering evergreen plants around a cooling fountain.

4. THE CONTEMPORY GARDEN – Replacing and purposely challenging/ changing nature. Old dry stone walls faced with painted concrete and large pebbles in wire cages as substitutes for plants.

5. THE MYSTICAL GARDEN – Using the concepts of Chinese and Japanese gardens. Raked gravel or a large pond as the sea of life, with rocks as islands and large stepping-stones to an afterlife, and carefully trained trees as the haunted forest.

6. THE OASIS GARDEN – Based on a collection of palms and yuccas around a central swimming pool or pond.

7. THE POOL RESORT – One large terrace, perhaps up to the boundary with no room for planting a hedge. An elegantly tiled swimming pool, loungers, umbrellas, and dining table and chairs providing all the necessary colour. A corner flowerbed and a few geraniums in pots.

8. THE NATURE GARDEN – Semi wild, semi tamed. Maximum of wild plants, many of which are wind-blown or introduced by birds and spring up naturally. Maximum effort to attract and preserve wildlife. Could be on a terraced hillside or in a woodland setting – an old meadow or a rocky hillside.

9. THE FINCA – The priorities being growing vegetables and fruit, keeping poultry and rabbits and a small cottage garden by the front and back door. Perhaps a bougainvillea or grapevine over an arbour for shade outside the south facing door.

Patio garden

10. THE MINIMALIST GARDEN – The garden for the non-gardener who wants none of the mess of plants. Interest created through the textures and colours of walls, the surface of a wall-to-wall terrace, choice of terrace furniture, ornaments and groups of unplanted pots. Perhaps a sculpture or two. Could be very stylish or very bare.

11. THE MODERNISTIC GARDEN – A simple but very effective garden around a pure white cubic-designed house. White unplanted boundary walls. A line of well-clipped citruses with whitewashed trunks set in a perfect sward of green grass, white marble chippings or grey green tinted cobbles or sets. Sophisticated and without the mess of shrubs or potted plants. Could have a pristine pool set in a white terrace surround. Every line straight and geometrical, matching the design of the house.

12. THE WOODLAND GARDEN – Created within a copse or corner of a forest. Soft natural leaf mould pathways between glades that serve as terraces with full and semi shade. Planted with shade-loving plants in keeping with the setting.

13. THE COLOURFUL DOG RUN – A bare earth yard to house the dog or dogs. The walls or high fences festooned and overgrown with thick and colourful perfumed climbers. A quick sweep up and it's all cosy and attractive for an evening barbecue.

14. THE WATER GARDEN – Set around a number of ponds, fountains and brooks. Perhaps fed from a natural spring. The sound of music, colourful flowers, flowing water and bog plants being the main ingredients for success.

15. THE HOLISTIC GARDEN – With the benign Spanish climate and the time available to many retired expatriates it is very possible to develop a total or holistic garden. A garden that integrates a colourful perfumed flower and herb garden with productive areas for growing fruit, vegetables and livestock – hopefully by natural, ecological and organic methods.

Each of the concepts is very different and not all will be to everyone's taste, but each can be made very attractive with a little creativity and dedication. Be individualistic in deciding on the garden that will suit you best. There is no right answer, no right design for the 21st century but, for long-term enjoyment, do choose a garden that is compatible with your lifestyle and your house.

2.3 MAKE THE BEST USE OF NATURAL FEATURES

Whether you have just purchased a plot to build on, a new house on a bare plot or an existing unsatisfactory garden, decide at an early stage whether there are any natural features worth retaining and enhancing as focal points of your final garden. If your house is not yet built, or only partly built, persuade your builder to protect these features. They have a habit of disappearing when plots are bulldozed prior to starting construction or they can get buried under piles of building materials or rubble during construction.

The following features might be gardening treasures:

1. Dry stone terraces, perhaps a millennium or more old. Retain them to create an

interesting multilevel garden, and plant the holes in the walls and above as a natural rockery.

2. Walls of old buildings that can be cleaned up and stabilised as features covered with climbers and as useful windbreaks.

3. An old crumbling building or pigeon house that could be restored as a garden shed or hen house.

4. A spring that could become the centrepiece of a water garden or the source of water for a naturally constructed swimming pool.

5. A small ravine or barranca that could have a path up the middle, surrounded by a Mediterranean rock garden.

6. A dried up streambed that could be enhanced with waterfalls to create a magical effect during infrequent flash floods. Either bank could be planted with drought resistant plants and, if the bed is wide, it could be raked as the heart of a Japanese style garden.

7. An ancient gnarled tree that could be topped and trained to grow sideways as a natural sunshade.

8. A self- or bird-seeded flowering tree.

9. A copse of pine or oak trees, which, if in good condition, can be developed as a woodland garden with vital summer shade.

10. A rocky outcrop that could be left natural or developed into a rockery.

11. A natural slope that could be terraced into a more interesting, plant covered hillside garden.

12. A number of large rocks that could be bulldozed or craned into an interesting group.

13. An old well head, drinking trough or wash place. Each can be made the centrepiece of a terrace of potted plants, especially if in the semi shade of an old tree.

14. A natural hollow just right for a sunken, sheltered terrace and a circular bowl rockery.

15. Old water channels used previously for transporting irrigation water. You may be able to tap into an un-chlorinated, agricultural water supply as an inexpensive source of water for the garden, or use as the basis of a water garden or a way of collecting rain water to feed a storage tank.

16. An area of old stone terracing that will look much more attractive than a new crazy-paved stone terrace.

2.4 ESTABLISH A FRAMEWORK OF TERRACES AND PATHS

If your garden is to be designed for an outdoor lifestyle, then terraces need to be carefully sited and constructed as pleasant places for a host of outdoor activities, and surfaced paths with interesting routes need to join up the terraces and the doorways of the house.

TERRACES

Terraces are essential features of Spanish gardens and need to be given much thought before laying a first slab or area of stone chippings. Using a systematic approach and taking initial decisions on the following points will help you achieve the best result:

• What you will need terrace areas for and when you will use them most. Recognise that it is often more practical and interesting to have a number of terraces spread around the garden rather than one large one.

• Where each terrace would be best situated. Near or away from the house? With good internal or external views? In the sun or shade? Some in full view and others quietly tucked away?

• How to fit in terrace areas for different activities. Ensure you allow space for fiesta days when you may have a large group of visitors.

• What shapes would be most interesting and practical – square, oblong, round, oval, hexagonal, or irregular.

• Where they would be best located for convenience in relation to the kitchen door, garage, drive, pool, front door, etc.

Once you have made these tentative decisions, prepare a summary along the lines of the box below, indicating the purpose of the terrace, its minimum size and preferred location.

SUMMARY OF REQUIREMENTS FOR GARDEN TERRACES

TERRACE REQUIRED FOR:	MINIMUM SIZE IN SQ. METRES	PREFERRED LOCATION	ON PATH TO
Breakfasts in sunny sheltered spot for two	15	With a good view	Not important
Winter lunches and summer dinners in sunny spots for 4 to 14	60	Near pond for sound of fountain	Kitchen
Summer lunches in shade for 4 to 14	60	Under large tree	Kitchen
Quiet winter siestas	15	Quiet sunny spot	Unimportant
Quiet summer siestas	15	Quiet shady spot	Unimportant
Cooking with barbeque, paella pan or oven	20	Sun for winter, semi shade for summer	Adjacent to eating areas
As surround to pool	130	At side of house so as not to dominate garden	Naya, covered terrace
Carport for two cars	40	Alongside drive	Front door
Greenhouse, potting table, compost heap and sink	20	In semi shade for half the day	Garage where tools are kept
Mini table tennis	30	Away from siesta areas	Not important
Setting for fountain or other water feature.	10	At an attractive location within network	Not important
Rotary clothes drier	10	Near utility room	Utility room

MIX OF TERRACES, PATHS AND FLOWERBEDS

TYPE OF GARDEN	% TERRACES AND POOL	% PATHS	% FLOWER BEDS NOT WITHIN TERRACES
MINIMALIST	90 - 100	In terraces	0 - 10
AVERAGE with pool	60 - 80	5 - 10	20 - 30
KEEN GARDENER no pool	30 - 40	10 - 20	45 - 50

Aim towards the mix of terraces, paths and flowerbeds you would like to have, with the help of the box above.

The above percentages do not include areas of larger gardens allocated to a dedicated orchard, vegetable plot, tennis court or a large mown or wild area of grass. Small formal lawns within the flower garden area are regarded as lawned terraces.

Now draw a largish site plan, marking:
- House, boundaries and gates
- Direction of the prevailing winds
- Areas that get the morning, midday and evening sun
- Location of natural features you have decided to retain
- Possible location of special features you are considering fitting into your garden design
- A strip around the boundary for hedges and boundary shrub/tree beds. (Allow a metre in small gardens and up to three to six in large gardens)
- Direction of the best external views from the garden

Cut out pieces of cardboard to represent each of your planned terraces to scale and start to lay them out on the site plan. Work out a tentative layout and sketch in a possible network of paths connecting the terraces.

Then cut out full-size pieces of black plastic to represent all but the larger terraces and lay them out according to your plan on the soil, weighing them down with rocks or piles of sand. Mark the larger terraces with a line of sand. Adjust the layouts by trial and error until you are satisfied. Now mark out the sides of pathways between terraces with lines of pebbles or sand.

Walk through your network of terraces and paths. Sit on a chair in each area where you anticipate you will be eating or resting and take in the views. If it feels right, start to lay the paths and terraces, if not, adjust the draft plan by sliding the plastic terraces around, and change the shapes and sizes of the large layouts by adjusting stone or sand lines until you achieve what you want.

PATHS

Before rushing out to buy materials or asking the builder to construct a simple concrete path around the house, it is important to first do some basic design work. Start by asking yourself the following questions: Why do we need paths and how wide should they be? Would they look best straight or curved and what surface would look most attractive and interesting? Am I capable of doing a good job or should I find someone to construct them for me?

WHY PATHS?

Here are some reasons for establishing a network of paths around the garden:

1. To enable persons of all ages to move around the garden easily and safely in any weather, whether or not they are healthy and fit.

2. To move trays of food or drinks, wheelbarrows, gas bottles, garden machinery and furniture around the garden without fear of tripping or unnecessary strain.

3. To link the different areas, mini gardens and features in an interesting way.

4. To create and approach views within and beyond the garden that are interesting and even spectacular.

5. To reduce garden maintenance and water use by lowering the percentage of the garden planted as flower beds, vegetables or lawn.

6. To shelter and provide a moisture reservoir for the roots of plants lining the paths.

7. To make the garden look longer or wider by designing paths which become narrower from the beginning to the end.

8. To establish the style and aesthetics of the garden.

Most garden paths are straight, even when alternatives would be more interesting and practical. The reasons for this are various. Straight paths are easier to envisage, design and construct than ones that are curved. Paving stones are usually square or oblong, and the laying of curved paths with natural stone slabs as crazy paving is seen as time consuming and expensive.

But here in Spain the reasons are no longer relevant for most gardeners. Many now have the time to spend on laying out an ideal garden, stone slabs are often relatively inexpensive, stone chipping even less so, and good cheap labour is often available. So consider the possibilities of curved, twisting, zigzagging and narrowing paths to add interest and depth. For instance, use stones to lay out a path with parallel sides then change the design so that the near end is widened and the far end narrowed. You will find that an optical illusion makes the narrowing path look longer than the previous one with straight sides. You can enhance the effect by placing a large pot or rock at the beginning of the path and a half size

49

one at the other end.

Many paths are constructed against the wall of a house or outside walls and fences. What a pity that no space is left to plant interesting climbers, shrubs and other plants that can prevent the splash back of dripping rain just as effectively as a path and is much more attractive. However, if an old property has questionable foundations it is wise to concrete up to the walls and avoid close plantings. In all cases, plants with thick trunks and penetrating roots are to be avoided.

Keep slopes very gentle. All surfaces can become slippery with rain or frost. If you need to lose height, use steps or a wheelchair type slope with railings. If possible, use slopes of paths and terraces to channel rainwater to where it is most needed.

Main paths should be 90 to 120cm wide (150 if for persons with wheel chairs or walking frames). Secondary paths should be 50 to 70cm wide, and tertiary paths 30 to 40cm.

For safe steps risers should be 15 to 17cm (10 to 12cm for shallow steps, to create a special effect or to make it easier for infirm persons). The depth of steps is typically 30 to 50cm but a metre or more can be used on long, gentle gradients.

SURFACE MATERIALS FOR TERRACES AND PATHS

Here are some suggestions for terrace and path surfaces (consider using a number of different surfaces for interest):

1. Light coloured stone chippings laid over plastic are the fastest way of constructing interesting terrace areas and paths on level surfaces or on gentle slopes. We favour the pink tinted and 15-20mm graded chippings, as they look attractive, keep clean and soon bed down to give a firm surface. A fortnightly rake or sweep will keep them looking tidy and torrential rain will soon soak away. On steeper slopes you may need channelling to run off surface water and prevent erosion.

2. Dark coloured chippings create a contrast, but they can look drab in large areas and become more heated by the sun than lighter colours.

3. Square or oblong stone slabs or blocks are excellent in both formal and informal situations, however they can be expensive and very time consuming if you are chipping or cutting the rocks to size yourself. A variety of colours are available. Lay them on a well-prepared concrete foundation to get the levels right to ensure they do not become uneven when heavy rains make the ground underneath soggy. Prepared natural stone can be expensive, so it may be appropriate to consider less expensive concrete slabs that now come in a variety of colours and a range of surface designs.

4. Crazy paving is a less expensive rock slab solution. In most situations, don't be tempted to lay them directly on the soil or on loose sand as they will soon become uneven after storms and the gaps between slabs are more likely to become home for deep rooted weeds than low growing herbs and succulents.

5. Cobbles constructed from well-rounded river pebbles and stones can be very attractive, especially if different sized and coloured pebbles are used to create interesting patterns in the surface. Look out for design ideas next time you visit an old monastery or cobbled village. Work on a square metre at a time to ensure that you get the levels correct.

6. Old bricks laid in a variety of patterns create charming effects and are hard wearing. The traditional herringbone design can be especially pleasing to the eye. Coloured concrete patterned surfaces are a modern alternative, but normally are not as attractive, although some contractors now offer more than twenty designs and can lay many square metres in a day.

7. Grey concrete paths and terraces are uninteresting, so consider using them as the base for a more interesting alternative. Luckily there are now hard wearing polyurethane paints that can be used to paint existing concrete areas. Tints can, of course, be mixed into new concrete and can be very useful in brightening up and adding interest to an economy minimalist garden. Asphalt is also available in a range of colours but tends to look a little urban.

8. Bark chippings can be used to good effect in woodland settings or between raised beds in the vegetable garden.

9. Grass paths can be attractive, especially in the orchard and vegetable areas, but they tend to be scorched or untidy, depending on the weather, unless a regular watering, cutting and edge cutting programme is kept to. For many who do not have a gardener, this will be unnecessarily time consuming.

10. Stone or round concrete stepping-stones can be used for little-used paths across flowerbeds or lawns and large terracotta tiles are another alternative to consider. Choose the rougher finished variety for effect. They are also less slippery when wet than the smooth surfaced tiles, but both tend to gather moss in shady situations. Contractors now advertise non-slip treatments. Shiny-surfaced interior tiles are easier to sweep and wash down, but are not safe or aesthetically pleasing.

11. Railway sleepers have been used to create paths and steps in many informal gardens, but the sale of railway sleepers is now officially banned within the European Community, as the chemicals used to treat the wood are regarded as unsafe.

12. Low-growing herbs such as creeping thyme, camomile and dichondra repens can be used, but are more practical in semi-shaded areas. They will need regular watering and are unlikely to be very hard wearing if used for a main terrace or thoroughfare.

13. Wooden slatted paths and terraces can look very attractive in both formal and informal settings. Although very hot to walk on barefooted during the summer, they can be very useful in boggy or sandy areas.

14. The pea shingle, often used in the UK, is not normally available along the Costas, and builders use graded crushed rock as an alternative in concrete mixes.

15. Broken-up building rubble can obviously be used to create temporary paths in hidden parts of the orchard and vegetable plot or around the potting shed, but is not an attractive long- term solution.

16. Deep compost and well-rotted manure can be used to create weed inhibiting and moisture saving paths between rows of vegetables. In dry weather they are fine but rubber boots will be required for a few days after storms.

17. Bare earth is practical in very dry areas where weeds and heavy rainfalls are not major problems.

EDGINGS

Edgings are useful to contain stone chippings and also to add interest and a formal finish to both paths and terraces. Pebbles, small rocks, natural or glazed terracotta edging tiles or white painted concrete humps can all be used to good effect. Paths are softened when edged with ground cover plants or low clipped box or herb hedges.

MAINTENANCE

Sweep or vacuum paths and terraces regularly and repair any cracks or loose slabs as they occur. If in the shade, remove moss build-ups once or twice a year to prevent them becoming slippery when it rains. Washing up liquid and a stiff brush will remove most. If a tougher build-up has been allowed, use a pressure hose or a proprietary moss remover.

FURNISHING

Treat terraces as outside rooms and furnish tastefully, according to their use and situation.

2.5 DESIGN MANAGEABLE FLOWER BEDS

The number, location, type and style of flowerbeds are important decisions in all gardens. A number of practical possibilities are described on page 54/55 to help you decide on the most attractive and appropriate for your garden. The table summarises some typical situations, shapes and plantings. Recognise that the number, size and complexity of plantings will be the main determinants of the hours of garden maintenance work you or a gardener will need to do each week and the extra work involved in the annual winter cut-back. If you plan to be an absentee gardener, without a gardener during your long absences, minimise the number of flowerbeds and keep plantings simple.

TYPES OF FLOWERBEDS

In each situation a number of types of bed are possible, including:
- Beds level with the surrounding areas.
- Banked beds – for instance, round a raised pool or as dividers between different levels.
- Raised beds to add height and reduce bending. The practical height is between 30 and 90cm. The width should be 75cm (or 1.5 metres if you are able to work from both sides).
- Beds for planting directly, or beds in which to sink planted pots.
- Sunken beds which allow you to flood thirsty plants.
- Rockeries, as detailed in section 3.1.

EDGINGS

The edge of beds can be the edge of paving or the lawn, or they can be edged with small rocks, large pebbles or terracotta pieces. Raised edgings are essential if they are located within areas of stone chippings.

SURFACES

The surface of planted beds can be mulched or left as bare earth. With mulched beds fewer weeds grow, less water evaporates, and stone or wood chippings can be attractive in their own right.

CHOICE OF PLANTINGS

Your choice of plants and trees will need to take into account the colour schemes you wish to create, your need for a single height or banks of progressively taller plants, the desirability of flowers 365 days a year, the need for perfume and your local micro climate.

Full details of some 400 popular plants and trees for a wide range of garden situations are included in Part Four. Read the details regarding eventual heights, widths, and drought and frost resistance carefully before making your final choice.

Wander round your neighbourhood and visit local municipal or botanical gardens to gain an idea of how large mature plants can become. You will have a few surprises!

Decide on whether you want dedicated or mixed beds, a subtropical or Mediterranean garden, and what tropical plants, if any, will have a good chance of surviving your worst winter weather.

Where possible, plant closely for maximum impact, to create shade for the roots of plants and to hide irrigation pipes. Also, weeds have difficulty growing if they receive no direct sunlight. Plant some sacrificial plants, recognising that as they grow they will need to be thinned to avoid overcrowding. Annuals can be used in this way in early years.

Read section 2.6 Painting with Plants to help you decide on whether you prefer single or multi-coloured beds, harmony or vivid contrasts between areas of the garden, and whether you wish to create some cool beds, using whites, blues and greys or hot beds using vivid reds, oranges and yellows.

FLOWERBEDS – SOME TYPICAL LOCATIONS, SHAPES AND PLANTINGS

WHERE	POSSIBLE SHAPES	POSSIBLE PLANTINGS
Around the border of the garden for hedges	Long oblong strip	Just the hedge or with a perennial or shrub bed in front.
	Long oblong strip with oval front edge.	As above with low growing ground cover or annuals at the front.
	Long oblong strip with wavy edge.	As above, with bulbs mixed in.
	Wider corner beds.	As mini copses of trees or a major shrubbery.
Along the drive	Long strip following edge of drive.	A low or high hedge depending on the length of the drive. Roses, cacti, irises etc.
	A series of small round or square beds set in an area of stone chipping or grass.	A single variety or mix of flowering or evergreen trees, or shrubs. Collections of cacti or succulents. Annuals if in the cooler north.
Between the house walls and surrounding paths or terraces	Long oblong, minimum 50 cms wide.	Climbers up the walls or medium height shrubs to protect walls from splash back from rainwater running off the roof.
	Square or oblong in corner recesses or with a curved edge.	As above or a mini shrubbery, rockery or plant a specimen tree
Around terraces	Narrow or wide following contour of terrace.	In principal, anything of any height, including climbers on trellis.
In the centre of terraces	Square, oblong, round, oval, hexagonal or irregular.	In principal, anything including a tree or trees to give shade. Plant plants that enjoy the semi shade under the tree as it spreads.
Around the drip line of mature trees	Circular or special shape to match situation.	Whatever creates an attractive transition from the shade under the tree to the open garden and brightens up the shady area as a place to have a siesta or eat out of the sun.
Around the trunks of trees	Square or round.	Plants that will survive well in the shade of a tree with dense foliage or the semi shade of a more open tree.
Around the pond	Generally best to follow contour of pond or have a square or oblong bed with pond set in centre.	Low growing perennials and ground cover plants that will ensure a clear view of the flowers of pond plants and any fish. If the planned view is from one side only, plant taller plants on the far side as a backcloth.
Within the open space of the garden	Any shape with a flat surface.	In principal anything, taking into account the size of your garden and the internal vistas you want to develop.
	Circular or square with a domed surface to show off plants.	Use for a special display of annuals, bulbs, herbs or low growing perennials or shrubs.

FLOWERBEDS – SOME TYPICAL LOCATIONS, SHAPES AND PLANTINGS

WHERE	POSSIBLE SHAPES	POSSIBLE PLANTINGS
Alongside paths	Strip beds following contour of path	Low hedges of clipped herbs, shrubs or box, annuals, perennials, roses, shrubs, or bulbs.
	Wide beds on either side with path through middle.	Plant, shrub beds or copses.
Around the pool terrace.	Follow the contour using the outer shape that looks most pleasing.	Plants that have a low flower and leaf fall to minimise the chance of debris being blown into the pool. Plant other plants further back using the idea of concentric plantings described in section 3.3.
In the face of a dry stone wall.	Aim to cover the wall with cascading plants planted in the holes between rocks.	Drought resistant succulents and herbs.
On the vertical walls of the house or patio.	Break up with climbing plants or hanging pots.	Climbing plants selected from sectiom 4.7 or as below.
On balconies, terrace walls or railings.	Window boxes or rows of pots.	Geramiums, petunias and succelents are the most traditional. Refer to section 2.4and 5.4..

Take into account the colour and texture of leaves and the architectural form of plants, not just the colour of the flowers.

If you plant isolated specimen trees or shrubs for their individual beauty, don't spoil their effect by using competing under plantings. The planting and care of plants is covered fully in the sections of Part Six, and the selections of plants for a wide variety of geographic locations within Spain are listed within the sections of Part Four.

At each autumn garden review, decide on the successes and failures of your various flowerbeds and change accordingly for the following year. Achieving a wonderful long-term garden is always an iterative process.

There are many plants that survive in Spanish gardens without ever showing their best, so do ensure that you improve the soil in all flowerbeds before you start to put in plants. You will need to dig well-rotted compost and manure into some, and others will need improved drainage by working in coarse sand or grit. See section 6.1.

2.6 PAINTING WITH PLANTS

The basic design of your garden will give it shape, space and privacy and included those features that you consider essential to your use and enjoyment of the garden throughout the year. But beyond the basics it is the choice, and placing of plants relative to each other, that will achieve the mystique, magic, 3-D effect and interest of a great garden, however small or large.

The 400 plants presented in Part Four provide you with an amazing choice of colours and colour combinations. Their varying heights and widths enabling you to assemble masses of a single colour or intimate mixes of calming or exciting colours.

A. USING COLOURS

The main form, perspective and depth of the garden will be achieved by the bold and subtle use of the many shades of green. The dominant colour of most gardens through out the year. Something Clodagh has no problem remembering coming from Ireland. The colours of flowers providing the hot and cold spots, the sparkle, the vitality, the brilliance of fiestas and the calming siesta effects.

We sketched out this chapter over breakfast on a June morning. In the part of the garden we could see we counted 60 shades of green including lime greens, blue greens and grey greens. We counted only 40 other colours – 15 pinks and reds, 10 yellows and oranges, 10 blue and mauves, 5 shades of white plus the creams, greys and yellow ochre of rocks and stone chippings. Beyond the garden the varied hues of roof tiles and mature trees filled the foreground while the browning mountainside beyond was a mix of misty browny and bluey greens. The sort of combined internal/external vista that caused Dick to some years back start to regard gardening as 'Painting with plants'.

The art of choosing, co-planting and combining into a pleasing whole;
• The seven colours of the rainbow – red, orange, yellow, green, blue, indigo and violet.
• The colours of the artists pallet including many shades of whites and creams.
• The hundreds of hues and shades of individual flowers, leaves and trunks. Some occurring naturally and others developed by plant breeders by cross pollination.
• The colours of young new growth and maturity, especially on evergreens.
The effectiveness of the final colour scheme will depend on how you decide to separate or combine plants.
Basic choices include:
a. A mixed bed of annuals, perennials, shrubs and bulbs designed to achieve the most vivid late spring kaleidoscope effect.
b. A mixed bed planted to give year round colour. As one type of plant stops flowering another picking up the baton.
E.g. Freesias, followed by irises then by gazanias and purple lantanas.
c. Beds, banks and walls of colour in a variety of combinations and moods.
The following chart offers some thought starters for a number of differently conceived displays.
The choices are yours. Nothing is right or wrong and after all its your garden.

THE SEVEN 'C's' OF COLOUR COMBINING

1. COMMON COLOURS	Planting a single type or mix of plants with a single common colour of flower and similar foliage colours to create a mass effect.	e.g. A bank of purple lantanas; a wall covered with purple bougainvilleas; a bed of single colour gazanias; a single pink oleander hedge; a bed of bright red geraniums; a pine garden with only pink hydrangeas.
2. COMPATIBLE COLOURS	Planting plants with different but close shades or hues of a colour in the flowers and foliage.	e.g. A bed of varied coloured gazanias; a bed of San Diegos; side by side pastel coloured pink and yellow water lilies alongside the delicate mauve of the water hyacinth; a bed of soft pink and mauve small pin-cushion zinnias.
3. COMPLEMENTARY COLOURS	Co-planting several different plants with vivid contrasts but harmony between the flower or flower and leaf colours.	e.g. A view of yellow heliopsis, red geraniums, blue agapanthus, bright green geranium leaves, orange leonotis, red/orange lantana and a pink flowering oleander hedge in the background.
4. CLASHING COLOURS	Purposely close planting a number of plants with violently different colours at either side of the artists pallet and the rainbow.	e.g. An orange leonotis underplanted with bright red geraniums and bright red crocasmias in front of a purple bougainvillea and orange bignonia on a wall. A bed of mixed colour large spiky headed zinnias.
5. CALMING COLOURS	Purposely co-planting plants whose flower and foliage colours create no clashes but rather a sense of restful harmony between flowers and foliages or foliages.	e.g. Purple lantana under planted under an old tree stump covered in a white/blue passion flower; the dark greens in a mixed corner of oleander, bay and pistachio and grey green foliage of curry plants.
6. COLD COLOURS	An extension of '5' with a mix of cold white and mauve flowers and grey blue leaves that look cool even at midday on a mid summers day.	e.g. White bugle lilies, agapanthus and gladioli in front of a wall of white solanum;white irises alongside a white flowering echium with white alyssum in front.
7. CALIENTE (HOT) COLOURS	Purposely mixing the most vivid reds, oranges and yellows to create a garden hot spot.	e.g. Red, yellow and orange lilies, beneath a red and yellow devils tongue. alongside yellow lantana and orange leonotis with a background wall of purple and red bougainvilleas and an orange bignonia.

Consider some bold daring colour schemes as well as more subdued traditional ones. Consider colour schemes for each season of the year. Map out the colour scheme of each bed, wall and internal vista as if you were completing a jigsaw puzzle while still drawing the picture.

Use your imagination. Use plants already in the garden, the charts in previous sections and in a garden centre to help you start to develop ideas.

Try the following experiments

1. Wander round the garden with a tray or flat basket. Collect a leaf of every colour you can find and a flower of every form, size and colour.

Then attempt to produce two examples of each of the 7 C's. Finally consider whether your ideas can be implemented by transplanting some plants or reducing or increasing the number of others.

2. As a simplification of '1' collect the four or five brightest coloured flowers in the garden and then decide where they could be co planted to create a dramatic effect. Likewise collect twigs of the coolest grey or grey green leaves and see where a calm bed would best fit in if it does not already exist.

3. Before you repaint a wall or the house next time try out a number of colours to check which set up your favourite wall plants or tall self standing plants best. Include yellow ochre in your colours it can be even better than white.

4. Next time you visit a garden centre think about buying plants in groups rather than individually. Pick out some plants that interest you and place them in a group. Add others and remove some until you achieve a pleasing effect. Consider which of the seven C's you have followed or achieved and where the combination of plants would best fit into the garden. The garden centre may take an interest in what you are doing and may even offer to help. After all they may have a happier customer this way and end up selling more plants.

They might even start displaying plants in unusual but practical groupings.

B. ARCHITECTURAL SHAPES

Architectural plants can be as interesting as colourful flowering plants. Like a still life painting or live sculptures in the garden.

A wonderful garden, or mini garden, can be produced with just one or a mix of the following.

a. An oasis of palms.

b. A glade of cordylines.

c. A stone chipping area or rockery planted with a collection of euphorbias.

d. A corner or boundary of tall flowering agaves.

e. An area of mature cacti and aloes.

f. A tall hedge of prickly pear cacti.

g. A row of aeoniums in pots or planted as a dedicated bed.

Lastly have fun with painting with flowers whatever the size of your garden. Your selections don't have to be complex. In a small garden your hottest (caliente) spot may be a pot of orange oriental lilies in front of a scarlet bougainvillea and the coolest a container of white petunias. The plants listed in the Part Four are the most popular and accessible plants so you should have few major problems.

2.7 IS A LAWN FOR YOU?

Lawns are not as popular in Spanish gardens as in Northern Europe, for a number of good reasons.

A well-kept lawn needs much water and, except in some mountainous regions, rain is infrequent. Water is also in short supply and expensive in some areas, especially in the hot summer months.

Many lawns look their best in the winter and spring, not during the summer. Even with a watering system, growth will be uneven and the lawn will look untidy, unless a perfectly balanced spray irrigation system is achieved.

Wild lush meadows are not natural except in the north and northwest of Spain and creating a lawn is therefore often fighting with nature. The work involved in the preparation, planting and aftercare of a good lawn is extensive, onerous and costly. Mowing it can be time consuming and regular edge trimming can be a chore. Wind-blown or machine-distributed cuttings and seed can self-seed in adjacent flower-beds, and be carried by feet into the swimming- pool.

THOROUGH PREPARATION OF THE SEED BED

1. Clear the area well, digging out all rubble and rocks down to around 30cm or the depth of a fork.
2. Rotovate and harrow the chosen area, working in well rotted chicken manure and compost from an eco park composting plant, and TerraCottem soil improver/water retaining gel. (www.terravida.com).
3. If you cannot obtain the manure, or have a soil depth of less than 20cm, import some rich soil to top up to that depth.
4. Decide how you are going to water the lawn. A convenient method is to sink a network of water pipes and pop-up spray heads into the soil at this stage. Install the system so that it can be used as soon as the seed is sown – and you will not have to cut channels later in the established lawn.
5. Rake to a fine tilth, and level. Roll and check levels. Remove high spots and fill in hollows. Repeat until totally level on the flat or across your chosen slope.

For many gardeners, especially those with small and moderate gardens, the effort and expenditure is better spent on terraces, areas of interesting, coloured stone chippings, special features and flowerbeds.

A weedy, patchy lawn is a nightmare for the proud gardener. There are alternatives that look good, require less upkeep and use less water.

A lawn does have its advantages, of course, and many new gardeners in Spain are willing to take up the challenge. A green lawn can be a reminder of home in northern Europe. It can create a cool look in the summer, and a contrast to a surrounding dry landscape. It can also be a wonderful way to blend a garden into the surrounding hills and woods if you are living in a higher-than-average- rainfall mountain area.

Grass is cooler to walk on than stone slabs in the summer, provides somewhere soft for the children and the dog to play as well as a handy surface for practicing your golf putting.

A lawn gives a feeling of tranquillity without the stimulus of seasonal flowers or colour changes and, if immaculate, can be a joy.

DO IT PROFESSIONALLY

If you do decide to include a lawn in your garden layout, make sure that you do it professionally, whether you do it yourself or use an outside contractor. A good lawn requires even more care here than in northern Europe. Success can depend on the following factors.

THE RIGHT TYPE OF GRASS

When your lawn area is thoroughly prepared, you need to select the appropriate seed, plantlets or turfs you are going to use, taking into consideration the type of grass you want and its watering and maintenance needs. For some practical options, see the box below.

A good horticultural shop will be able to offer you a wide range of practical seed mixes and help in selecting the one most   suitable for your: location and conditions, such as a sunny area, shady or semi-shaded position, near the sea with salt spray, in an inland valley, your average local rainfall season by season, minimum and maximum temperatures and type of use.

SOWING

The best sowing time is early spring or autumn. Sow seed evenly over the surface by hand or using a wheeled seeding machine. Sow first around the edge and then from end to end and finally from side to side to achieve as even a coverage as possible. Rake the seed lightly into the top of the soil and roll. Then water in well with a fine sprinkler. Avoid causing build-ups of water and the development of rivulets. If possible keep some seed back for later repairs. If ants appear dust the area with sulphur powder.

SELECTION OF AN APPROPRIATE SEED, PLANTLETS OR TURFS

TYPE OF LAWN AND PLANTS	NORMALLY PLANTED AS	WHEN TO PLANT	WATERING NEEDS	BEST SITUATIONS	MAINTENANCE NEEDS
Course e.g. Gramma	Seeds or plantlets	Spring/ Autumn	Moderate	Any, including high rough use, when left 5cms long	Medium. Cutting in proportion to watering
Semi course e.g. Rye	Seeds	Spring/ Autumn	High	Well-used areas	Medium
Fine -e.g. Bermuda grass	Seeds	Spring/ Autumn	High	Little-used areas	Very High
Fine/semi coursemix	Seeds, or turf	Spring/ Autumn	High	High or mode-rate use areas	High
A herb alternative e.g. Dichondra repens or Thymus serpyllum	Seeds	Spring/ Autumn	Moderate	Low usage in semi-shade and shade	Low, rarely need to trim and doesn't need mowing

PLANTING

The best time for planting gramma plantlets is the autumn. Plant them 8 – 10cm apart and then sow normal grass seed between. Eventually the gramma grass plantlets join up and replace the finer grass grown from seed. In mid summer the grass dies off and the gramma takes over.

WATERING

Keep the sown area damp with a fine spray until the roots are well established and it is ready for its first cut. Then water to keep the grass green but not overly lush. This will maximise the time the lawn will look at its best, minimise the frequency of mowing and control your water bill. A deep watering down to the lowest roots twice a week in mid summer will be more effective than a surface sprinkle twice a day. If you are unsure about the effectiveness of your watering, dig out two 20cm square turfs – one before and one after watering – to examine the soil/root conditions. Replace the turfs and firm, and then give them a good soaking and a second firming. Note that gramma grass may go brown during the winter but soon re-greens in the Spring.

AN APPROPRIATE CUTTING CYCLE AND LENGTH

The frequency of cutting will depend on the fertility of the soil, top-up fertilising, the extent of rainfall and watering, the wear and tear of the lawn – and your standards of tidiness and perfection. A short cut will dry out and burn quicker but kill off any weed seedlings as they occur. A long cut will dry out more slowly, be more hardwearing but will allow weeds to become established. If you want an area of meadow rather than a civilised lawn, just let the grass grow and make hay twice, in the spring and late summer.

SEASONAL MULCHING

All lawns benefit from an annual spring scarification – to remove dead grass and moss – and a light mulching with a sand/compost or sand/peat substitute mix. Sprinkle the mulch evenly over the grass after scarification and then brush into the grass. If it does not rain within a week, water it in.

FEEDING

Lawns are hungry. Give the lawn a dressing of a balanced lawn fertiliser each spring and autumn. Don't over feed, and ensure that it is washed down into the soil as soon as applied with a copious watering to avoid burning the lawn.

REGULAR WEED CONTROL

Remove deep-rooted perennial weeds by hand and weed kill with selective weed killer each spring. If you have decided to treat your grass area as a pasture with wild flowers, just let the weeds grow.

CONTROL OF USE

The intended use of the lawn would have determined the type of grass sown or planted. If you want a perfect lawn, ensure that no hard wearing activities are allowed.

REPAIRS

If patches develop, dig up the area to a depth of 10cm, rake to a fine tilth, firm and re-sow the patch with the same seed as used originally, or in the case of gramma grass plant new plantlets to cover the bald patches.

Over a period of time visible and annoying bumps, hollows and broken edges may develop. Make an 'X' cut through the turf over each bump. Roll back the turf from the centre of the 'X' and then scrape out the excess soil. Roll back the turf one or two times and take out more soil until you are happy that all is level. Put the turf back, firm and water well. Hollows are easier. Just fill them with a sand/compost/soil mix, and firm.

To remake the curved or straight edge of the lawn, cut out the offending area and turn the turf round. Cut to shape. Fit odd pieces into the interior gap. Fill any holes with a sand/compost/soil mix and finally firm and water well.

SOME PRACTICAL ALTERNATIVES TO A LAWN

If you don't want the bother and expense of a lawn, there are plenty of alternatives to choose from.

1. A swimming pool and terrace.

2. An orchard with or without an underlay of wild grass and flowering wild flowers, allowed to grow naturally with a once or twice-a-year cut/strim.

3. Large terraces surrounded by mature trees for summer shade.

4. Areas of attractively coloured stone chippings. Larger areas can be broken up with flower-beds surrounded by rocks, a rockery, specimen palms, cacti and succulents. They can also be laid with contrasting areas of differently tinted chippings, or even raked into designs as in Japanese gardens.

5. A simulated dry riverbed.

6. A copse of evergreen or flowering deciduous trees with paths of stone or wood chippings meandering through.

7. A simulated oasis with a central swimming pool or water lily pond surrounded and shaded by a circle of palms.

8. An organic vegetable plot.

9. Just more of a colourful Spanish garden.

10. If you have a very large garden to provide privacy, or as investment with the intention of selling off one or two building plots, fence unused areas off and leave them wild.

2.8 LARGE AREAS OF STONE CHIPPINGS

Many gardeners have laid large areas of stone chippings as paths, formal terraces, patios, courtyards and as a general cover for bare sun-baked soil or sticky mud after torrential rains. The benefits, problems and ways of livening them up are outlined below.

THE BENEFITS

1. You can quickly produce a clean tidy surface, which is especially important if you are an absentee gardener.

2. Chippings laid with the minimum thickness of 10cm over black plastic will suppress weeds.

3. Chippings serve as a good mulch for shrubs and trees planted through plastic into the earth below.

4. A reservoir of moisture builds up under the plastic if holes are made in the plastic sheeting, or woven plastic material is used. This is very beneficial when plants are planted through the chippings/plastic or alongside in an adjacent flower-bed.

5. The surface can soon be swept or vacuumed, even under trees.

6. A large circle, square or oblong of chippings can be a good substitute for a lawn. Less preparation and maintenance is required and in many cases, chippings frame or set off plants better than the green of a lawn. Also, most importantly, your watering bill will be very much lower.

7. A good contrast to the dominant green of the rest of the garden.

8. Shows off central features well.

9. Chippings are relatively inexpensive.

10. Easy to lay and rake flat.

11. Can be used on gentle slopes or as a series of low terraces behind low dry stone walls.

12. A minimalist garden can be quickly established as a permanent garden or as a base from which to develop a full garden. At each stage the chippings can be raked back and the plastic rolled back to expose the soil for preparing the next flowerbed, vegetable garden, pond, etc.

13. Flooding from heavy rains quickly drains away, and chippings provide a mud-free environment.

COLOUR AND SIZE

Our favourite is a 1 1/2 or 2cm graded light-coloured chipping with a pinkish tint because it looks bright, clean and does not absorb and reflect the heat as much as the darker colours. However, there are a wide range of sizes, colours and tints available from quarries by lorry load and in smaller quantities from garden centres.

PROBLEMS

1. The need to sweep or rake to give a perfect finish for special occasions – but it doesn't take long.

2. The need to sweep, rake or vacuum leaves, especially under trees – but you don't have to cut the lawn.

3. The building up of humus in chippings under trees if they are not cleaned frequently.

HOW TO LIVEN UP LARGE AREAS

1. Surround the area of chippings with flower or shrub beds.

2. Plant specimens – such as palms, cordylines, flowering trees, aloes or a mini orchard – through the chippings.

3. Create a cartwheel herb bed, perhaps with a bay in the centre – surrounded by four segments of rosemary, sage, lavender and rue between the spokes and with an outer tyre of variegated thyme.

4. Make a raised bed, in the centre or offset, to house a collection of succulents, cacti or bulbs.

5. A bed of yellow lantanas surrounded by purple ground cover lantanas.

6. A fountain or pond.

7. An aviary.

8. A seat in the sun or under a tree.

9. A raised bed vegetable garden.

10. A pattern of square beds planted with herbs and perhaps edged by a low box hedge, as sometimes seen in monastery gardens.

2.9 PROVIDE FOR SHADE

Why shade? One could well ask the question when one sees developers bulldoze mature trees or copses to create clear building sites; or expatriates who buy a traditional Spanish property with a shady garden and chop down most of the trees in order to build a larger terrace around the pool, enlarge the lawn for sunbathing, or do away with the bother of sweeping or raking up leaves.

Such actions are a great shame as shade has always been an essential ingredient of successful gardens in Spain. It provides personal protection from the burning sun. The cool deep shade of an ancient tree is a wonderful place to hang a hammock or sky chair for a restful siesta, or to lay out a table for a midsummer luncheon party.

Shade or semi-shade is the natural haven for many naturalised Spanish garden plants that originated in the jungles of the South and Central Americas and Asia – and many seedlings and young propagated plants develop best in dappled shade.

There are several ways to provide for   shade, some are natural and others are special constructions that have become popular over the years.

SHADE FOR PERSONS AND PLANTS

1. Large, spreading, mature specimen trees or groups of younger or smaller trees.

2. The natural shade along the north side of the house, and tall hedges along the southern boundary.

3. The natural shade of enclosed patios, especially with a centrally planted tree.

4. A deep naya (arched covered terrace) – an important feature of many old Spanish properties and now luckily incorporated in the design of many new houses.

5. Wooden or metal pergolas draped with vigorous climbing plants.

6. Shady passage ways filled with shade-loving plants as often seen in villages in the Alpujarras.

7. A grape vine trained along a metal   frame. The traditional front or back porch in many Spanish villages.

8. Pergolas covered with canvas, canes or tiles.

9. Large umbrellas. The range of shapes and colours now available ensure that one can find something to fit in with any garden setting.

10. The traditional swing chair with a canopy.

11. The increasingly popular open tent- like gazebos and Coolashades now available in a variety of sizes cloths and colours.

12. A traditional Spanish outdoor kitchen with room for a dining table.

13. Awnings and blinds outside nayas, arches or doorways – especially useful for apart-ment and upstairs terraces and balconies.

With such a choice, no garden should be without shade. Personally, we believe nothing beats the shade under the natural umbrella of a spreading tree. Carobs, oaks, figs, olives, tall varieties of citrus, avocados, palms, pines, acacias and many other flowering trees can provide useful shade.

2.10 HEDGES, WALLS, FENCES AND GATES

EXTERNAL BOUNDARIES

High hedges, fences and walls around the entire perimeter of the garden are becoming increasingly popular, although restricted by urbanisation regulations and local bylaws in some areas.

Their benefits are as follows:

1. The provision of privacy from neighbours, passing pedestrians, lorries and, of course, builders if you are living on an expanding urbanisation. Privacy allows all parts of the garden to be used unseen.

2. A windbreak from hot summer winds and cold winter winds. In many situations it will be impossible to grow tender sub-tropical and tropical plants without such year-round shelter.

3. Shade on the north side for summer terraces and plants that are best out of direct sunlight.

4. A continuous outer wall of green from a hedge or climbers trained up walls, panels or a wire mesh fence. Some are in flower for many months of the year.

5. A natural transition from your garden to external vistas.

6. A contribution to personal security if combined with high gates, but do select gates that enhance the appearance of your house and the neighbourhood.

7. Reduction of the noise transmitted to or from adjacent properties.

8. Encourage wildlife, especially birds that roost or nest.

INTERNAL DIVIDING HEDGES

Hedges or fences of various heights can be useful within the garden for the following reasons:

1. To help divide the garden up into a number of zones or mini gardens.

2. To provide internal screens and windbreaks, for instance around the pool, the Jacuzzi, an eating terrace, cosy corners, a seat for winter days, the tennis court, carport, orchard, the children's garden or the vegetable garden.

3. To line the drive. A long curved drive lined with a well-clipped hedge can be an impressive entrance to a larger property.

4. To add interest and intrigue as one wanders from one part of the garden to another, passing under green arches and through verdant – perhaps perfumed – passage ways.

5. To provide the basis of a maze in a large garden.

6. To surround formal flower-beds. Rose, hibiscus and perennial beds can be well presented in this way.

7. To edge pathways or around a lawn.

8. To give shelter for wildlife such as birds, lizards, insects, etc.

SOME POSSIBLE HEDGING PLANTS

There are many plants available for different types of hedges, including the following:

1. For thick high boundary hedges – cypress, thuja, oleander, pittosporum, privet, gandula, bay, berberis, lantana, oranges and hibiscus. A three-metre high prickly pear cactus hedge will really keep people and animals out.

2. Colourful climbers for fences – bignonias, bougainvilla, jasmine, plumbago, honeysuckle, Brazilian flame vine, solanum, morning glory, and ivies.

3. For medium height internal hedges/screens – box, bottlebrush, euonymus, pittosporum, lantana, teucrium and hibiscus.

4. For low internal hedges – box, lavender, rosemary, euonymus, rue and euphorbia milii if in a sub-tropical area.

SHAPING HEDGES

Hedges need to be regularly trimmed to stimulate dense foliage. Once dense, some of the hedging plants listed lend themselves to topiary and can be clipped into interesting shapes – sloping sides, curving tops, arches, balls, birds sitting on the hedge, etc. Hedges flower less if kept tightly clipped.

GATES

The choice of gate has a major impact on the appearance of a property from the road and also on the style of garden inside the gate. The choices include the following:

1. Stylish – traditional cast and wrought iron gate in a whole range of simple or artistic designs.

2. Urban – the solid sheet metal gates now in fashion. They can be constructed from a single sheet – or eight smaller interwoven bowed sheets – to create a pseudo woven effect. Some single sheet gates have raised designs that add interest and style.

3. Wooden – the four or five-barred gate most suitable for natural surroundings, or an elegant solid wood gate set in an archway. Normally they have a small inset pedestrian door. Traditionally varnished, they can add style, security and the image of entering a large townhouse or country estate.

Choose what goes best with your property and the style of garden.

2.11 CREATE WINDBREAKS AGAINST STRONG WINDS

Many Spanish gardens are in exposed positions and windbreaks are required to cope with regular strong gusty winds that can spoil your enjoyment of an otherwise attractive garden by making it chilly to sit out in the winter or on a summer evening after a scorching day on the beach.

Winds can quickly dry out the garden soil and flowerpots and evaporate water off the surface of a pond or pool, make it difficult to control the barbecue, roll pots over and cause damage to plants – even uprooting or snapping off, mature trees.

Strong winds can make it impossible, or at least very difficult, to grow more tender plants, so think about the need for windbreaks at an early stage in your garden design.

POSSIBILITIES

Here are 15 suggestions for both natural and constructed windbreaks:

1. Build boundary walls rather than installing wire mesh fences, and make sure they are strong enough to withstand the buffeting of gales and heavy rainfall.

2. If the builder has provided wire mesh fences, cover them with shrub, cane, wood or plastic slat fencing panels or strong closely woven cloth. This creates an instant windbreak while climbers on the fence – or a hedge in front – are growing.

3. Site the eating and resting terraces on the down-wind side of the house.

4. Retain any existing trees. Trim the tops and train them to grow sideways. If one or two windswept trees survive, consider keeping them as attractive features even though they give little shelter. Their shape may add atmosphere to the future garden and a reminder of why the estate is called windy ridge.

5. If a small copse of holm oak or pines has survived, keep them as a valuable windbreak. If you consider felling trees on the perimeter to create space, or in the centre of the garden to create a woodland glade, recognise that you might be changing the aerofoil characteristics of the copse and even creating a chimney effect in the centre. Both may cause trees to fall in a strong gale especially if the soil is soft after heavy rains. The shape and leaning of natural trees in the vicinity of your house will give an idea of the severity of past gales.

6. If you have a large garden with no natural windbreak, consider planting a two, three or even four rows of trees along the windward boundaries. Plant either evergreens alone or evergreens with deciduous flowering or fruit trees on the down wind side of the evergreens. Ensure that all trees are well staked and guyed from day one. If they are in a very exposed position, re-guy as they grow.

7. Construct Dutch-style reinforced glass windbreaks at strategic points in the garden that you can sit behind and still enjoy the best garden views. Plant some aromatic and colourful plants downwind of the screen.

8. Similarly, glaze in open covered terraces on the windy sides of the house so that you can sit in the sun and enjoy views on the windiest of days.

9. Plant internal hedges to give shelter to terraces, seats, tender plants and the swimming-pool.

Lanzarote sheltering vines

10. Build internal screen walls as alternatives to hedges.

11. Build a garden naya or an outdoor kitchen (much loved by Spaniards).

12. If you have a pool or Jacuzzi, invest in a strongly constructed cover to conserve the heat and reduce water evaporation. If you can afford an all-weather swimming cover, you can also try to grow some semitropical plants inside.

13. Low growing plants can be protected by a semicircle of rocks. One sees ancient vineyards and melons protected in this way around the Mediterranean costas and islands.

14. Protect young plants with cloches. Five or seven litre-capacity water bottles with the bottom cut out and held down by canes in the middle and around the outside are an inexpensive solution.

15. If totally demoralised, move to a more sheltered situation! Gardening should be a joy as well as a challenge, and some challenges can eat up retirement years rather than enhance them.

2.12 ENHANCE VISTAS BEYOND THE GARDEN

If you are lucky you will have one or more good views of the sea, a lake, mountains, rolling countryside, forests, a distant village, a castle or across a picturesque valley – or your best view might only be of interestingly shaped and coloured roofs. Whatever they are, ensure that you make the best of them when designing and constructing the garden. Here are a few suggestions:

1. Lop or remove trees that block the view if you are certain the middle view will not be spoilt soon by high-rise building.

2. Offer to pay for the felling of a tree or two on adjacent land if they block out what could be your best view.

3. Plant and trim boundary hedges and trees to create a frame that draws one to the best views.

4. Site regularly-used terraces and garden seats where you will be able to enjoy the views for many hours each day, throughout the year, and from both sunny and shaded situations.

5. Plant the garden so that the internal vistas become harmonious foregrounds for the distant views.

6. If the land falls away beyond your property and nothing sticks up from below to mar the view, plant nothing. Perhaps even make one edge of your pool the effective link between your garden and the sea, valley or seascape beyond.

7. Don't forget that the view from the pool is important. If you cannot look into un-built territories, then plant the surrounding hedge or shrubs so that they block out surrounding buildings but enable tree or mountaintops to be seen.

8. Do what you can to persuade later developers or owners to site new houses and keep rooflines low, so as to not destroy or seriously spoil your best views, especially if you have enjoyed them for many years.

Yes, it can be difficult, but with a little thought we have managed to improve two views and keep one. Unfortunately, a new house now blocks out the fourth and the western sunsets that we enjoyed for 15 years. However, a fast growing acacia soon blocked out most of the house.

2.13 CHOOSE COMPATIBLE AND COMFORTABLE GARDEN FURNITURE

Chairs, seats, tables, drinks trolleys, sun loungers, hammocks, sky chairs, umbrellas, lights and drying frames are all essential features of a garden and penthouse terrace designed for outside living. Buy the best that you can afford, recognising that the quality, style and colour of garden furniture can enhance or mar the aesthetics of a wonderful garden. Ask yourself the following questions:

Does the furniture we brought with us really look good in the garden or do we need to think about replacing all or part of it? What style, material and colour of furniture would best suit the part of the garden where it is required? Within your budget what would be the most comfortable, last the longest, weather the least and require minimum maintenance?

Visit a few garden centres and furniture stores that specialise in selling Spanish and imported ranges of furniture. Look at wood, metal, wicker, rattan and plastic chairs, seats, tables, etc. Recognise that:

• Alloy furniture needs less maintenance than that constructed from steel tubing. Some are designed to look like traditional cast iron work.

• White wicker furniture might look elegant by the pool but clash with the more informal areas of the garden.

• Winter-weathered plastic can soon be cleaned but teak takes longer to sandpaper and re-oil. Cane and wicker are least resistant to damp conditions. Paints are now available for plastic and wooden furniture in the shade of green that blends in best with your garden.

• Surfaces of plastic tables can be plain or designed. The surfaces of wooden or metal tables can be tiled, of marble, mosaic, stone or glass.

• A table for six can easily be expanded to one for 10,12 or even 14 by cutting out an oval shaped tabletop from plywood or chipboard. Split in half, it is easier to transport around the garden and store in the garage.

• Hammocks and sky chairs for hanging between or in trees can be of cotton or synthetic material. A double hammock is generally more comfortable for single use than a single hammock.

• Garden umbrellas now come in a wide range of sizes, with metal or wooden posts. Some have a winding mechanism for raising and lowering the umbrella.

• Shade can be provided not only by large umbrellas but also by awnings, roofed wood- or metal-framed gazebos, and roofed or thickly plant-covered pergolas.

• Garden seats in cosy corners can be easily constructed from natural rock with a comfortable seat.

• A softly upholstered swing seat may be more useful than a rigid, harder seat.

• A seat round the trunk of a tree can be more useful and look better than a raised flowerbed, which would be difficult to keep colourful in the deep shade.

• Elegant iron-framed pavilions found in old majestic Spanish gardens are again becoming popular, especially where a wonderful coastal or mountain vista can be seen from a vantage point in the garden.

• The colour of the cushions for chairs and seats, the covers of pavilions, gazebos, umbrellas and table clothes are seen more than the frames – so take as much care over the colour scheme in your garden as you would over your lounge.

• The most expensive is not always the best to look at or the most comfortable. It is most important to test the comfort of all chairs and seats in the shop before buying.

• Lastly, the washing line! An umbrella frame takes up the least room and can be easily removed and stored during party days.

2.14 USE POTS AND CONTAINERS CREATIVELY

Pots and containers can add much to the ambiance and completeness of a Spanish garden and are, of course, the basis of gardening on apartment and penthouse terraces, in enclosed patios and in minimalist gardens designed to have few or no plants.

Luckily, a wide choice is available with different materials, colours, designs, glazing, and sizes – some for hanging on walls or from ceilings, others for standing firmly on the ground, from tiny pots to terracotta wine and water storage jars standing several metres high. Self-watering pots with a built-in water reservoir are now widely available.

Pots and containers can look attractive, either filled with plants or empty, strategically placed as individual pots or in interesting groups.

There are, however, some general do's and don'ts as summarized below:

SOME DO'S

Before you go out to buy the first pot or container, decide why and where you need them, which will be used for plants and which will be used empty, what varieties of plants you plan to use and whether you prefer internally or externally glazed pots. The latter when filled with plants will dry out less quickly than traditional, basic, terracotta pots.

You should then size the pots you need and know the numbers of each size required. Consider whether you want to put a single plant in each pot or create a more dramatic display by planting several similar plants or a mix of compatible plants in a single container.

Before buying, visit a garden centre to check on the sizes of pots your chosen plants will be in. Be sure your new pots are large enough to give the roots of the plants room for growth when transplanted.

Then visit one or two pot shops and consider what colours, finishes and shapes would best blend in with the rest of the garden in their planned positions, which pot finishes will reflect sunlight and surrounding colours and which will be non-reflective and show their pure colours. Then consider whether a single design would look best or whether you should try and mix the heights, widths, shapes, surface designs, etc.

If the display of pots you are selecting from is at a garden centre, place some plants in them before making your final decision. If you are buying in a pot shop, take a few plants with you to try out there..

Consider the question of seasonal or permanent plantings. Both may well have a place in your garden. Seasonal plantings include:

Autumn – pansies, kalanchoas and carnations.

Winter – poinsettias, azaleas, bulbs or cyclamen

Spring – primulas, begonias and bulbs.

Summer – petunias, portulacas, begonias.

Permanent plantings embrace a wide range of plants that do well in pots, provided they are placed appropriately. Our favourites include the following:

In the sun, for instance on a terrace or low wall – zonal and ivy leaved pelargoniums/ geraniums, succulents, argyranthemums, herbs.

In the semi shade, for instance in the naya or on a north facing front step – fuchsias, aechemia, begonia rex, streptocarpus, gardenias, camellias, azaleas and hydrangeas.

In the shade – ficus, philodendron, plectranthus, pothos, hostas, spider plants and calathea.

Make sure you fill pots and containers with a compost that is water retaining but well draining. It is a good idea to add a little water absorbing gel into the bottom third of the compost before planting up.

Don't forget that planted pots will need regular watering – once or twice a day if placed in the sun during the summer. A typical compost can absorb its own weight of water but lose it within 24 hours by evaporation from an unglazed terracotta pot. They are therefore not suitable for absentee gardeners unless planted up with drought resistant plants, such as succulents and cacti, or replanted on the first day of each visit.

Obviously, there is no problem if an absentee gardener is prepared to run a drip irrigation watering system to each pot. There is only a limited amount of natural food in potting compost, so feed potted plants once a month in the winter and once a week in the summer.

It's a good idea to place empty pots in groups to create artistic features. Such groupings can look especially attractive on penthouse roofs, around the pool, on large areas of stone chippings, on walls, in corners or niches of patios or on the elegant tiled courtyard of a minimalist garden. Be sure to weigh them down to stop them from blowing over in strong winds. Consider making a water feature out of an urn or pitcher on a terrace or flowing into a pond.

Plant pots don't have to stand vertically. They can look very attractive when laid on their side – with a plant coming out of the mouth – on a terrace, a flowerbed or rockery.

SOME DON'TS

Most plants in pots need regular watering. If this will be a chore or something you are liable to forget, then control the number of pots or select larger glazed pots that will dry out less quickly than unglazed terraco-tta pots. Other don'ts include:

Don't create clashes between adjacent plastic, terracotta, and glazed pots. Why not place plastic pots inside other more attractive pots, making sure they have drainage holes? Your display will look better and the pots will not dry out as quickly.

Don't leave annuals in pots in the full sun. They will survive better in dappled shade, and brighten up such areas at the same time.

Don't forget that the heat reflected off terraces can dry the underneath of the leaves of plants at the same time that the heat from the sun dries the tops – especially when pots are placed on dark coloured terraces.

Don't place pots of bulbs in deep shade as they will go leggy and grow weak. Start them off in a totally dark cellar and then bring them out into semi-shade.

Don't forget to drill holes in pots that will be left empty to prevent them filling with rainwater that can go sour and attract mosquitoes.

Don't forget to give all pots a spring clean.

Don't allow plants to become root bound in pots. Check them annually and pot on when roots reach the inner sides of the pots and are growing out of the bottom.

Don't leave diseased plants in pots, especially when near others. Remove them to a nursery area if you think that they can be saved, or put them in a plastic bag in the rubbish bin (not on the compost heap).

Don't leave plants to die in pots or containers visible from the road when you leave the house for long periods. It is an obvious sign of an absent owner.

2.15 CHOOSE ORNAMENTS CAREFULLY

Carefully chosen and placed ornaments add interest and charm to many gardens, enhancing the natural beauty of plants or even replacing them in minimalist absentee non-gardener gardens. However, tasteless ornaments can turn an otherwise charming garden into an eyesore.

An amazing range of sculptures and concrete figures are on sale at garden centres and pottery shops. It is obvious that tastes and the skill of the sculptors, mould makers and painters vary widely. No doubt ornaments turn up in gardens as presents, instant holiday buys, arm twisting by children or additions to an addictive collection.

Our advice is to try and select ornaments that do something for you – and be sure to place them in situations where they truly add to the overall charm, mystique and aesthetics of your garden and, most importantly, enhance rather than overpower nature.

2.16 PROVIDE FOR THE ELDERLY, IMFIRM AND IMPAIRED

Many foreigners retire to Spain and take up gardening as an active hobby – hoping to tend their gardens into their eighties or even nineties. But as each decade passes, many find it harder do all the propagation and maintenance work unaided and need the help of a gardener.

Even so, they can still continue to potter, if only to care for a special plant collection in the garden or greenhouse and, with less time spent physically working in the garden, there is at last more time to just wander around and sit in the garden and enjoy the results of many years of dedicated labour.

It could be your partner is unable to garden for one reason or another. He or she – as well as a family member or visitor – has impaired sight or movement but would love to enjoy the perfumes, beauty and feel of the garden as much as possible. Keep this in mind when designing your garden, and incorporate special features to make it amenable to the elderly and impaired – or construct the garden in a way that would allow such features to be added at a later date without having to totally redesign it.

Consider the following actions and features:

To enable safe movement around the garden:
- Ensure that the surface and slopes of all paths are safe.
- Make paths wide enough for wheelchairs, walking frames and two persons walking side-by-side.
- Add edges to paths to help sight impaired walk with a stick.
- Construct shallow riser steps or gentle slopes.
- Fit handrails to both sides of slopes and steps, around the most colourful and perfumed flowerbeds, and the fishpond.
- Repair any looseness or cracks as soon as they occur.
- Remove any prickly or spiky plants well away from paths and terraces, or preferably have none.
- Cut back all branches of bushes and trees that could cause eye injuries or catch on clothing.
- Remove trees and posts in or alongside paths or terraces to prevent collisions.
- Position hose reels away from the main thoroughfares, and always leave coiled up.
- Position flower pots off the edge of terraces so they cannot be tripped over.
- Sweep up fallen leaves and fruit daily. They can be slippery even in dry weather.
- Ensure that garden tools and children's playthings are not left around.
- Have the garden electricity circuits checked to ensure that they are safe and the wire cannot be grabbed onto and pulled loose.

To enjoy smells and textures:
- Plant perfumed and aromatic plants that sight-impaired persons would especially enjoy.
- Include jasmine, lemon, rosemary, thyme, curry, alliums, lavender, mint, scented lilies, but avoid poisonous plants such as datura.

To enjoy sounds:
- Install fountains and bird tables, baths and boxes that attract birdsong and add interest to all gardens, especially for persons who have the time to sit and listen. Visually impaired persons often have especially sensitive hearing.
- Hang wind chimes that make pleasing sounds in a gentle breeze, but be sure to test the sounds in the shop before buying!
- Install loudspeakers on a cosy terrace or in the greenhouse so that favourite tunes can be played and the sound adjusted by the listener.

To enjoy the best vistas:
- Construct or place safe, non-tipping, heavily-constructed seats at various vantage points around the garden – preferably in the shade for hot days and in un-shaded spots for overcast days.
- Provide sturdy tables for drinking and eating, reading, writing, and doing hobbies.
- Install a two-way walky talky system from the house so that beverages can be requested, messages passed on or assistance called for.

To be able to continue doing some gardening:
- Recognise that even gentle gardening helps keep one physically and mentally fit – but equally that one needs to keep fit for gardening. Take regular walks within your limitations and do some stretching exercises before commencing to garden.
- Purchase lightweight, ergonomically designed tools, such as Fiskars designs.
- Build raised beds in the garden and in the greenhouse at a height that will enable work to be done while sitting down. Make the tops of the sidewalls easy to sit on. Even consider building beds as a raised table with room for legs beneath, with a potting table the same height alongside or a raised bed in the shape of a horse shoe that allows the entire surface to be worked by turning on a seat or in a wheel chair.
- Stock the garden with small - and medium - height plants that can be tended without undue stretching.
- Move to a smaller property or apartment and start to specialise in container and window box gardening – or have the gardener maintain the garden and enjoy your personal container/window box area.
- Increase the area of terraces and reduce the number of large shrubs.
- Revert to small - scale vegetable and fruit growing in pots, window boxes and containers and don't attempt to continue to work a large vegetable plot or orchard.

2.17 PROVIDE FOR COLLECTING AND CHANNELLING RAINWATER

Gardeners in Spain are very glad when the rain comes. Plants in the garden immediately look refreshed, potted plants on the naya can be moved out into the rain for a cleansing shower, and the hours spent on watering is reduced for a time.

However, unless the garden is designed to collect and channel rain water to where it is most needed, much water is wasted when there is a heavy downpour, especially during the autumn and spring gota frias. Precious water seeps down to the water table, runs out through the gate and pipes in the garden wall or over a boundary terrace. This is a great loss as plants are better when watered with rainwater than with chlorinated domestic water, and rainwater is free.

To save rainwater, you can do the following:

1. Fix guttering on at least part of the roof and run the water to a storage tank or a large water butt.

2. Slope paths and terraces to channel water to flower beds, the vegetable plot and pond.

3. If necessary, build a raised edge along paths to improve the channelling.

4. Edge receiving flower-beds with small rocks so as to distribute the water evenly, rather than allowing a torrent to make a channel and cause erosion.

5. Edge the entire garden area with at least a 30cm wall to keep excess water on your plot and avoid overflowing into the neighbour's plot or the street. Yes, it will flood a little, but this will soon soak down into the soil when the rain stops, providing you take the following precautions:

• Construct some paths and terraces with stone chippings laid on porous plastic sheeting. The water will soak away quicker than through sun-baked, hard earth.

• Mulch shrub beds and around trees.

• Keep bare soil loose by hoeing. This will allow the earth to take up rain-water more quickly and reduce the evaporation during the dry spells.

• Plant closely to reduce the areas of earth that is baked by direct sun light.

6. If the land slopes, construct a network of channels and pipes to move rainwater to where it is most needed.

7. If you plan to have a long, hard-surface drive, consider designing it to channel water to a storage tank. Slope the drive from either end to the middle and sideways so that water runs down the middle – or into a channel along one side – first into a settling tank and then into a storage tank. From there you can irrigate the garden by gravity or by using a pump.

2.18 AVOID UNNECESSARY MAINTENANCE WORK

Maintenance is largely self-imposed. It is directly related to the complexity of your garden design and the extent of your interest in gardening. What a dedicated gardener will accept as

25 MOST TIME-CONSUMING MAINTENANCE TASKS

The 25 most time-consuming maintenance tasks	Is this required in your garden?			Tick your top 10 areas for reducing maintenance work
	Yes	Partially	No	
1. Cutting and caring for lawns.				
2. Weekly sweeping up of pine needles.				
3. Regular deadheading daisy-like flowers.				
4. Cleaning up fallen carob beans and olives.				
5. Pruning and spraying fruit trees and cleaning up fallen fruit.				
6. Cleaning weeds from cracks in unsealed crazy paving and poorly laid chippings.				
7. Trimming hedges.				
8. Cleaning large terraces around swimming pools, especially if surrounded by dirty plants.				
9. Weeding a large organic vegetable plot.				
10. Annual clean up of an intensely planted garden.				
11. Cutting back spring/summer flowering perennials.				
12. Daily watering summer annuals.				
13. Caring for a large number of plants in pots.				
14. Painting walls not covered by plants.				
16. Hand watering with a watering can or hose.				
17. Weeding rockeries.				
18. Trimming herbs after flowering.				
19. Growing plants from seed.				
20. Propogating from cuttings				
21. Weeding sparsely planted and un-mulched flower beds.				

25 MOST TIME-CONSUMING MAINTENANCE TASKS (continued)

The 25 most time-consuming maintenance tasks	Is this required in your garden?			Tick your top 10 areas for reducing maintenance work
	Yes	Partially	No	
22. Keeping on top of the compost heap.				
23. Weeding driveways, paths and chippings.				
24. Cutting fronds off palm trees.				
25. Heavy pruning of fast growing trees like acacias.				
NUMBER OF TICKS IN COLUMN				

a reasonable amount of work in return for a colourful and perfumed garden will be regarded as an unacceptable amount of work by a non-gardener.

It is important to consider the maintenance work you are creating for yourself at an early stage in the design and development of your garden – as well as at the time of your annual garden audit – as even dedicated gardeners will be looking to reduce the amount of work required as they grow older

How maintenance intense is your current or future garden and how might you reduce the maintenance work required? Complete the following questionnaire and take note of the general observations given for various scores. Reflect on the garden that you are designing – or already have – and go back to the questionnaire to confirm or decide on the top 10 areas for reducing the amount of ongoing maintenance work. Finally, decide how you could achieve that by redesigning some aspects of the garden.

To assess the extent of the maintenance work in your garden, add up the number of times that you have answered 'yes' and multiply by two. Add this score to your number of 'partially' answers. Finally compare your scores with the statements below.

FINAL SCORE	OBSERVATIONS FOR ABSENTEE GARDENERS	OBSERVATIONS FOR RESIDENT GARDENERS
37 - 50	Take on a good gardener fast!	Probably the garden of a dedicated gardener. If you are not one, find a good gardener fast.
25 - 36	Decide what can be delayed until you retire or take on a reliable jobbing gardener.	Probably a balanced garden for you if you like gardening, and not too onerous for most employed gardeners.
13 - 24	Probably a manageable and satisfying garden.	Probably a very manageable but basic garden.
1 - 10	An ideal garden for a non-gardener but perhaps unexciting.	An ideal garden for a non-gardener but perhaps unexciting.

Remember that there always needs to be sensible balance between the colour, perfume and beauty of your garden and the work required to achieve it if you are to enjoy life in Spain to the full.

2.19 ECOLOGICAL FRIENDLY PRACTICES

There is one further decision to be made before you lay out the garden, prepare the soil or add the first plants, and that is – to what extent will you manage your new garden along ecological/organic lines? There are three options.

1. Inorganic Practices, using manufactured inorganic chemical fertilizers, insecticides, fungicides or weed killers that gradually replaced traditional methods of improving soils and combating pests and diseases from the 1950's onwards.

2. Organic Practices, using environmentally friendly traditional natural methods or the now widely available biological/ecological products for enriching and improving the structure of soils, preventing and controlling pests and diseases and controlling weeds. Search out the safer products in garden centres, horticultural shops, agricultural cooperatives or on web sites such as the very useful (www.trabe.net).

3. A part way house between the above two approaches.

We follow natural practices in our holistic garden for growing flowers, fruit, vegetables and poultry. The benefits include a safer environment for the family, pets, beneficial insects and reptiles.

The choice is now there, but if you decide to go down the inorganic chemical route you should be aware that you will destroy beneficial insects and micro organisms as well as those that cause problems. There is evidence that once you start to use chemicals in a major way, the natural food chain balance will be disturbed, which could result in:

- Fewer bees in the garden to pollinate flowers.
- Fewer butterflies.
- Fewer beneficial insects that normally feed off other insects.
- Fewer frogs and toads and lizards that feed off slugs and insects in the garden pond and rockery.
- Fewer birds that keep down unwanted insects in the flowerbeds and hedges, visit the garden to forage for food or nest in the shrubs or hedges.
- Fewer worms in the soil to work in fallen vegetable material, manure and compost.
- Fruit and vegetables can be contaminated by residual chemicals.

So decide now, in principle, whether or not your garden will be a chemical free zone. Will pests and diseases be normally treated with ecological/organic solutions? Will wildlife be actively attracted to the garden? Will excess land be allowed to develop as a natural area?

Fortunately, every year more and more products are available for the gardener who decides to go the eco/organic route. See sections 6.6 and 6.7.

PART THREE

ADD INTERESTING FEATURES

Features such as ponds, swimming pools, rockeries, vegetables plots, orchards, cooking facilities and natural areas can enhance the enjoyment of your garden.

3.1 A COLOURFUL ROCKERY

A rockery *(un jardincito rocoso)*, a popular feature of many Spanish gardens, is a sloping or flat mini-garden constructed of rocks and earth and with plants planted between the rocks. The rocks retain moisture and provide shade for the roots of the plants.

A rockery can be interesting and colourful throughout the year as a wide range of flowering and foliage plants grow well in the microclimate of a rockery, whether by the seashore or high up on a mountainside, though naturally some of the plants will change.

It is a good way to use the existing rocks of an area of a natural hillside, an old dry stone terrace wall or the rocks churned up by the builder. Of course, if you have no free rocks on site a lorry load can be easily purchased. A rockery is also a good way to hide a pile of inherited builders rubble.

If you have a split-level garden, a rockery can provide a natural transition from one level to the other and, when well constructed and planted, a rockery requires relatively little watering, weeding and no feeding.

TYPES OF ROCKERY

Rockeries can range from a mini-rockery in a stone basin to a large-scale rockery in a mountainside garden. The following are possible and all can be attractive:

1. A planted front of a dry stonewall. If the wall already exists, push earth and succulents that are drought resistant into the holes. If you are building a new dry stonewall, plant up between rocks while building. In this case you can ensure a bed of soil for each plant within the wall.

2. A rockery on top of a dry stonewall. Plant the front as above.

3. An interesting sloping surround for a raised up swimming-pool.

4. A clean surround for the swimming pool terrace – as most rockery plants do not drop leaves and flowers that could blow into the pool.

5. Either side of steps or a zigzagging path if you have a major difference in levels at some point in the garden.

6. A natural outcrop of rock.

7. A rock garden that you can walk around or even over. This would be a good way of covering over a large heap of builder's rubble. In such cases, start by covering the rubble with 10cm of soil and then watering well to work soil into the spaces within the pile of rubble. Then add a further 25cm of soil before starting construction.

8. A covering for the natural slope of the garden – not only for attractiveness and colour but also to use natural features, control rain water run off, and as an alternative to less interesting terrace walls.

9. The easiest treatment for a wild rock strewn-mountain slope that may also be covered with natural herbs, alpines, bulbs and shrubs.

10. A natural surround for a pond, particularly one with a cascade or waterfall.

11. A rockery spiral or snail that offers a greater depth of soil at the centre – and the north side will provide a degree of shade for the roots of plants.

12. A miniature rockery built up in a stone trough or sink as an interesting stand-alone feature on a terrace.

SUCCESS FACTORS

Decide where a rockery will have most impact and interest in relation to the rest of the garden. Will it be a stand-alone feature, a mini- garden, or a transition between one part of the garden and another. Decide on the width and vertical fall to be built up or used if on an existing slope.

• Have a clear vision of the style of rockery you intend to build before you start construction, whether you intend to create a terraced effect with lines of rocks, have a wild mountainside-effect with randomly placed rocks, enhance a rocky outcrop or construct a combination of compatible styles.

• Weed the area thoroughly before you start, otherwise the weeds will thrive in the microclimate of the finished rockery. Construct with natural-looking rocks. In general, weathered rocks look more natural than clean virgin rocks just blown out of the rock face of a quarry. Try and obtain a mix of sizes. Check that you can move the largest safely or obtain help.

• Build up the rockery from the bottom. Work the base of each rock into the earth until it looks natural as an individual rock and in relation to adjacent rocks. Ensure that each rock is stable and then level the earth between rocks.

• Add or remove soil until you achieve the best effect. If you have a heavy clay soil, mix sand and compost into the soil as you progress. Most rockery plants thrive in a moist but well-draining soil and are often reasonably drought resistant.

• Aim to plant appropriate plants in every gap between rocks. Plant as you go, in order to place the end of roots or cuttings under rocks or when the construction work is complete or a combination of both.

• Stand back every so often and consider the rockery as a whole. Ask yourself, "Does it already begin to look good? Does it look like a miniature natural landscape? Am I making the best of the lie of the land and enhancing natural or built features such as steps, a pond or waterfall? What will it look like when the plants start to spread and mature?"

Answer these questions yourself and adjust accordingly. The fine-tuning of your rockery will inevitably be a process of trial and error.

Cover the earth around plants with a mulch of small rocks, fine stone chippings or volcanic ash. Many rockery plants can rot if waterlogged around the stem and surface roots.

Be prepared to be ruthless with expansive plants every few years, especially on small and medium- sized rockeries.

WHAT PLANTS ARE APPROPRIATE?

A wide range of plants, as shown in the box below (see sections 4.4, 4.5 and 4.14):

TYPICAL TYPES OF PLANT	LOW LEVEL ROCKERY (below 400 metres)	HIGH LEVEL ROCKERY (above 400 metres)
Short and limited spread.	Succulents, dwarf irises, thyme and gazanias.	Frost resistant succulents jonquils and herbs.
Short and spreading.	Creeping thyme, verbena, lotus, messems and oregano.	Purple and white trailing lantana.
Medium height and limited spread.	Cacti, sage, succulents and ajania.	Frost resistant cacti and common sage
Medium height and spreading.	Some rock roses, arctotis, cascading rosemary, chamomile, santolina, freesias and cacti.	Dwarf junipers, azaleas, Heathers and rock roses
Taller but limited spread.	Some rock roses, irises sages, aeoniums, rue, and alliums.	Dwarf conifers.
Taller but spreading.	Lavender, lantanas and pelargonium graveolens.	Agave and brooms.

Decide on the type and size of rockery you want. Do you prefer a level, mixed or graded from front-to-back height of foliage (for example, low succulents at the front and taller cacti or herbs at the back)? Do you want a semi-wild or neat rockery?

Would you like to achieve broad sweeps of colour, using one variety of plant, or a kaleidoscope effect by mixing a large number of types of plants? Do you want your plants to smother the rocks or remain in the spaces between? Do you want to develop a collection of one type of plant, for example succulents or cacti.

Whatever your choice, aim for a range of interesting forms, colours, flowers and textures of leaves.

MAINTENANCE REQUIRED

As with the rest of your garden, a rockery needs regular care. Below is a maintenace list:

1. Seasonal deadheading and cutting back of dying flowered stems.

2. An annual cut back or trim of plants that are starting to outgrow their allotted space or remove/reposition one or two rocks to give the most attractive plants space to spread. Ensure that you use cuttings to propagate new plants.

3. Removal of plants that have just become too large and dominate or upset the balance of the rockery.

4. Weeding, but relatively little if you have used plenty of rocks and close planting. Remove weeds while small. It will be more difficult if their roots are allowed to become established under rocks or between the roots of established plants.

5. A twice-a-year clear out of any accumulated debris – dead leaves, twigs, etc. – from between the plants and rocks. Add to the compost heap.

6. Remove and replace any dead plants.

7. Top up the rock or volcanic chippings still visible around plants.

8. Take cuttings to propagate new plants to use as in-fills, replacements, to use on a new rockery area or to swap with a friend for a rockery plant that you do not have. There are an enormous number of interesting succulents and herbs.

9. Watering of least drought resistant plants during prolonged dry spells.

3.2 PONDS, FOUNTAINS AND SPRINGS

Ponds, fountains and springs can add a special dimension to all gardens in Spain – from the smallest terrace or patio to the large landscaped garden. They are relatively simple to install, have a number of benefits that no other features can offer and can be fascinating features throughout the year.

They create an interesting focal point, one that draws your attention – especially if situated in a quiet area or set against a pleasing backdrop. The sight and sound of running and splashing water has a calming and cooling effect, and watching wildlife such as fish, frogs, toads, damsel flies, dragonflies and visiting birds can be very stimulating to all ages. There is also the added satisfaction of breeding fish and terrapins, although the latter are voracious vegetarians and pond plants can disappear overnight.

The creation of a humid area gives you the opportunity to grow water plants, some of them very beautiful and spectacular, and with care and a little luck many can be grown from seeds in the Spanish spring and summer climate. In some gardens ferns will grow in shady situations.

WHERE TO PLACE THEM

They can provide very effective centrepieces for a terrace, a mini garden, an inner patio, or a total garden. They have immediate visual and mental impact, especially when the water is playing or running.

For maximum impact and benefit site them:

- Where they can be seen from the spot where you regularly eat, rest, read, take a siesta or work – especially from the kitchen or study.
- In less visible places where they will add interest to a stroll around the garden – perhaps within an enclosed mini garden or patio.
- Alongside or within a secret haven within the garden.

If you are lucky enough to have a natural spring flowing for part or the whole of the year, make this the centrepiece of a special mini water garden.

FORMAL OR INFORMAL DESIGNS

Chose a design that matches or compliments the style of your house, garden and overall environment. A design in this context, whether simple or complex, includes shape, size, colour of rock and other materials, a natural or manufactured look.

We have a well head with an internal fountain and a pond – with three spout fountains coming out of dry stone walls at either end of the pond – as the eye-catching centre piece of the main part of our garden. Each is built and surrounded by natural stone from the local mountain. The designs are natural and rustic, stimulated by traditional artisan constructions seen in rural Spanish villages.

Nearby neighbours have just the opposite. Being absentee non- gardeners, their garden is wisely Spartan – with large areas of stone terraces and raked stone chippings that match the light cream colour of the house. There are no climbing plants around the house because the pathways constructed by the builders have left no gap for planting. A formal, simple, no-fuss, cast-simulated stone fountain set in the centre of a terrace adds interest to an otherwise boring front garden. Anything fussy would look out of place. Around the corner, a carved marble fountain looks equally at ease in a more heavily-planted garden with mature conifers and shrubs. It´s pump is solar powered.

A hillside finca that we recently visited was lucky enough to have a natural spring dripping out of the mountainside. This was channelled into an old earthenware pipe that fed a large pool and then overflowed into a natural rock channel feeding a bog garden – very simple, natural and effective.

Another house, 600 metres up in the hills, had a large shady terrace under large palm and rubber plants. In the centre, a weathered, imitation, animal drinking trough, with a continuous trickle of water from a spout at one end, looked perfect set in a sea of healthy ferns in pots.

Many garden centres are well stocked with a very wide range of fountains, prefabricated ponds and cascades and self-contained water features for the garden, small terrace or patio. Study them carefully and consider what you could construct yourself before making a purchase. In either case, construct or buy what will fit naturally and harmoniously into your garden.

SPRINGS

An imitation spring can be constructed with water coming out of a bank, a dry stonewall or a patio wall. The water can either fall into a catchment tray, a channel or stony stream bed that then runs through part of the garden or into a pond from where a submersed pump recycles the water.

PONDS

Attractive ponds can range from a small, one-square-metre pool in the flowerbed of a small garden to a mini lake in a 3000-square-metre garden.

The three most popular ways of constructing a pond are as follows:

a. Buy a moulded glass-fibre or pressed plastic pond that can be sunk into the ground or be built up around. This is easy and speedy to install. The drawbacks are the limited range of shapes, sizes, and depths available. Also, the imitation rock effects of some of the surrounds and inbuilt or matching cascades are not very aesthetic.

b. Dig out a hole of any size, depth and shape and line with a sheet of butyl   pond liner laid over a sand base to stop any jagged stones in the earth from puncturing the liner when it is filled with water. The drawbacks are the folds that develop in the sheet in irregular shaped ponds and the life expectancy of the liner, typically quoted as ten to fifteen years.

c. Construct a reinforced concrete pond. This is the most expensive and time-consuming method and most gardeners would want to contract the work. Cracks and leaks can develop if the concrete shell is insufficiently thick, waterproofed and reinforced – especially around curves.

Each type of construction needs to be edged with terrace slabs for a formal finish, wooden duckboards for a semiformal finish or large rocks and a rockery to give a natural effect.

CASCADES AND WATERFALLS

The sight and sound of a sheet or spout of water dropping down from one pond to another can add special magic and interest. Single or multi drop falls can be constructed, with the water landing directly onto the surface of a lower pond or onto weathered stones at the bottom of the falls.

FOUNTAINS

The following are three popular designs for fountains:

d. Horizontal fountains with one or more spouts coming out of a wall into a catchment tank or the surface of a pond.

e. Vertical fountains out of the surface of ponds. Pump sets normally come with a range of jet heads to create a variety of spray shapes.

f. Traditional stand-alone fountains. Prefabricated single or multiple tier designs are readily available.

MINI WATER FEATURES

In recent years an amazing array of mini water features have become available for gardens, patios, apartment or penthouse terraces with the pump and water sump normally integral.

Solar powered pumps are becoming more available. Some operate only when the sun is out, while others have integral batteries that power the fountain and attractive lights for several hours after dark. Prices seem to be coming down and they are safer than mains electricity around the garden.

PLANTS FOR SPECIAL MICROCLIMATES

You need to use different plants for different microclimates. For instance, ferns and irises are suitable for a humid microclimate beside a spring and in the shade, while the following variety of plants are essential to a well-balanced, healthy pond (see section 4.15).

• Oxygenating plants, some of which have flowers.

• Floating plants that give colour, shade and have long trailing roots that harbour insects on which fish can feed.

• Plants with deep roots that put up broad leaves and spectacular flowers.

• Perimeter plants grown in pots or in on a marshy shelf.

Fountains can look attractive with no surrounding clutter, but equally they can be enhanced by the careful placing of pots of geraniums if the fountain is in the sun or by ferns if in the shade.

FISH AND REPTILES

A good aquarium shop or water-garden centre should be able to supply you with healthy goldfish, koi carp, sturgeon or terrapins. Frogs and toads will find their own way there.

MAINTENANCE

Regular maintenance is important if you want to keep your water feature attractive and healthy. Below are some guidelines:

a. Keep trays and pond bottom clear of leaves and dead flowers.

b. Clean off algae in spring or leave natural according to situation.

c. Top up water level regularly and keep jets and filters clean.

d. Clean pump filters and solar panels regularly.

e. Thin out heavy weed growth in summer to leave room for fish to be seen and fed.

f. Thin out plants and prune roots if vigorous during the winter clean up.

g. Add a little Eco Bio Algicide or a small bundle of fresh straw if the water goes green. Once ponds are a balanced eco system you should have little problem with the condition of the water and any residual mud stirred up should soon settle. If you empty and refill a pond you will be back to square one, as most ponds develop algae during their first few months.

h. Add a little pond disinfectant every couple of months as per instructions to maintain health of fish.

i. Don't overcrowd the pond. Too many fish will stunt their growth and cause health problems.

j. Don't overfeed your fish or terrapins, as uneaten food will rot on the bottom. Three times a week in summer and once a week in winter should suffice.

k. Remove dead leaves and flowers to reduce the build up of decaying matter on the bottom of the pond. Net out decaying matter from the bottom of the pond during winter clean up.

l. Don't use the special fertiliser blocks sold for water lilies in small ponds. If you do, new leaves and roots will smother the pond.

m. Don't worry about mosquitoes and gnats, as the fish quickly devour any larvae.

3.3 SWIMMING POOL OR JACUZZI

A swimming pool or/and jacuzzi can be a popular feature of Spanish gardens. But the use of a swimming pool can be restricted to five or six months a year if not heated and/or covered with a sliding roof. A jacuzzi being smaller is less expensive to heat and large jacuzzis with the possibility of swimming against a fast jet of water are now available. In both cases solar water heating is now an economic reality.

Which you install and how large will depend on:

a. The largest number of regular visitors you expect.

b. Whether you like to swim or wallow.

c. The size of the garden or penthouse terrace.

d. Your budget.

The options include:

1. A large pool as the main feature of the largest area of garden set within a large terrace or lawn..

2. A smaller pool or jacuzzi as a secondary feature tucked away within a hedged mini garden.

3. A long narrow pool just wide enough to swim to one side of the house or patio.

4. A jacuzzi built into or placed on the terrace surrounding the pool.

5. A jacuzzi placed where the best view of the garden or sea can be seen.

6. If the land slopes away beyond your boundary, and there are no buildings beyond, a jacuzzi or pool at the edge of the property can create a wonderful scenic effect.

When finalising your garden design recognise that if a pool is the main feature of the garden it can become boring within a year or two, will need to be kept meticulously clean – preferably all the year round- and will seriously constrain the overall layout of the garden.

A jacuzzi or children's paddling pool are less obtrusive options for smaller gardens.

SIZING THE TERRACE AROUND THE POOL OR JACUZZI

Ensure that you provide sufficient space for the greatest number of visitors you expect. Allow for sunbathing and resting under umbrellas. Remember, the wider the terrace the less chance there is of dead flowers and leaves being blown into the pool.

PLANTING AROUND THE POOL

You can avoid leaves being blown into the pool by designing the garden in a series of three concentric circles or oblongs around the pool, depending on the shape of the pool and garden – the inner area being the pool terrace.

If you want plants on the terrace around the pool have them only in pots and exclude any plants which drop leaves or dead flowers on a regular basis. It is best to restrict yourself to interesting succulents.

In the next area, outside the pool area, have a densely planted bed of interesting, colourful and perfumed plants that have minimum leaf and flower falls, for instance succulents; herbs such as rosemary, sage, thyme and lavender; daisy-like plants which, although they need dead heading, do not drop their flower heads (argyranthemum/marguerite, dimorphotheca, euryops and felicia.); and summer lilies of various sorts.

If you want shade around the pool, there are very few trees that do not drop leaves, flowers or fruit. The cleanest and most attractive are Canary Island palm and washingtonia fan palms. Corners of pools can be shaded with canvas sails.

Surround the flowered area with a dense internal hedge, either a metre-high hedge as a dividing filter between the clean plants listed above and less clean plants in an area beyond, or a two-metre hedge – perhaps lavender, pittosporum, teucrium fruticans, or cupressus leylandii – separating the pool garden from the other areas.

In the outer area, plant your favourites such as lantana, hibiscus, bignonias and bougainvilleas that do drop flowers and leaves that blow around.

MAINTAINING THE SWIMMING POOL AND JACUZZI

During months of use

1. Whether you have a salt, chlorine or electrolysis system for maintaining the hygiene of the pool follow the recommended procedures several times a week especially if used frequently and by a large group of persons.

2. Clean twice a week removing leaves and insects from the water and swimming pool skimmers.

3. Keep the surrounding terraces clean so that dirt is not transferred into the pool or jacuzzi by dirty feet or gusts of wind.

4. If dirty rain muddies the pool let the fine particles settle to the bottom of the pool and then vacuum the pool to waste. If water remain murky a flocculent will help.

5. Keep the jacuzzi cover on when not in use, especially overnight.

During winter months of no use

1. The best practice is to keep a pool full and clean. The two most popular approaches are to add copper sulphate crystals to the pool or cover with a wide insulated cover or black plastic sheet weighted down so that no light enters.

2. If the jacuzzi is not to be used for several months it is best emptied and covered with a waterproof cover.

Preparation for spring

1. Give the terrace and surrounding flower beds a good clean up.

2. Give the walls and bottom of the pool a good clean and adjust the free chlorine content of the water to safe swimming levels in time for a first swim as soon as the water temperature is bearable.

3. Clean the jacuzzi, fill, add chemicals, and bring water up to temperature.

3.4 FACILITIES FOR *AL FRESCO* COOKING

Cooking and eating outdoors is possible for most months of the year. It is one of the real delights of living in Spain, particularly if one has a delightful garden. For variety and a good diet think beyond just a fixed or portable barbecue.

The following are easy to provide for in your garden design and offer the possibility of al fresco cooking and eating in different parts of the garden according to your mood or season.

- An easily built or purchased wood fired oven to prepare roast meats and vegetables, pizzas and home baked bread.
- An earthenware Mexican oven that doubles up as a barbecue and oven is especially useful for roasting meat, fish and vegetables in foil.
- A pair of Moroccan tagine dishes for the slow cooking of spicy North African recipes over charcoal.
- A paella pan and gas ring on legs for cooking traditional paellas and fideuas.

- An earthenware cooking plate for cooking pita bread on a barbecue or tagine burner.
- A traditional migas pan for cooking chilly flavoured migas and spicy sausages Andalusian style.
- A fondue, raclette or hot stone meat cooker.
- A solar cooking box or grill.

The ultimate, of course, is a Spanish style outside kitchen incorporating a barbecue including a spit for roast lamb and suckling pig, an oven, paella ring, sink and worktops.

3.5 A HERB GARDEN

There is a wide range of herb plants that are native to Spain and add perfume, flowers, colour and texture to formal or informal areas and in general, enhance the overall garden.

A good herb garden should display a collection of herbs in an interesting manner, making good use of the various heights, colours, leaf textures, flowers and seed heads. It should also make harvesting herbs easy, provide space for adding new herbs that you come across and allow spreading herbs to be controlled.

The following practical designs are suggested:

1. Plant between the spokes of an old wagon wheel or a similar bed constructed with terracotta tiles forming the dividing spoke.
2. A square or oblong dedicated garden with an outer bed and a number of inner mini beds. Additional interest can be achieved by constructing raised outer or inner beds.
3. As an herb border alongside or around the vegetable plot.
4. As a raised spiral or snail shell bed – the different depths of soil and sunny and shady side being planted according to the preferred habitat of different herbs.
5. As a border to a path near the kitchen
6. As a collection of pots and containers, either all the same size or more interestingly of different sizes and heights. This could be fitted in at the end of an apartment terrace.
7. A middle ages knot garden with interesting shapes achieved by growing and trimming herb plants into a variety of interweaving low hedges and infills.
8. As internal clipped hedges. Rosemary and lavender are especially useful in this respect.
9. As an informal collection of herbs worked into a rockery or flowerbeds.
10. As a lawn of creeping thyme or dichondra in a semi-shaded area. These herbs could also be used for the pathways within a formal herb garden.
11. A long raised bed with a handrail at the front as an interesting bed for persons with impaired sight who can gain pleasure from smelling the variously perfumed leaves.

WHAT TO PLANT

What you plant will depend on how you intend to use herb plants in the garden and after being harvested. They can add perfume to the garden. Strong-smelling herbs include rosemary, lavender, thyme and the curry plant. Herbs such as marjoram, mint and lemon verbena have more subtle smells. Separately and in combination they can create a pleasing aromatherapy effect while you are working, eating or resting in the garden.

Herbs, especially lavender, rosemary and thyme, attract butterflies and can be arranged attractively in pot-pourri bowls for the terrace and house.

They also, of course, can be used in cooking to flavour all kinds of dishes, to make refreshing and healthy infusions as an alternative to tea and coffee as well as a base for distilling essential oils.

Several herbs are also very useful on the vegetable plot in producing ecological feeds and insect deterrents, and as beneficial companion plants.

PROPOGATING FROM CUTTINGS

Many herbs, including sages, thymes and mints, can be multiplied by taking root cuttings and planting them directly in the garden or growing them first in pots to achieve a strong root ball before planting. Rosemary, sage, rue, lavender and others can be propagated from stem cuttings.

GROWING FROM SEED

We find that April and May sowings of herbs are the most successful. We sow sun loving herbs that can withstand a degree of dryness directly into the garden where required. These include dill, coriander, aniseed, fennel, dandelion and borage. We grow herbs such as parsley and basil, which need to be kept constantly damp, in pots or trays before planting seedlings into larger pots to be kept in the semi-shade.

To ensure your herb garden will be successful, do the following:

1. Plant in water-retentive but well-draining, fairly rich, gritty soil. Herbs generally dislike heavy, clayey, waterlogged soils.

2. Keep all new plants damp until deep tap roots have been put down. This may take one or two years. Once established, most perennial herbs need little watering except during prolonged very dry spells.

3. Purchase and plant small or medium sized plants in preference to large ones, especially if planting in the late spring or summer rather than in the autumn or winter. It is important that the root ball is large enough to support the sometimesforced top growth.

4. Herbs in the ground need little if any feeding, however, annual herbs in pots can benefit from a weak feed every so often.

5. Keep herbs tidy by trimming between harvests. Trimmings can be immediately used, dried or used as cuttings for propagation.

HARVESTING LEAVES, ROOTS AND SEEDS

Harvest daily as required or cut and dry for later use. Dry in the sun, cool oven or proprietary tray drier with fan blown warm air (www.conasi.biz) and store in airtight containers. Herbs for cooking can be conveniently stored in ice cubes in the freezer.

3.6 VEGETABLE PLOT

Wouldn't you like to walk out onto your apartment terrace or into the garden and pick your own fresh vegetables daily? Well it's very possible in many areas of Spain. Section 4.18 describes thirty popular vegetables for terraces and gardens and when they are best sown and normally harvested.

The sister book 'Growing healthy vegetables in Spain' explains in detail how to grow more than a hundred types.

Part two of that book is dedicated to growing vegetables in less than one square metre as illustrated in the first three photographs below.

A seed sprouter takes up no more space than two pages of this book, a mushroom sack the weekly newspaper, the collection of containers only a square metre. Last summer we grew more than fifteen different vegetables in the collection of containers shown.

Once you move from an apartment terrace to a garden the possibilities are endless as well as more than a 100 on our vegetable plot. You can develop a traditional vegetable plot of a hundred metres or more, build five to twenty square metres of deep raised beds, grow vegetables in strip beds between rows of trees in the orchard or along the boundary fence, mix vegetables into flower and shrub beds cottage garden style or even take on an allotment in the agricultural land surrounding your village. We have done all and it's fun, satisfying and healthy not just for the diversity of vegetables but also if grown organically – which is not difficult – knowing that they are not tainted with residual chemicals.

3.7 ORCHARD AND SOFT FRUIT PATCH

There are good reasons why everyone with a property in Spain – even if only to visit for holidays – should plant a few fruit trees and vines. If resident for most of the year then soft fruit bushes and plants can be added. A selection of the most popular fruits trees, bushes, plants and vines are described in section 4.8. More extensive lists and how to care for each are provided in the sister book 'Growing healthy fruit in Spain'.

The main reasons for growing fruit are as follows.

1. The subtropical, Mediterranean and more temperate climates of the various parts of Spain settled by expatriates each allow a diversity of fruits to be grown.

2. Many types are reasonably drought and frost resistant once established.

3. Many can be grown in large containers. Something very convenient and interesting for penthouse and apartment terraces and town house roof gardens and patios. No one need be without a perpetually fruiting lemon tree, fig tree, grape vine, strawberry barrel and peach tree for instance.

4. In small and moderate sized gardens fruit trees can be arranged around the garden in the same way as flowering trees. Some are indeed among the most spectacular flowering trees and additionally have the benefits of the decorative effects of ripening fruit – for instance citrus fruits can stay on trees for months – and seasonal harvests of fresh fruit picked when at their best. If grown ecologically/ organically you will have less risk of residual chemicals from insecticide and fungicide sprays. There are now many biological/ecological products on the market that make this possible.

5. If you have a larger property a full scale orchard, orange grove and vineyard are possible. Many expatriates have taken to making their own wines.

6. Grape vines, blackberries, kiwi fruit and other vines can be trained on walls or fences or over gazebos in any sized garden.

7. Soft fruit bushes and plants take up relatively little space so why not at least have a corner patch if you are in the cooler valleys and mountains.

8. A collection of relatively few varieties will enable you to harvest your own fruit 365 days a year. Sections 4.9 indicates typical harvest times.

9. If you have purchased a property with a large number of citrus , avocado, olive, walnut, almond trees or vines consider taking some out and planting a few other types of fruit after first improving the soil.

10. There are a large number of ways for using and storing fruits beyond just eating them raw or drinking their juice. Look up fruit based fish and meat dishes, pickle your olives, use gluts for bottling or making jams and chutneys or dry for flavour/energy packed snacks when out walking or playing golf.

3.8 A CHILDREN'S CORNER

A children's garden can provide much to interest and absorb children. They should have a large enough area to plant a mix of plants that they can later on:

- **Pick and dissect** – for example, margarites, marigolds, sunflowers, portulacas, petunias, nasturtiums and zinnias.
- **Smell** – sweet peas, jasmine, San Diego, and herbs such as rosemary, thyme and curry.
- **Make an infusion from** – peppermint and lemon verbena.
- **Eat with a meal** – radishes, courgettes, tomatoes, lettuces, carrots, spinach and melons.
- **Eat when they like** – wild strawberries, peas, perpetual lettuce and rocket.
- **Have a competition with** – pumpkins for weight and sunflowers for height.
- **Dry and paint** – gourds.
- **Care for a few years** – seedling trees such as oak from acorns, avocado from the stone of a ripe fruit, olive from a fallen olive and citrus from orange or lemon pips. Allocate them an area of easily worked soil in the semi shade. Perhaps help them lay it out as a wagon wheel so that they can plant different seeds between the spokes or a raised snail bed.

Provide them with a garden hose or mini irrigation system, plant pots, potting compost, mini tools and some of your seedlings. Give them some pocket money to buy their own small plants when you visit a garden centre. Let them do what they like. Just let them know that plants die if they are not watered and then give just enough support to ensure a few successes.

If you help children start a garden, you should also take them around the garden and explain which plants can be poisonous and which are dangerous because of the prickles and spikes. Poisonous plants include anemones, arum lily, box, cyclamen, datura, iris, ivy, lantana, lilies, morning glory, daffodils, oleander, poinsettia, solanum, tobacco plant and wisteria.

In an age where children spend much time indoors on the computer, doing homework, watching television or on a mobile telephone, it makes sense to encourage outdoor activities with interest and challenge. Additional ideas are included in the sister books 'Growing healthy fruit in Spain' and 'Growing healthy vegetables in Spain'.

3.9 ATTRACTORS FOR BENEFICIAL WILD LIFE

Wildlife in the garden is beneficial for a number of reasons. Their movement, colours, noises and breeding cycles add interest. Their pollinating activities help fruit trees and flower plants to pollinate. Seeds in the droppings of recently migrated birds may germinate interesting and unusual plants. Their foraging for food loosens the surface soil, which in turn lessens water evaporation. They devour many unwanted insects and slugs. Worms in high humus soils cultivate the soil effortlessly hour after hour.

The wildlife that can be attracted includes butterflies, birds, crickets, lizards, frogs, toads, bats, worms, and hedgehogs. Do so consciously. Develop your garden as a haven from the polluted modern urban environment, for wildlife as much as for yourselves.

Wildlife is under constant threat with the continual cutting down of mature trees and copses, the filling in of ponds and barancas (gulleys), the clearing of natural mountainsides and heath lands, the construction of wind generators, the drying up of ponds due to changes in the water table and the removal of top soil.

All this is being done to enable the construction boom to continue, including the resi-dential estates in which most expatriates and Spaniards live. Outside urban environments, the ever-increasing threats of plastic horticultural land and the use of concentrated pesticides, herbicides and fertilizers don't help. However, there are many practical things that can be done, all of them bringing almost immediate benefit to your garden. When developing a new garden or improving an existing one, consider the following ways to attract and retain wildlife:

1. Plant thick hedges and shrub beds that will attract sheltering and nesting birds.

2. Replace trees cut down by builders or felled because they were unsightly, unsafe, dead or diseased.

3. Put up nesting boxes for birds in trees or on high walls. Fix them in situations that are difficult for cats to reach. If possible, put up a number of boxes with different size entry holes for different species. Many garden centres now stock a wide range of boxes.

4. Leave a pile of straw and twigs in an out-of-the-way corner of the garden as handy nest-building material. A totally tidy garden presents little of interest to birds and they will soon move on.

5. Preserve or build dry stone walls. Plant some holes between the stones and leave the others as homes for lizards and insects.

6. Put up a bat box under the eves. When bats move in you have nightly eaters of mosquitoes and gnats.

7. Hang up a bunch or two of herbs high up on the naya wall to give shelter for geckos, those lizards with suction feet that allow them to walk across ceilings and do such a good job of catching any mosquitoes, gnats, flies and moths that settle.

8. Install a birdbath in a quiet part of the garden, preferably where you can see it from your favourite eating or resting places. You will be surprised by the variety of birds it will attract. If possible, top up the birdbath with unchlorinated rain water from a butt or with water from a local fountain or spring.

9. Set up a self-standing or hanging bird table. We prefer a hanging one out of the way of marauding cats. Stock it with a variety of seeds and nuts, preferably not dry chunks of bred as these can swell up in their stomachs and can be especially harmful to fledglings.

10. Hang up half coconuts and peanut/ seed feeders from the boughs of trees where cats will not be able to jump up or down onto feeding birds.

11. Construct a pond, where frogs, toads, dragon and damsel flies, and birds will soon add to the continuous interest of the fish in the pond.

12. If you have a water butt, add some oxygenating pond weed and a couple of gold fish to eat any mosquito and gnat larvae that might hatch.

13. Construct a compost heap that will attract worms and other insects beneficial to the composting process as well as providing food for blackbirds that love to peck

around the base of the heaps. Use the compost to plant and mulch around trees, shrubs and vegetables. This will attract breeding worms as well as shelter roots from the sun, preserving moisture and providing essential nutrients.

14. If you have a lawn, leave one corner to grow long, preferably allowing a few wild flowers to develop. Butterflies need such an area for laying eggs, and other insects will also be attracted. A controlled clump of nettles is also beneficial.

15. If you have room, go a stage further and allow a natural wilderness corner to develop. Encourage natural grasses, herbs and wild annuals and perennials to take over. If starting with a clear area or previously rotovated corner of the orchard, accelerate the process by planting a mix of wild plant seeds. Poppies, fennel, scabious, marigolds, dandelion, wild garlic, wild chichory, clover, lupins, buttercups, valerian, irises, san diego, decorative thistles and lavatera would all be good starters. Among shrubs, add brooms, buddlejas, thyme, rosemary, and rock roses.

Before you sow seeds or plant plants, take a spring drive through rural areas and observe what is growing and flowering wild alongside motorways. Some of the totally natural wind-blown, bird- dropped flower displays are amazing by any standards. The challenge is to do as well as nature in your own nurtured patch. It won't be easy but patience will be rewarded.

16. Stop using chemical pesticides, insecticides and herbicides in the garden. Seek out natural ecological products and solutions as discussed in section 6.7.

17. Plant some sunflower seeds or plants. The open flowers will attract pollinators and the seed heads can be hung up to attract seed-eating birds in the winter.

18. Make a point of including plants that are especially attractive to butterflies, which we refer to as the "flying flowers" of Spanish gardens for the beauty they add. Without appropriate plants only the odd butterfly will pass by – but with the right plants a garden can team with hatches of butterflies of all colours and hues.

The right plants provide a continuous supply of easily accessible nectar as well as stems and leaves on which the butterflies can lay eggs and the hatching caterpillars can feed.

The best nectar supplying plants are those with bright coloured, fragrant open flowers. Their favourite flowers include bougainvilleas, lantanas, margaritas, marigolds, purple buddleia (our yellow one just doesn't work), ice plants, rosemary, lavender and thyme. If you do not have a wild area and if fields or mountainsides that used to surround your garden are now under concrete and bitumen, plant up a few pots of tall wild grass, thistles and nettles. A few decorative cabbages in pots or a flowerbed will also provide food for some varieties of caterpillars.

19. The humming bird hawk moth is also an interesting summer visitor to watch. It feeds by sticking its long proboscis into deep necked flowers such as nicotiana (tobacco plant), honeysuckle, stephanotis and devils tongue (caesalpinia).

20. Grow evergreen climbers up fences, into trees and over sheds to give winter shelter for the chrysalises of butterflies.

21. When you do the winter cleanup, leave a metre cube of leaves, twigs and dried weeds in a quiet rarely visited corner of the garden. With luck you will attract a hedgehog that feeds on slugs and a variety of nuisance insects.

Action on even only a few of the above ideas will add interest to your garden and arrest the disappearance of species from your neighbourhood.

3.10 A NATURAL AREA

A wild, naturalised area has a number of benefits if you have a large plot or a site set on a wild moorland, mountainside or in woodlands. Retaining its wild beauty may be the best garden for your location.

There are several practical benefits to retaining or developing a naturalised area or garden:

1. The preservation of a diversity of wild plants that may be disappearing fast from your area of Spain due to new roads, urbanisations and the wide use of weed killers.

2. Preserving the continuity from your natural garden to unspoilt surrounding heathland, mountainside or woodlands.

3. A low-maintenance, maximum-interest area of the garden, orchard or otherwise unused part of the site. Increasingly, 15,000 square metre sites are being sold in rural areas to enable a house to be legally built. Few new owners, especially if retiring to Spain, will have the motivation, energy or budget to turn the whole site into a cultivated garden, and there is a limit to how much fruit can be usefully harvested from an orchard.

4. An appropriate wilderness or naturalised area will require little, if any, irrigation once established. Any established plants have already survived the rigours of being parched in the summer and perhaps waterlogged and frozen in the winter.

5. Many wild plants thrive in poor shallow soils and flower profusely in the spring before many cultivated annuals, perennials and shrubs come into flower or are at their best. However, many die off in the summer.

6. A small-scale wilderness area can be an attractive way of dealing with a very impoverished or rocky corner of a smaller garden, covering a large heap of builder's rubble, an unploughed, uncut area of an orchard or a rough bank around the flower or vegetable garden.

7. A truly natural area will require little maintenance, as by definition it is an area that will be left to grow naturally, only thinning out the wilderness when the balance between grasses, flowering plants and shrubs looks wrong or if it becomes an uncomfortable fire risk.

8. In time a naturalised garden will become a haven, a small but important nature reserve for a whole host of birds, butterflies, insects, reptiles, small mammals and even larger ones such as rabbits, wild boar and deer.

The area you have that is suitable for a naturalised garden could be one of four typical sites: a rocky heath land or mountainside, a flowering bank, a mound of builder's rubble or a wild meadow.

A ROCKY HEATH LAND OR MOUNTAINSIDE

With this type of site you can either leave it as it is, if you want it to be totally wild, or you can clean up the area to discover what plants you have and make the best of them. Even if you wish to leave it totally wild, we suggest that you clean up part of the area as follows:

a. Decide which mature trees, strong saplings or stunted but attractively shaped trees you want to keep. If necessary, prune them to pleasing natural shapes, cutting out dead wood and retaining any windblown effects. The trees may be oaks, junipers, pines, carobs, olives, almonds, birches, pomegranates etc.

b. Cut back overgrown evasive shrubs such as gorse, broom, holly oaks, mountain palms, etc. Decide which are in good situations and cut the others back to the ground and treat the stumps with acid applied on a paint brush to avoid harming other plants or the soil structure.

c. The spaces between rocks are probably rich in flora but not all of interest. So, space by space, clear all the grass and low-priority plants such as dandelions and wild chicory. Also cut back the dead stems of bulbous plants.

d. Trim large rockroses, thistles, euphorbias, rosemary and lavenders, thymes, etc., to shape and to stimulate new flowering side shoots.

e. Now do nothing more until the spring, when you can really see what plants will flower, especially bulbous plants that appear from nowhere. You may be pleasantly surprised by the natural collection of wild narcissi, grape hyacinths, tulips, gladi-oli, orchids, irises, lilies etc that you have inherited. You will also discover the extent and colours of naturally occurring flowering plants, of which there can be many. We suggest you purchase a book of Mediterranean/mountain wildflowers to identify them all.

f. Once you know what you have, decide where you need to have infills by planting seeds, transplanting, taking cuttings or purchases. The best source of wild plant seeds is probably Semillas Silvestres S.L., based in Córdoba (informacion@semillassilvestres.com).

g. Choose the best route for paths. The choices are bare earth or stone chippings laid over plastic to keep them clear of weeds. Meander the paths between widely spaced rocks and past some of the best clumps of plants.

A FLOWERING BANK

The aim is to create a mass of colour that matches the best you have ever seen driving along motorways or country lanes in the spring. And that's some challenge. Try the following for a good chance of success:

a. Choose a semi-shaded bank or one that is in full sun for half the day.

b. A plant-covered bank will have had years of natural soil improvement. Each year worms and ants will have been working dead vegetation into the soil, enriching it and improving its moisture retaining properties. Check that the soil is reasonably friable and well draining. A solid bank of clay is unlikely to be successful but if that is what you have, mix compost, sand and some fine stone chippings into the top 10 to 15cm of earth.

c. In the autumn and spring, plant a mixture of seeds of plants that can thrive on banks, such as marigolds, wild sweet peas, broom, poppies, lupins, antirrhinums, stocks, fennel, wild garlic, borage, valerian, decorative thistles, decorative grasses, holihocks, euphorbias, daisies, lavatera, scabious, etc. Some will be available from the address given above and packets of mixed wildflower seeds will be found in some seed display racks. Wildflower plants should not be dug up and transplanted, but some seeds are easy to collect during the summer.

d. Dampen the bank after planting and keep damp until strong plants are established. Then leave the bank to grow wild.

e. Pull out clumps of grass if they start to take over from the flowering plants.

You should have a self-perpetuating colourful bank of perennials and self-seeded perennials within a couple of years.

A MOUND OF BUILDER'S RUBBLE

Create an interesting shaped heap and then cover with ten centimetres of a rich sandy soil mix. Hose the embryo bank well to wash as much soil as possible down into the spaces in the rubble, then cover with a second ten centimetres of earth and continue as for a flowering bank.

A WILD MEADOW

You can create your own wild meadow by taking the following steps:

a. Stop cutting an area of a lawn, meadow or spare piece of land.

b. Stop using any weed killer or chemical fertilizers on the area.

c. Allow the existing flowering plants and grasses to grow, flower, seed and die back naturally. As the meadow thickens, more birds will be attracted and drop other seeds. Wind-blown seed will also gradually add to the diversity of natural plants. Yes, some will be what you normally call weeds in the flowerbeds, but so were all now-useful herbs and bedding plants before seed men and natural medicine experts discovered they had useful benefits.

d. Plant additional seeds from your own garden and the roadside as well as seeds from mixed wildflower packets. These will have more chance of taking off if the meadow is semi shaded and naturally damp in the late winter and spring. Obviously, an area near a spring, river and high up on a misty slope is likely to be more successful than one in an arid area. Include the seeds mentioned for banks, together with salvias, clavels, hollyhocks, buttercups and san diego.

e. Before planting new seeds, cut the meadow in September or October and rake off all the cuttings. Then aerate the surface of the soil and spread a centimetre of soil over the surface. Brush the soil into the aeration holes.

f. Then scatter your mix of seeds over the surface in patches or evenly, according to the picture you want to create.

g. Sieve a poor soil and sand mix over the seeds and firm.

h. To achieve the optimum germination conditions it may be worth splitting   your seeds into two or three containers and making successive sowings two or three weeks apart in both the autumn and spring. As occurs in nature, some seeds will probably germinate in the autumn and some in the spring.

i. Spray the planted area with water to keep it damp but not waterlogged. This should help achieve a higher germination rate than in nature. You can also raise seedlings in trays or pots for planting out.

j. Then just leave the meadow to grow and develop naturally.

k. In most areas, cut the meadow in early autumn and remove the cuttings. By not haymaking in the hottest months the grasses will protect the roots of plants from the sun. In the lusher areas of the Pyrenees and the northern coasts of Spain, you can probably cut twice and get two lots of flowers.

l. Don't waste scarce water on the area unless you are planning to produce fodder for animals and need as high a crop as possible.

To encourage wild life, consider placing a bird table and bird bath, a pond with natural surrounds and a small pile of logs within your wild areas.

3.11 AN AVIARY OR POULTRY HOUSE

An area of only four to nine square metres is sufficient for housing a small flock of breeding budgerigars, a pair or two of mini doves, a pair of parrots, two to four egg laying chickens, or a small flock of pedigree bantams for eggs and breeding. A larger aviary/poultry run would allow the keeping of geese, guinea fowl or peacocks, which have the additional benefit of being good watchdogs in country areas. Whatever the size, ensure that part of the structure is roofed to provide sufficient summer shade.

The benefits of having birds in your garden are many. Their chirping and antics inter-est all ages, the chickens provide fresh eggs and wildlife are at-tracted by the prospect of a free meal of scattered grain. They eat the outer leaves of brassicas, their manure is a natural ferti-lizer for the vegetable garden or orchard and it acts as an ac-celerator for the compost heap. But ensure that you negotiate the keeping of a cockerel with the neighbours if living in the middle of an urbanisation.

3.12 TOPIARY FEATURES

There are many shrubs and trees that can be trimmed and trained into interesting shapes as hedges or freestanding specimens. Training is achieved by attaching a wire frame to the tree, around which to trim or hold a branch in a special shape, or weighing branches down with weights. In many ways topiary for the garden is using the skills of the bonsai specialists on normal- size trees and shrubs. Incidentally, a collection of Bonsais on a north facing terrace, or in the shade of tree, can add considerable interest and be a wonderful hobby for a gardener in later years.

The easiest trees for practicing the art of topiary include box, yew, cypress and bay. The easiet shrubs include pittosporum, euonymus, privet and rosemary.

Standard shrubs are a mild form of topiary and can be effective in many garden layouts. Those available in garden centres include bottle brush, hibiscus, lantana, oleander, plumbago, wisteria, bougainvilleas, roses, polygala and fuchsias.

PART FOUR

400 POPULAR SPANISH PLANTS

This collection of the most popular and practical plants for Spanish gardens will enable you to select those most appropriate to your summer and winter microclimate, soils and reliability of water supply.

4.0 AN INTRODUCTION TO 400 POPULAR PLANTS

This section provides a practical guide to some 400 of the most popular and practical plants used in Spanish gardens. They are selected on the basis of being readily available and easy to care for in typical micro climates.

In the tables that follow in Sections 4.1 to 4.18 we summarize the most important characteristics of these plants. The tables include the Botanical, English and typical Spanish names. Where there are several varieties we have selected our favourite.

Below is a summary of the main uses, benefits, greatest problems and soil needs of the plants included.

1. ANNUALS

A. USES
Can be grown in containers, large pots, hanging baskets, window boxes and flower beds.

B. BENEFITS
1. Instant colour.
2. Numerous varieties to choose from.
3. Able to create continuous twelve months of colour by sequential planting of seasonal varieties.
4. Most have a long flowering season.
5. Many can be raised from seed.

C. GREATEST PROBLEMS
1. Thirsty plants that need regular watering, once or twice a day on hot days.
2. Need regular deadheading to stimulate continuous flowering.
3. Can be flattened by heavy rains and winds.
4. Can be difficult to maintain a constant temperature for germination and growing on.
5. Most not frost hardy.

D. SOIL NEEDS
Very fertile, rich in humus, water retaining but well draining.

2. PERENNIALS

A. USES
Normally grown in dedicated beds or mixed beds with shrubs.

B. BENEFITS
1. Large number of varieties. Jointly they can give colour all the year round.
2. Many produce cut flowers for the house.

3. Easy to propagate by separation or from root and stem cuttings.
4. Many do well in the inland frost belt.
5. Many can do well in pots.

C. GREATEST PROBLEMS
1. Need regular deadheading to keep neat and stimulate a long flowering period.
2. Major annual cut back required, normally in the winter.
3. Can grow leggy and woody after a few years. Need to maintain a backup of young propagated plants as replacements.
4. Need to be on a drip watering system in the summer to prolong flowering.
5. Some grow into large clumps that need dividing every few years.

D. SOIL NEEDS
Generally fertile, rich in humus, water retaining and free draining

3. HERBS

A. USES
Grow in a dedicated herb garden, pots or containers, around the vegetable plot, on the rockery or in mixed beds.

B. BENEFITS
1. A wide range of varieties grow well in Mediterranean conditions as well as higher up on mountainsides.
2. Many drought and frost resistant.
3. Provide a wide range of flower colours, perfumes, formats and leaf colours and textures.
4. Wide range of culinary, aromatherapy and natural medicinal uses.
5. Mostly perennials that can be propagated from cuttings plus some useful annuals that can be grown from seed.

C. GREATEST PROBLEMS
1. Annuals require regular watering.
2. Annuals grown from seed require continual nurturing.
6. Annuals can go to seed fast in the high Spanish temperatures.
7. Perennials require annual pruning to stop them going leggy and woody.
8. Pots and containers need regular watering. Once herbs go dry they often do not recover.

D. SOIL NEEDS
Fertile, free draining, non clayey and gritty.

4. GROUND COVER

A. USES
1. Carpet planting at front of flower beds, under shrubs and trees, within rockeries and cascading down banks and walls.

B. BENEFITS

1. Rapidly fill up bare spaces with a mass of greenery and flowers.
2. Smother weeds.
3. Reduce surface evaporation.
4. Many are drought resistant.
5. Natural mulch around taller shrubs and trees.

C. GREATEST PROBLEMS

1. Many need deadheading to keep them neat.
2. Need trimming back regularly to stimulate new side shoots and prevent the heart becoming leggy/woody.
3. Can become the home of slugs and snails.
4. The more vigorous need controlling.
5. Can smother less vigorous plants.

D. SOIL NEEDS

Enriched soil, moisture retentive and well draining.

5. FLOWERING SHRUBS

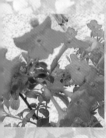

A. USES

The backbone of Spanish gardens as individual specimens and planted as shrubberies, in mixed beds and as hedges.

B. BENEFITS

1. A wide choice of endemic and naturalised plants.
2. Come in all heights from a few centimetres to many metres.
3. Many slow growing so don't outgrow gardens for years.
4. Most grow well in full sun.
5. Some grow well in the shade and semi shade.

C. GREATEST PROBLEMS

1. Need watering until well established.
2. The more vigorous need regular pruning to control their size.
3. Some need dead heading to stimulate follow on flowering.
4. Tropicals and tender sub-tropicals can be wiped out by a single frost.
5. Some can be become very large after ten or fifteen years if they are not pruned hard during each year's winter cut back.

D. SOIL NEEDS

As for perennials, except for acid loving shrubs such as camellias, heathers, blue hydrangeas, rock roses and azaleas.

6. CLIMBING SHRUBS

A. USES
To cover walls, fences, pergolas, dead trees, old buildings and to climb up through trees or cascade down banks.

B. BENEFITS
1. Wide range of flowering varieties that can give year round colour.
2. Can be a mass of flowers for months.
3. Many are pleasantly perfumed.
4. Many are fast growing and trainable.
5. Interesting tropical species will grow in warmer and sheltered situations.

C. GREATEST PROBLEMS
1. Some can get out of control, especially in an absentee garden.
2. Need to regularly check and loosen ties round trunks and branches.
3. Roots of many varieties, especially clematis, need to be shaded to avoid being burnt by the sun.
4. Heavy flower and leaf falls.
5. Many not fully frost resistant.

D. SOIL NEEDS
As perennials.

7. FLOWERING TREES

A. USES
As specimen trees for their flowers, shade, architectural shapes and varying heights. Also as part of boundary hedges to frame the best views and hide the worst.

BENEFITS
1. Attractive seasonal flowerings. Mainly in spring and summer.
2. Mainly deciduous therefore giving good shade in the summer and allowing the sun to shine through in the winter.
3. Grow relatively fast in the right conditions.
4. Once established most are fairly frost and drought resistant.
5. The wide range of leaf, flower, fruit and bark colours and textures brighten up the garden and add interest.

E. GREATEST PROBLEMS
1. Dead flower, leaf and fruit falls need sweeping up. But they are useful on the compost heap.
2. Flowering seasons generally short.
3. Some can become too large for their situation, especially in small gardens, where they may need pruning each winter.
4. Vigorous roots can undermine foundations.

5. Heavy heads can snap off thin trunks unless well staked for some years after planting.

F. SOIL NEEDS
As perennials.

8. FRUITING TREES, BUSHES AND PLANTS

A. USES
Blossom, fruit and autumn leaf colours and harvests.
Can be planted as individual specimens, in groups or orchards and in large containers. Vines can be trained on fences or walls.

B. BENEFITS
1. Diversity of types, forms and sizes.
2. Harvests of fresh ripe fruit.
3. Many fairly frost and drought resistant.
4. Can live for a long time.
5. Evergreens as well as deciduous types.

C. GREATEST PROBLEMS
1. Sub tropical types are frost tender.
2. Regular spraying required against pests and fungal diseases.
3. Correct watering to achieve good crops.
4. Annual pruning essential.
5. Some grow large.

D. SOIL NEEDS
Deep fertile, rich in humus, moisture retaining but free draining.

9. EVERGREEN TREES

A. USES
Can be planted as interesting specimen trees, in small groups or copses, as hedges or in containers on terraces, penthouse roofs, patios or the naya. Provide year round shade.

B. BENEFITS
1. Are in leaf all year round and can be trimmed to shape. Some good for topiary and hedges.
2. Give shade all year round.
3. Add architectural form to gardens.
4. Many are suitable for growing in poor soils.
5. Many are frost and drought resistant once established.

C. GREATEST PROBLEMS

1. Many have very spreading vigorous root systems so do not plant near the foundations of buildings.
2. Can be felled by strong winds unless well staked.
3. Generally have shallow root systems searching long distances for moisture so difficult to grow other plants around them.
4. When used as hedges need regular trimming to keep neat and tidy.
5. Some can become very large within ten years and therefore not for small gardens.

D. SOIL NEEDS

Generally as perennials except some prefer a more acid soil.

10. PALMS, YUCCAS AND CORDYLINES

A. USES

Architecturally attractive plants that add interest, form, movement, shade and a tropical touch to any garden.

B. BENEFITS

1. Many varieties available with differing forms of fronds.
2. Generally drought resistant once well established.
3. Large mature palms can be transplanted with care.
4. Rustling fronds create a restful ambiance.
5. Can be grown from seed. Good in a small garden as slow growing.

C. GREATEST PROBLEMS

1. Many have dangerous spikes on the trunk end of the fronds.
2. Can outgrow a small garden within ten years.
3. The trunks of Canary Island palms can break up walls and paths as they expand with age.
4. Pruned fronds cannot be put on the compost heap as they take a long time to rot down.
5. Nor do they readily go through a shredder as they are very stringy.

D. SOIL NEEDS

Rich in nutrients, high in humus, sandy and free draining.

11. BULBOUS PLANTS

A. USES

To brighten mixed flower beds, rockeries, terraces and nayas throughout the year.

B. BENEFITS

1. A wide range with varying flowering seasons available. Some have very spectacular flowers.
2. Can under plant deciduous shrubs with early spring varieties.

3. Many grow into large colourful clumps.
4. Many can be grown successfully in pots and containers.
5. A good source of cut flowers.

C. GREATEST PROBLEMS

1. Shortish flowering seasons.
2. Summer slug damage especially to soft skinned bulbs.
3. Too easy to dig up and damage when dormant if not marked.
4. Can be expensive compared with other plants.
5.When flowering is over the leaves
need to be left to die back and can look unsightly.

D. SOIL NEEDS

Generally high in humus and free draining. Best to place a thin layer of grit under bulbs when planting.

12. SUCCULENTS

A. USES

To add interest to rockeries, dry stone walls, the edge of flower beds and paths and nayas and terraces when planted in pots and containers.

B. BENEFITS

1. An amazing number of interesting varieties.
2. Some lovely and interestingly shaped long lasting flowers.
3. Easy to propagate from cuttings.
4. Most are drought resistant.
5. Do well with little care.

C. GREATEST PROBLEMS

1. Some, especially the messems, can go leggy and woody.
2. Need to deadhead those that have flowers on long stems.
3. Thin skinned sappy varieties can be susceptible to frost damage.
4. Spreading varieties can smother small plants.
5. More delicate varieties can rot off if over watered.

D. SOIL NEEDS

Rich in humus, free draining, open, gritty/sandy. Benefit from mulch of chippings or ground volcanic rock to keep stems dry.

13. CACTI, AGAVES AND ALOES

A. USES

To create Mediterranean effects in flower beds, rockeries or in pots on terraces or walls.

B. BENEFITS

1. Drought resistant once established.
2. Can be easily propagated from cuttings or by removing young suckers.
3. Many have spectacular flowers even though some   last for only a day.
4. The majority can be best grown in full sun.
5. A good choice for absentee gardeners.

C. GREATEST PROBLEMS

1. Prickly and spiky. Need careful handling and weeding.
2. Most need light watering until roots are established
3. Some not frost resistant.
4. A 10cm wide aloe can be a metre across within 5 to ten years.
5. Dangerous in gardens with small children.

D. SOIL NEEDS

As succulents.

14. GRASSES AND CANES

A. USES

1. Grasses - To stabilize a bank or sand dune or as an interesting dedicated or wild corner.
2. Canes – As an external hedge or internal screen.

B. BENEFITS

1. Come in a wide range of single and variegated colours. Some have interesting flowering plumes.
2. Short and tall varieties available. Canes from a half to ten metres high.
3. Spread into large clumps within a few years.
4. Clumps can be split for transplanting.
5. When established drought resistant.

C. GREATEST PROBLEMS

1. Canes and pampas can spread rapidly in damp conditions. Once in the garden difficult to get rid of.
2. Spreading cane roots can break into terracotta water pipes.
3. Edge of some grass leaves can cut deeply, especially pampas grass.
4. If allowed to dry out can go brown before maturity.
5. Difficult to grow other plants close to canes.

D. SOIL NEEDS

A high moisture retaining soil.
Canes can take off in constantly damp conditions!

15. POND PLANTS

A. USES
To create a balanced, colourful, interesting and healthy water based eco system.

B. BENEFITS
1. Easy to grow.
2. Maintain the oxygen level essential for healthy fish.
3. Some wonderfully exotic flowers.
4. Floating leaves give shade for fish.
5. Little care required.

C. GREATEST PROBLEMS
1. Grow very fast in ideal conditions. Will need thinning and pruning each year.
2. Some die back in winter adding to decaying pond debris.
3. Mostly flower in spring and summer.
4. Clumps of rooted plants can eventually take over a pond if not taken out and split every few years.
5. The clumps can become very heavy and unmanageable.

C. SOIL NEEDS
If in pots fertile and rich in humus.

16. HEDGING PLANTS

A. USES
To create external and internal hedges for privacy, windbreaks, shade and edges for paths and parterres.

B. BENEFITS
1. Wide variety of suitable plants available.
2. Can be pruned to give open or solid screens.
3. Many flower and create colourful boundaries.
4. Many are evergreen.
5. Many can be wired and trimmed into topiary shapes on top of the hedge and arches cut out.

C. GREATEST PROBLEMS
1. Can become straggly and woody if not regularly trimmed.
2. Spreading shallow roots make it difficult to plant other shallow rooted thirsty plants within half a metre.
3. Height and breadth need controlling to minimise work.
4. Generally need a lot of water in the early years.
5. Evergreens can be attacked by fungi.

D. SOIL NEEDS
As shrubs and trees.

17. NAYA PLANTS

A. USES
To brighten up and add interest to semi shaded and shaded nayas, porches and areas under trees.

B. BENEFITS
1. Generally grow best in semi shade and shade.
2. Are evergreen perennials or shrubs.
3. Many flower, some spectacular.
4. Varied range of leaf colours and textures.
5. Some are winter flowering.

C. GREATEST PROBLEMS
1. Fungal diseases if over watered.
2. Pores in waxy leaves can become blocked by dust unless dusted and washed.
3. Can grow out towards light unless occasionally rotated.
4. Some varieties prone to mealy bug.
5. Varied watering needs make watering complex.

E. SOIL NEEDS
A free draining, high in humus, water retaining but gritty compost.

18. VEGETABLES

A. USES
Daily harvests of fresh healthy vegetables.

B. BENEFITS
1. Wide diversity of types and varieties.
2. Harvesting possible 365 days a year.
3. Many easy to grow.
4. Can be grown in containers as well as in open ground.
5. Free of residual chemicals if organically grown.

C. GREATEST PROBLEMS
1. Pests and diseases if forced with excessive fertilizers and water.
2. Gluts in good years, but many uses.
3. Weeding of young plants.
4. Not drought resistant, need watering.
5. Climbers need staking.

D. SOIL NEEDS
Deep fertile, high in humus, moisture retaining but free draining.

4.1 ANNUALS

NAMES Botanical English / Spanish	Height and spread	Typical Flowers Colours	S	S	A	W	WHERE	GHB	GIP/W	PERF	DR	FR
1. AGERATUM Floss Flower / Agérato	L L	Blue	•	•	•		S SS		•		M	L
2. ANTIRRHINUM Snapdragon / Boca de Dragón	M M	Many	•	•	•		S SS		•		M	L
3. CALENDULA Marigold / Calendula	M M	Orange, yellow	•	•	•	•	S SS		•	•	M	H
4. CATHARANTHUS Periwinkle / Vinca	L M	Pink, white		•	•		S SS		•		M	L
5. CELOSA Cockscomb / Celosia	M L	Red	•	•			S		•	•	L	L
6. ERYSIMUM/CHEIRANTHUS Wallflower / Alhelí	M M	Many	•			•	S SS			•	M	H
7. HELIANTHUS Sunflower / Girasol	H M	Many		•			S				M	L
8. IBERIS Candytuft / Iberis	L/M M	Pink, white	•	•			S SS				M	L
9. IMPATIENS Busy Lizzie / Impatiens /Alegría	L/M M	Many	•	•	•		SS SH	•	•		L	L
10. LATHYRUS Sweat Pea / Guisante de Olor	H M	Many	•	•			S			•	M	H
11. LOBELLA Lobelia / Lobelia	L M	Blue, white, red	•	•			S SS				M	M
12. LOBULARIA Alyssum / Alisum	L M	White, yellow, pink	•	•			S SS	•	•	•	M	L
13. MATTHIOLA Stock / Alhelí	M M	Many	•	•	•		S SS		•	•	M	M
14. NICOTIANA Tobacco Plant / Tabaco	H M	Many		•	•		S SS		•	•	M	L

1. Ageratum
2. Antirrhinum
3. Calendula
4. Catharanthus
5. Celosa
7. Helianthus
9. Impatiens
10. Lathyrus
11. Lobella
12. Lobularia
14. Nicotiana

4.1 ANNUALS

NAMES Botanical English / Spanish	Height and spread	Typical Flowers Colours	S	S	A	W	WHERE	GHB	GIP/W	PERF	DR	FR
15. PAPAVER Poppy / Amapola	M M	Many	•				S				H	M
16. PERICALLIS Cineraria / Cineraria	M M	Many	•	•	•		S SS		•		L	L
17. PETUNIA Petunia / Petunia	M H	Many	•	•	•		S SS	•	•	•	L	M
18. PHLOX Phlox / Flox	M M	Many	•	•			S SS				M	L
19. PORTULACA Sun Plant / Portulaca	L M	Many	•	•	•		S SS	•			M	L
20. SALVIA Annual Sage / Salvia	M L	Red, white, blue	•	•			S SS		•		M	L
21. SCABIOSA Scabious / Scabiosa	M L	Many		•			S			•	M	L
22. TAGETES PATULA French Marigold / Tagetes	L M	Yellow, orange, red	•	•	•		S SS		•	•	M	L
23. TROPAEOLUM Nasturtium / Capuchina	M H	Yellow, orange, cream	•	•	•	•	S SS		•	•	L	L
24. VIOLA Pansy / Pensamiento	L L	Many	•	•	•	•	S SS	•			M	H
25. ZINNIA Zinnia / Zinnia	M L	Many	•	•			S				M	L

COLUMN CODES:
HT = Height: **L** = Low (less than 20cm); **M** = Medium (20 – 40cm); **H** = High (over 40cm).
Sp = Spread: **L** = Little (less than 10cm); **M** = moderate (10-20cm); **H** = Spreading wide.
WHEN FLOWERING: S = Spring; **S** = Summer; **A** = Autumn; **W** = Winter.
Where: S = Likes full sun; **SS** = Likes semi shade; **SH** = Likes full shade.
GHB = Good in hanging baskets.
GIP/W = Good in pots and window boxes. **PERF** = Indicates that the plant gives out a pleasing smell.
DR = Drought resistance: **L** = Low; **M** = Moderate; **H** = High. **FR** = Frost resistance: **L** = Low;
M = moderate; **H** = High.

15. Papaver
16. Pericallis
17. Petunia
19. Portulaca
20. Salvia
22. Tagetes patula
23. Tropaeolum
24. Viola
25. Zinnia

123

4.2 PERENNIALS

NAMES — Botanical English / Spanish	Height and spread	Typical Flowers Colours	When Flowering				WHERE	BYEA	GHIB	GIP/W	PERLF	FOLG	EVG	DRR	FRR
			S	S	A	W									
Daisy like flowers Nos. 1 to 5															
1. ARGYRANTHEMUM Marquerite / Margarita	H H	Pink, red, yellow, white	•	•	•		S			• pot only		•	•	M	M
2. OSTEOPERMUM/ FRUTICOSUM African Daisy / Dimorphotheca	H H	White, purple, yellow	•	•	•		S	•					•	H	H
3. EURYOPS CHRYSANTHEMOIDES Paris daisy / Euryops/Marguerite	H H	Yellow	•	•	•	•	S			• pot only		•	•	H	H
4. CHRYSANTHEMUM Chrysanthemum / Crisantemo	H H	Many			•	•	S	•		• pot only	•		•	M	H
5. FELICIA Blue daisy / Agatea	H H	Blue	•	•	•		S				•			M	M
6. ABUTILON Chinese lantern / Abutilon	H H	Many	•	•	•		S SS			• pot only		•	•	L	L
7. AJANIA Ajania / Ajania	H H	Yellow			•	•	S					•	•	M	H
8. ARCTOTIS African daisy / Arctotis	M H	Many	•	•	•		S	•				•	•	M	M
9. BIDENS FERULIFOLIA Burr marigold / Bidens ferulifolia	L M	Yellow	•		•		S SS					•	•	M	M
10. COREOPSIS Tickseed / Coreopsis	M H	Yellow	•		•		S SS	•					•	M	H
11. CUPHEA Cuphea / Cuphea	H H	Many			•	•	S SS					•	•	M	H
12. DIANTHUS Carnation / Clavel	M H	Many	•				S	•	•		•			M	H
13. DICLIPTERA SUBERECTA Dicliptera / Dicliptera	M M	Orange	•		•		S			• pot only		•	•	M	M
14. GAZANIA Gazania / Gazania	L M	Many	•	•	•		SS	•			•		•	M	M
15. GERANIUMS Cranesbill / Geranio	M H	Many	•	•	•		S SS		•	•		•	•	M	L
16. HELIOPSIS Orange sunflower / Heliopsis	M H	Mustard, yellow	•	•	•		S	•					•	M	M

1a. Argyranthemum
1b. Argyranthemum
2. Osteoperum
3. Euryops Chrysanthemoides
4. Chrysanthemum
5. Felicia
6. Abutilon
8. Arctotis
9. Bidens Ferulifolia
11. Cuphea
12. Dianthus
14. Gazania
16. Heliopsis

4.2 PERENNIALS

NAMES Botanical English / Spanish	Height and spread	Typical Flowers Colours	S	S	A	W	WHERE	BY BEA	GHIB	GIP/W	PERF	FOL	EVG	DR	FR
17. HELLEBORUS Hellebore / Heleboro	M M	White	•			•	SS						•	L	H
18. IBERIS SIEMPERVIVENS Everlasting Candytuft / Iberis Siempervivens	M H	White	•	•			S							M	H
19. LEONOTIS Lion's ear / Leonotis	H H	Orange		•	•	•	S						•	H	H
20. MALVA Holyhock / Malva	H	Many	•	•	•		S	•						H	H
21. PAEONIA CAMBESSEDESII Majorcan Peony / Paeonia cambessedesii	H H	Many	•				S				•	•		L	M

PELARGONIUM/GERANIUM (Nº 22-25)

NAMES Botanical English / Spanish	Height and spread	Typical Flowers Colours	S	S	A	W	WHERE	BY BEA	GHIB	GIP/W	PERF	FOL	EVG	DR	FR
22. ZONALE Zonal / Zonale	H H	Many	•	•	•		S SS			•		•	•	M	M
23. PELTATUM Ivy leafed trailing / Murciana	M H	Pink, red, orange	•	•	•		S SS		•	•		•	•	H	L
24. REGAL Regal / Regal	H H	Many	•	•			S			•		•	•	H	M
25. GRAVEOLENS Scented / Perfumada	H H	Mauve	•	•	•		S		•	•		•	•	H	H
26. PRIMULA Primrose / Primula	L M	Many	•			•	SS			•				L	H
27. RUDBEKIA Coneflower/Rudbekia	H H	Many		•	•		S		•					M	M
28. SENECIO CINERARIA Dusty millar/Senecio maritime	M H	Yellow		•	•		S SS					•	•	M	H
29. STRELITZIA Bird of Paradise/Strelitzia	H H	Orange	•			•	S			•			•	H	L

COLUMN CODES:
HT = Height: **L** = Low (less than 20cm); **M** = Medium (20 – 40cm); **H** = High (over 40cm). **SP** = Spread: **L** = Little (less than 10cm); **M** = Moderate (10 – 20cm); **H** = spreading wide. **WHEN FLOWERING: S** = Spring; **S** = Summer; **A** = Autumn; **W** = Winter. **WHERE: S** = Likes full sun; **SS** = Likes semi shade; **SH** = Likes full shade. **BY SEA** = Plants suitable for gardens near the sea. **GHB** = Good in hanging baskets. **GIP/W** = Good in pots and window boxes. **PERF** = Plant has pleasant perfume. **FOL** = Plant has an attractive foliage. **EVG** = Plant is evergreen. **DR** = Drought resistance: **L** = Low; **M** = Moderate; **H** = high. **FR** = Frost resistance: **L** = Low; **M** = Moderate; **H** = High. * Primulas are also grown as annuals.

18. Iberis Siempervivens
19. Leonotis
20. Malva
21. Paeonia cambessedesii
22. Pelargonium Zonale
23. Pelargonium Peltatum
24. Pelargonium Regal
25. Pelargonium Graveolens
27. Rudbekia
28. Senecio
29. Strelitzia

127

4.3 CULINARY AND AROMATIC HERBS

NAMES Botanical English / Spanish	USES	WHERE	BY SEA	HT & SP	Le.	Fl.	Se.	When Flowering S S A W	Harvesting Season S S A W	GIP	PERF	PEREN	ANNUAL	DR	FR
1. ALLIUM Chives / Cebollino	C F S	S	•	L M	Green *	Pink	Pink	• • •	• •	•		•		M	H
2. ALOYSIA TRIPILLA Lemon verbena / Hierba Luisa	I C S	S	•	H H	Pale Green	Pale Pink		• •	• •		•	•		M	M
3. ANETHUM GRAVEOLENS Dill / Eneldo	C F	S SS		H L	Green *		Seeds *	•	• • •	•			•	L	L
4. ARTEMISIA Wormwood / Artemisia	I	S			Grey *	Small Yellow		•	• • •		•	•		H	M
5. BORAGO OFFICINALIS Borage / Borraja	S V	S	•	H H	Green *	Blue White *		• •	• • •			•	•	H	M
6. CHAMAEMELUM NOBILE Roman chamomile / Camomile / Manzanilla	I A	S		M M	Green	White daisy like*		• •	• •					M	H
7. COMFREY Comfrey / Consuelda	I*	S		H H	Green *	Blue		• •	• •			•		M	H
8. CORIANDRUM Coriander / Cilantro	C F S V	S SS		H M	Green *	White	*	• • •	• •				•	L	M
9. HELICHRYSUM ANGUSTIFOLIUM Curry plant / Curi	F	S		H H	Grey *	Yellow		• • •	• •					M	H
10. LAURUS Bay / Laurel	F	S	•	H H	Green *	Cream		•	• • •					M	H
LAVANDULA (Nª11-13)															
11. ANGUSTIFOLIA OFFICINALIS Lavender / Lavandula	A C	S	•	H H	Green/ Grey *	Purple		•	•		•	•	•	M	H
12. INTERMEDIA English / Inglesa	A C	S	•	H H	Green	Spikey Mauve *		•	•		•	•	•	M	H
13. DENTATA French / Dentata	A C	S	•	H H	Green	Soft Mauve Pink*		• • • •	•		•	•		H	H
14. MELISSA OFFICINALIS Lemon balm / Melissa	I F S	S SS	M M	M M	Green *	Pale White Pink		• • •	• • •		•	•	•	M	M

1. Allium
2. Aloysia Tripilla
4. ArtemIsia
5. Borago officinalis
6. Chamaemelum
7. Comfrey
9. Helichrysum Angustifolium
10. Laurus
12. Lavandula intermedia
13. Lavanda dentata
15 Mentha

129

4.3 CULINARY AND AROMATIC HERBS

NAMES Botanical English / Spanish	USES	WHERE	BY SEA	HT & SP	Typical colours & parts used (Le. / Fl. / Se.)	When Flowering (S S A W)	Harvesting Season (S S A W)	GIPRF	PERF	PEREN	ANNUAL	DR	FR
MENTHA / MINT / MENTA (N° 15-16)													
15. PIPERITA Peppermint / Hierba Buena	I A	S SS		M H	Green* Mauve	•	• • •	•	•	•		M	H
16. SPICATA Spearmint / Menta	F S	S SS		H H	Green* Mauve	•	• • •	•	•	•		M	H
17. OCIUM BASILICUM Basil / Albahaca	A F	S SS		M M	Green Purple White	• •	• •	•	•		•	M	
18. ORIGANUM Marjoram / Orégano / Mejorana	F	S SS		L M	Green* Purple White	•	• • • •	•	•			M	M
19. PETROSELINUM Parsley / Perejil	I F S	S SS		M M	Green*	• •	• • •	•	•		•	L	H
20. ROSMARINUS OFFICINALIS Rosemary / Romero officinalis	I A C F	S	•	H H	Green* Blue	• • •	• • • •	•				H	H
21. RUTA Rue / Ruda	I A	S		H H	Green* Yellow	• • •	• • • •	•	•			M	H
SALVIA / SAGE / SALVIA (N° 22-24)													
22. OFFICINALIS Common sage / Salvia officinalis	I A C F	S		H H	Green Grey* Purple	• • •	• • • • •	•	•			M	H
23. FARINACEA Mealy cup / Salvia farinacea	I S	S		M M	Green Blue	• • •	• •		•			M	L
24. ELEGANS RUTILANS Scarlet pineapple / Elegans Rutilans	I	S		H H	Green* Scarlet*	• • •	• • • • •	•	•			M	H
25. SANTOLINA Cotton lavender / Santolina	I S V	S	•	H H	Green Grey* Yellow	• •		•	•			H	H
26. TANACETUM PARTHENIUM Feverfew / Tanacetum parthenium	I A F	S SS		H H	Yellow Green* White daisy like	• • •	• • •	•	•			M	M
27. TARAXACUM OFFICINALE Dandelion / Diente de León	A C	S	•	M M	Green* Blue Root*	• •	• • •	•				M	H
28. THYMUS Thyme / Tomillo	I F	S	•	M H	Green Varied* Mauve Pink	• •	• • •	•	•			M	H
29. VALERIANA OFFICINALIS Cat's valerian / Valeriana officinalis	I	S	•	H H	Green* Pink Root*	• • •	• • •	•				H	H

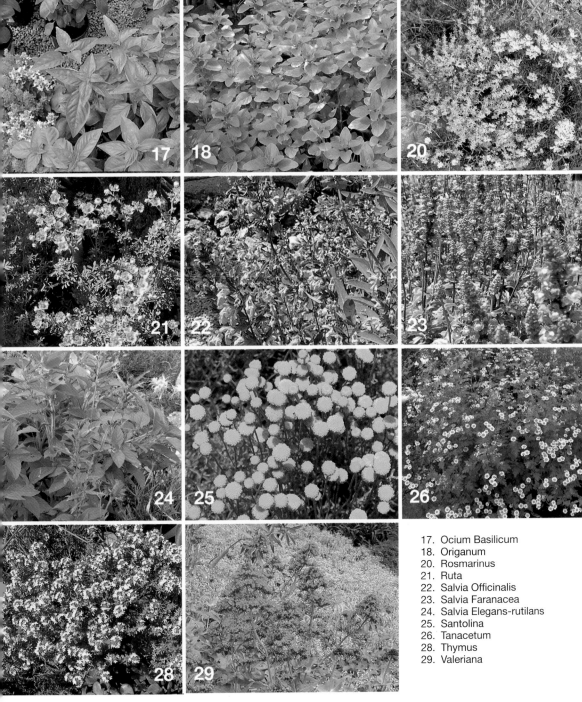

17. Ocium Basilicum
18. Origanum
20. Rosmarinus
21. Ruta
22. Salvia Officinalis
23. Salvia Faranacea
24. Salvia Elegans-rutilans
25. Santolina
26. Tanacetum
28. Thymus
29. Valeriana

COLUMN CODES:
USES – I = Infusion; **C** = Companion planting; **A** = Aromatherapy/cosmetic; **F** = Flavouring. **S** = Salads; **V** = Vegetable.
BY SEA = Plants suitable for gardens near the sea.Where: **S** = Likes full sun; **SS** = Likes semi shade;
SH = Likes full shade. **Ht** = height: **L** = Low (less than 20cm); **M** = Medium (20 – 40cm); **H** = High (over 40cm).
SP = Spread: **L** = Little (less than 10cm); **M** = Moderate (10 – 20cm); **H** = spreading wide.
Typical colours and parts used – Leaf, flower or seeds *.
When flowering: S = Spring; **S**= Summer; **A** = Autumn; **W** = Winter. Harvesting season: **S** = Spring; **S** = Summer;
A = Autumn; **W** = Winter. **GIP** = Good in pots. **PERF** = Plant has pleasant perfume.
PERE = Perennial. **ANNUAL** = Annual.
DR = Drought resistance: **L** = Low; **M** = Moderate; **H** = High. **FR** = Frost resistance: **L** = Low; **M** = Moderate; **H** = High.

131

4.4 GROUND COVER PLANTS

NAMES — Botanical English / Spanish	Height and Spread	Typical Flowers or (leaf) Colours	S	S	A	W	WHERE	Ground Cover	ROCKERIES	CASCADING	BY SEA	DR	FR
1. ARCTOTIS (See p.125) African daisy / Arctotis	M H	Many	•	•	•		S	•	•	•	•	M	M
2. ASTERISCUS MARITIME Asteriscus / Asteriscus	L H	Yellow	•	•	•		S SS	•	•		•	M	H
3. CARPOBROTUS Giant pig face / Carpobrotus	L H	Purple, yellow	•	•	•		S	•		•	•	M	L
4. CHLOROPHYTUM COMOSUM Spider plant / Cinta	H H	White (variegated leaf)	•	•	•		SS SH	•		•		L	L
5. CRASSULA MULTICAVA Fairy / Crassula multicava	M H	Tiny pink & white (pale green)	•			•	S	•			•	H	L
6. DICHONDRA MICRANTH (lawn substitute) Kidney weed / Dichondra micranth	L H	Green (dark green)	•				S SS	Lawn				M	H
7. FRAGARIA ALPINA Alpine strawberry / Fresa alpina	L H	White, small fruit		•			S SS	•				M	H
8. GAZANIA Gazania / Gazania	L H	Many	•	•	•		S	•	•		•	M	M
9. HEDERA Ivy / Hedera	L H	Green (variegated)					S SS	•			•	M	H
10. JUNIPERUS HORIZONTALIS Spreading juniper / Juniperus horizontalis	M H	Blue, green					S	•			•	M	H
11. LANTANA MONTEVIDENSIS Trailing lantana / Lantana montevidensis	M H	Mauve, white, yellow	•	•	•	•	S	•	•	•	•		H
MESSEMBRYANTHEMUM FAMILY (Nos 12-15)													
12. APTENIA Aptenia / Aptenia	L H	Pink/red	•	•			S	•	•	•	•	M	L
13. DELOSPERMA Mesem / Mesem	L H	Many	•	•			S	•					M
14. DROSANTHEMUM CANDENS Rosea ice plant / Drosanthemum candens	L H	Many	•	•			S	•		•	•	M	L
15. LAMPRANTHUS Ice plant / Lampranthus	L H	Red, pink, orange, yellow	•	•			S	•	•	•	•	M	M

2. Asteriscus Maritime
3. Carpobrotus
4. Chlorophytum
6. Dichondra Micranth
8. Gazanias
9. Hedera
10. Juniperus Horizontalis
11. Lantana Montevidensis

133

4.4 GROUND COVER PLANTS

NAMES Botanical English / Spanish	Height and Spread	Typical Flowers or (leaf) Colours	When Flowering				WHERE	Ground Cover	ROCKERIES	CASCADING	BY SEA	DR	FR
			S	S	A	W							
16. LOTUS MACULATES Lotus / Lotus	L H	Burnt gold, yellow	•	•	•		S	•	•	•		M	M
17. ORIGANUM (See Pag. 131) Marjoram/orégano / Mejorana / Orégano	L M	Pink, white	•	•			S	•			•	M	H
18. PLECTRANTHUS NEOCHILIS Plectranthus neochilis / Plectranthus neochilis	M H	Lavender	•	•	•			•		•	•	M	L
19. ROSMARINUS PROSTRATUS Ground cover rosemary / Rosmarinus prostratus	M H	Blue	•	•		•	S SS	•	•	•	•	M	H
20. SEDUM RUBROTINCTUM Christmas cheer / Sedum rubrotinctum	L L	Yellow (succulent leaves go red in dry conditions)	•	•		•	S	•	•		•	H	M
21. THYMUS (See Pag. 131) Thyme / Tomillo	M M	White, pink mauve	•	•			S	•		•	•	M	H
22. TRADESCANTIA Spiderwort / Tradescantia	M H	Pink	•				S SS	•		•	•	M	M
23. VERBENA Verbena / Verbena	M H	Many	•	•	•		S	•			•	H	M
24. VINCA MAJOR Greater periwinkle / Vinca major	H H	Violet, blue	•	•	•		S	•	•		•	H	H
25. VINCA MINOR Lesser periwinkler / Vinca minor	M H	White, pink, blue, violet	•	•			SS	•			•	M	H
26. VIOLA RIVINIANA Dog violet / Viola riviniana	M H	Blue, violet	•	•			S SS	•			•	M	H
27. GRASSES (see Section 4.13)													

COLUMN CODES:
HT = height: **L** = Low (less than 20cm); **M** = Medium (20 – 40cm); **H** = High (over 40cm). **SP** = Spread: **L** = Little (less than 10cm); **M** = Moderate (10 – 20cm); **H** = Spreading wide. **WHEN FLOWERING: S** = Spring; **S** = Summer; **A** = Autumn; **W** = Winter. **WHERE: S** = Likes full sun; **SS** = Likes semi shade; **SH** = Likes full shade. **CASCADING** – will cascade down over walls and banks. **BY SEA** = Plants suitable for gardens near the sea. **DR** = Drought resistance: **L** = Low; **M** = Moderate; **H** = High. **FR** = Frost resistance: **L** = Low; **M** = Moderate; **H** = High.
Other plants that can be used as ground cover include morning glory, nasturtiums and gourds.

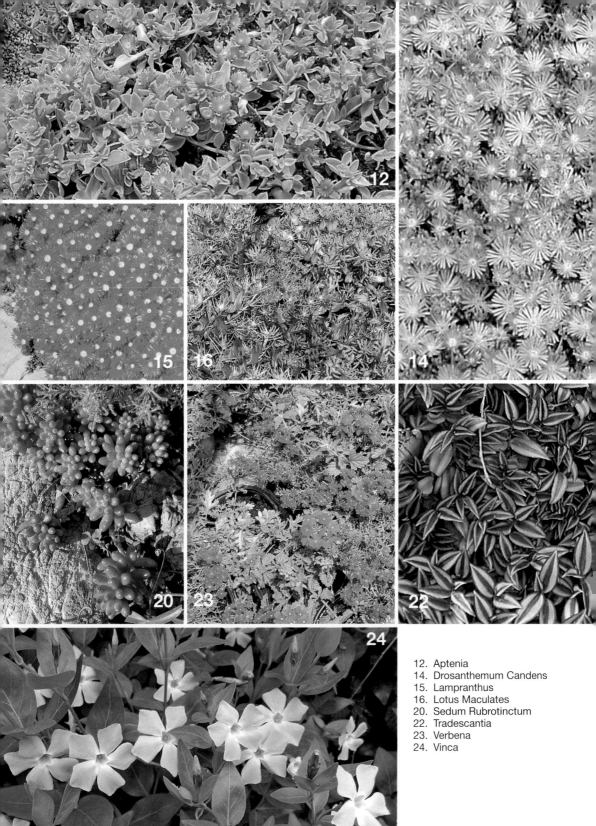

12. Aptenia
14. Drosanthemum Candens
15. Lampranthus
16. Lotus Maculates
20. Sedum Rubrotinctum
22. Tradescantia
23. Verbena
24. Vinca

4.5 FLOWERING SHRUBS

NAMES Botanical English / Spanish	Height and Spread	Typical Flowers Colours	S	S	A	W	WHERE	BY SEA	GIP	PERF	HEDGES	EVG	DR	FR
1. BUDDLEJA Buddleja / Budleia	H H	Mauve, yellow + others	•	•	•		S	•		•		•	M	H
2. CALLISTEMON Bottlebrush / Calistemo	H H	Red, yellow, white	•	•			S	•			•	•	H	H
3. CAMELLIA Camellia / Camelia	H H	Many	•	•		•	SS			•		•	L	H
4. CEANOTHUS California Lilac / Ceanoto	H H	Blue, violet, white	•	•	•		S SS	•		•		•	M	H
5. CESTRUM NOCTURNUM Lady of the night / Galán de noche	H H	White		•	•		S	•	•	•			M	M
6. CISTUS Rock rose / Cistus	H H	Pink, white yellow	•	•			S	•				•	M	H
7. CORONILLA Crown vetch/Coronilla	H H	Yellow	•				S	•				•	M	H
8. DATURA (Brugmansia) Angel's trumpet / Datura	H H	Pale yellow, pale pink	•	•	•		S SS	•		•			M	L
9. ECHIUM CANDICANS Pride of Madeira / Echium candicans	H H	Blue, white	•	•			S SS					•	M	M
10. ERICA Heather / Brezo	M M	Pink, white	•		•	•	S SS	•	•			•	M	H
11. HEBE Veronica / Hebe	L L	Many	•	•	•	•	S SS	•				•	M	H
12. HIBISCUS ROSA SINSENSIS Chinese hibiscus / Hibisco rosa	H H	Many	•	•	•		S	•	•		•	•	M	M
13. HYDRANGEA Hydrangea / Hortensia	H H	Many	•	•	•		SS	•	•				M	H
14. JUSTICIA ADHATODA Justicia / Justicia	H M	White with pink veins	•	•			S					•	M	L
15. IOCHROMA Tube flower / Iochroma	H H	Red, purple, blue		•	•		S SS	•	•		•	•	L	L

2. Callistemon
3. Camellia
4. Ceanothus
5. Cestrum Nocturnum
6. Cistus
7. Coronilla
8. Datura
9. Echium
11. Hebe
12. Hibiscus
13. Hydrangea
16a. Lantana mixed
16b. Lantana Bandera

137

4.5 FLOWERING SHRUBS

NAMES Botanical English - Spanish	Height and Spread	Typical Flowers Colours	S	S	A	W	WHERE	BY SEA	GIP	PERF	HEDGES	EVG	DR	FR
16. LANTANA CAMARA Common lantana /	H H	Orange/red (1)	•	•	•		S	•	•			•	H	M
Lantana camara	H H	Pink/yellow white/yellow white	•	•	•		S	•	•	•			H	M
(1) Spanish flag/bandera									•	•	•			
	M M	Yellow	•	•	•	•	S						H	M
17. LAVATERA Lavatera / La malva real	H H	Pink, white		•	•		S	•					M	M
18. MALVAVISCUS ARBOREUS Sleepy Malva / Malvaviscus Arboreus	H M	Red, pink, white	•	•	•		S SS	•					L	L
19. NERIUM Oleander / Adelfa	H H	Many	•	•	•	•	S	•	•		•	•	H	H
20. PITTOSPORUM TOBIRA Japanese mock orange / Pittosporum	H H	Cream	•	•			S SS	•		•	•	•	M	H
21. PHILADELPHUS Mock orange / Celinda	H H	White	•	•			S	•		•		•	M	H
22. PLUMBAGO Leadwort / Plumbago	H H	Blue, white	•	•	•		S	•	•				H	H
23. PLUMERIA Frangipani / Frangipani	H H	Cream		•			S			•			M	L
24. POLYGALA DALMAISIANA Sweet pea shrub / Polygala	H H	Pink	•	•	•	•	S	•	•				M	H
25. RETAMA - GENISTA Broom family / Retama	H H	Yellow	•	•			S	•	•	•		•	M	H
26. ROSA Rose / Rosa	H H	Many	•	•			S	•		•			L	H
27. RUSSELIA Coral plant / Russelia	H H	Red, pink, white	•	•	•		S	•				•	M	M
28. SENNA CORYMBOSA Cassia / Cassia	H H	Yellow		•			S	•					M	L
29. STREPTOSOLEN Marmelade bush / Streptosolen	H H	Orange/ yellow	•	•			S SS	•	•			•	M	L
30. VIBURNUM Viburnum / Viburnum	H H	White	•	•		•	S SS	•			•	•	M	H
31. ALYOGYNE HUEGELII Lilac Hibiscus / Alyogyne	H H	Lilac, violet	•	•	•		S	•					M	H

17. Lavaterra
19. Nerium
20. Pittosporum
21. Philadelphus
22. Plumbago
23. Plumeria
24. Polygala
25. Retama
27. Russelia
28. Senna Corymbosa
29. Streptosolen

COLUMN CODES:
HT = height: **L** = Low (less than 50cm); **M** = Medium (50 – 100cm); **H** = High (over 100cm). **SP** = Spread: **L** = Little (less than 50cm);
M = Moderate (50 – 100cm); **H** = spreading wide. **WHEN FLOWERING: S** = Spring; **S** = Summer; **A** = Autumn; **W** = Winter.
WHERE: S = Likes full sun; **SS** = Likes semi shade; **SH** = Likes full shade. **BY SEA** = Plants suitable for gardens near the sea.
GIP = Good in pots. **PERF** = Plant has pleasant perfume. **HEDGES** = Suitable for hedging. **EVG** = Plant is evergreen.
DR = Drought resistance: **L** = Low; **M** = Moderate; **H** = high. **FR** = Frost resistance: **L** = Low; **M** = Moderate; **H** = High.

4.6 CLIMBING SHRUBS

NAMES Botanical English / Spanish	Height and Spread	Typical Flowers Colours	S	S	A	W	WHERE	FENCES	BY SEA	VIG	GIP	PERF	FOL	EVG	DR	FR
BIGNONIA FAMILY - No 1-4																
1. PODRANEA RICASOLIANA Pink trumpet vine / Ricasoliana 'Contessa Sara'	H H	Pink		•	•		S	•	•	H					H	H
2. CAMPSIS GRANDIFLORA Chinese Trumpet creeper / Campsis grandiflora	H H	Waxy orange		•	•		S	•	•	H					H	H
3. TECOMARIA CAPENSIS Cape Honeysuckle / Tecomaria Capensis	H M	Orange, yellow		•	•	•	S SS	•	•	H				•	H	M
4. PANDOREA JASMINOIDES Bower vine / Pandorea Jasminoides	H M	Pink, yellow with dark throats		•	•	•	S SS	•	•	H			•	•	H	M
BOUGAINVILLEA / BOUGAINVILLEA / BUGANVILLA (Nos 5-7)																
5. GLABRA Glabra / Glabra	H H M M	Purple White	•	•	•	•	S S	•	•	H M					H M	M L
6. SCARLET O'HARA Scarlet O'Hara / Scarlet O'Hara	H H	Red	•	•	•	•	S	•	•	H					H	M
7. BUTTIANA Buttiana / Buttiana	M M	Orange, gold, pink	•	•	•	•	S	•	•	M					H	L
8. CLEMATIS Virgin's bower / Clematide	H L	Many	•	•			S SS	•	•	L					L	M
9. FALLOPIA Mile a minute plant/ Russian vine / Polygonum	H H	White	•	•			S	•		H			•	•	H	H
10. HEDERA Ivy / Hiedra	H H						S	•		H			•	•	H	M
11. IPOMEA Morning Glory / Ipomea	H H	Blue, purple		•	•	•	S	•		H					H	M

1. Podranea
2. Campis Grandiflora
4. Pandorea Jasminoide
5. Glabra
6. Scarlet O´Hara
7. Buttiana
9. Fallopia
10. Hedera
11. Ipomea

4.6 CLIMBING SHRUBS

NAMES Botanical English - Spanish	Height and Spread	Typical Flowers Colours	S	S	A	W	WHERE	FENCES	BY SEA	VIG	GIP	PERF	FOL	EVG	DR	FR
JASMINUM / JASMINE / JAZMÍN (Nos. 12-14)																
12. OFFICINALE Common - Blanco común	H H	White	•	•	•	•	S	•	•	H	•			•	H	H
13. POLYANTHUM Pink - Polyanthum	M M	White with pink buds	•	•			S	•	•	H	•			•	H	H
14. NUDIFLORUM Winter - Amarillo	M M	Yellow	•			•	S	•	•	H				•	H	H
15. LONICERA Honeysuckle - Madreselva	H H	White, pink	•	•	•	•	S	•	•	H	•			•	H	H
16. MANDEVILLA (Dipladenia) Mandevilla - Dipladenia	M L	Many		•	•		SS			M	•				L	L
17. PASSIFLORA Pasión flower - Pasiflora	H M	Many		•	•		S SS	•	•	M					M	M
18. PYROSTEGIA VENUSTA Brazilian flame vine - Pyrostegia venusta	M M	Orange	•			•	S	•	•	M					H	L
19. ROSA Climbing rose - Rosal 'trepador'	M M	Many	•	•	•		S		•	L				•	M	H
20. SOLANDRA Chalice vine - Solandra	H H	Creamy yellow		•	•		S	•	•	M		•			H	L
21. SOLANUM Potato vine - Solano	H H	White, blue	•	•	•	•	S		•	M		•		•	H	M
22. STEPHANOTIS Stephanotis - Stephanotis	L L	White		•	•		SS	•	•	L	•	•	•	•	L	L
23. THUNBERGIA - ALATA Black-eyed Susan - Tumbergia alata	H M	Yellow, orange	•	•	•		SS			M				•	L	M
24. VITIS VINIFERA Grape vine/Vid	H H	White	•				S	•	•	M					H	H
25. WISTERIA Wisteria - Glicinia	H H	Blue, white, mauve	•	•			S	•	•	H		•			H	H

COLUMN CODES:
HT = Height: **L** = Low (less than 2m); **M** = Medium (2 – 5m); **H** = High (over 5m). **SP** = Spread: **L** = Little (less than 1m); **M** = Moderate (1 – 2m); **H** = spreading wide. **WHEN FLOWERING: S** = Spring; **S** = Summer; **A** = Autumn; **W** = Winter. **WHERE: S** = Likes full sun; **SS** = Likes semi shade; **SH** = Likes full shade. **FENCES** = Suitable for covering fences. **BY SEA** = Plants suitable for gardens near the se[a]
VIG = Vigorous growth. **GIP** = Good in pots. **PERF** = Plant has pleasant perfume. **FOL** = Plant has an attractive foliage. **EVG** = Plant is evergreen. **DR** = Drought resistance: **L** = Low; **M** = Moderate; **H** = high. **FR** = Frost resistance: **L** = Low; **M** = Moderate; **H** = High.
Note: Other plants that can be used as climbers are included in the shrub table (4.6) e.g., plumbago and lantana.

12. Jasminum Officinale
13. Jasminum Polyanthum
14. Jasminum Nudiflorum
15. Lonicera
16. Mandevilla
17. Passiflora
18. Pyrostegia
21. Solanum
22. Stephanotis
23. Thunbergia
25. Wisteria

143

4.7 FLOWERING TREES

NAMES — Botanical, English - Spanish	Height and Spread	Typical Flower and Fruit Colours	When Flowering				WHERE	BY SEA	PERF	FOL	EVG	DR	FR
			S	S	A	W							
1. ACACIA — Wattle / Acacia	H W	Yellow	•			•	S	•			•	H	H
2. ALBIZIA JULIIBRISSIN — Silk tree / Albizia	H W	Pink	•				S	•				L	H
3. ARBUTUS — Strawberry tree / Madroño	M M	White flower (strawberry type fruit)	•		•		S	•	•		•	H	H
4. BAUHINA — Orchid tree / Bauhina	H H	Pink, red	•		•		S	•				H	L
5. CAESALPINIA GILLIESII — Bird of Paradise, Devil's tonque / Lengua de Diablo	M M	Yellow with red stamens	•		•		S	•				M	H
6. CERCIS — Judas tree / Árbol de Amor	M M	Pink	•				S	•				H	H
7. CHORISIA SPECIOSA — Floss-silk tree / Chorisia	H H	Salmon, burgundy			•	•	S	•				M	M
8. CITRUS LIMON — Lemon / Limonero	M M	White	•	•	•	•	S	•	•	•	•	M	M
9. CITRUS SINENSIS — Orange / Naranjo	M M	White	•				S	•	•	•	•	M	M
10. EUPHORBIA PULCHERIMMA — Mexican flame tree / Poinsettia	H H	Red bracts	•			•	S	•				H	H
11. HIBISCUS MUTABILIS — Cotton rose / Hibiscus mutabilis	M M	White changing to pink/red	•		•		S	•				M	H
12. JACARANDA — Jacaranda / Jacaranda	H H	Blue	•		•		S	•				H	M
13. JUSTICIA — Justice / Justicia	M M	Many	•		•		S	•			•	M	L
14. KOELREUTERIA PANICULATA — Golden rain tree / Koelreuteria	H H	Yellow	•				S	•			•	M	M
15. LABURNUM — Golden rain / Lluvia de oro	H H	Yellow	•				S					L	H
16. LAGERSTROEMIA — Crape Myrtle / Árbol de Júpiter	M M	Pink, mauve	•		•		S	•				M	M

1. Acacia
2. Albizia
4. Bauhina
5. Caesalpinia
6. Cercis
7. Chorisia
10. Euphorbia
12. Jacaranda
14. Koelreuteria

145

4.7 FLOWERING TREES

NAMES Botanical English / Spanish	Height and Spread	Typical Flower and Fruit Colours	S	S	A	W	WHERE	BY SEA	PERF	FOL	EVG	DR	FR
17. MAGNOLIA Magnolia / Magnolia	H H	Many		•			S	•	•			M	H
18. MELIA AZEDARACH Bead tree / Melia Azedarach	H H	Lilac (cream berries)	•	•			S	•	•	•		H	H
19. PARKINSONIA Jerusalem thorn / Parkinsonia	H H	Yellow	•	•			S	•	•		g	H	H
20. PRUNUS ARMENIACA Apricot / Albaricoque	H M	White	•				S					L	H
21. PRUNUS CERASUS Flowering Cherry / Cerezos de flor	M M	Pink, red	•				S					M	H
22. PRUNUS DULCIS Almond / Almendro	M M	White, pink	•				S	•				H	H
23. ROBINIA PSEUDOACACIA False Acacia / Robina Pseudoacacia	H H	Pink, white	•	•			S	•	•			H	H
24. SALÍX BABILÓNICA Weeping willow / Salix	H H	Cream	•				S	•		•	g	M	H
25. SCHINUS False pepper / Falso pimiento	H H	Cream	•	•			S	•			g	H	M
26. SYRINGA Lilac / Lilo	M M	Pink	•	•			S	•	•			M	H
27. TAMARIX TETRANDRA Tamarix Tetrandra/ Tamarix Tetrandra	M M	Pink	•	•			S	•			g	H	M

COLUMN CODES:
HT = height: **L** = Low (less than 2m); **M** = Medium (2 –10m); **H** = High (over 10m). **SP** = Spread: **L** = Little (less than 2m); **M** = Moderate (2– 5m); **H** = spreading wide. When flowering: **S** = Spring; **S** = Summer; **A** = Autumn; **W** = Winter. **WHERE: S** = Likes full sun; **SS** = Likes semi shade; **SH** = Likes full shade.
BY SEA = Plants suitable for gardens near the sea. **PERF** = Plant has pleasant perfume. **FOL** = Plant has an attractive foliage. **EVG** = Plant is evergreen.
DR = Drought resistance: **L** = Low; M = Moderate; **H** = high. **FR** = Frost resistance: **L** = Low; **M** = Moderate; **H** = High

Note: There are a number of other deciduous trees such as gingko biloba and white mulberry suitable for the average garden but they have insignificant flowers. There are also many trees in the Prunus family worth considering for their flowers and foliage. A number of fruit trees are included in the above list for the quality of their blossom. They are also included in the list of fruiting trees in section 4.8 along with some other trees that can give good shade in a garden but have less spectacular flowers.

16. Lagerstroemia
17. Magnolia
18. Melia Azedarach
19. Parkinsonia
21. Prunus Cerasus
22. Prunus Dulcis
23. Robinia Pseudoacacia
24. Salix
25. Schinus
26. Syringa
27. Tamarix

4.8 FRUITING TREES, BUSHES AND PLANTS

This is a selection from the eighty fruits included in 'Growing healthy fruit in Spain' which provides full information for their selection, planting, watering, feeding, pruning, spraying and harvesting.

NAMES Botanical English / Spanish	Form	TBT	THT	THT	Typical planting Heights Above Sea Level (metres)					DR	FR
					< 200	< 400	< 800	< 1200	> 1200		
1. PRUNUS AMYGDALUS Almond / Almendro	Tree	J, F, M	A-S	W	•	•	•	•		M/H	H
2. MALUS COMMUNIS Apple / Manzano	Tree	M, A	A-O	W	•	•	•	•	•	M	H
3. ARMENIACA VULGARIS Apricot / Albaricoquero	Tree	A, M	May	W	•	•				H	H
4. PERSIA GRATISOIMA Avocado / Aguacate	Tree	J, F, M	O, J	Sp.	•	•				M	M
5. MUSA PARADISIACA Banana / Plantanera		A, J	A, O	W.	•	•				M	L
6. PRUNUS AVIUM Cherry / Cerezo	Tree	M, A	M-M	W.	•	•	•	•		M	H
7. FICUS CARICA Fig / Higuera	Tree	-	A-O	W.	•	•	•			H	H
8. CITRUS PARADISI Grapefruit / Pomelo	Tree	M, A		Sp.	•	•				M	M/H
9. VITUS VINFERA Grapevine / Vid	Vine	A, M	J, O	W.	•	•	•	•	•	H	H
10. CITRUS LIMON Lemon / Limonero	Tree	Cont **	Cont	Sp.	•	•				M	L/M
11. CITRUS RETICULATA Mandarin / Mandarino	Tree	M, A	O, J	Sp.	•	•				M	H
12. MANGIFERA INDICA Mango / Mangero	Tree	A, M, J	A-S	Sp.	•	•				M	L
13. PRUNUS PERSICA Nectarine / Nectarina	Tree	A, M	May - July	W.	•	•				M	H

1. Almonds
2. Apple
3. Apricot
4. Avocado
5. Banana
6. Cherry
7. Fig
8. Grapefruit
9. Grapevine
10. Lemon
11. Mandarin

149

4.8 FRUITING TREES, BUSHES AND PLANTS

NAMES Botanical English / Spanish	Form	TBT	THT	THT	Typical planting Heights Above Sea Level (metres)					DR	FR
					 200	 400	 800	 1200	> 1200		
14. ERIOBOTRYRA JAPONICA Nispero / Níspero de Japón	Tree	O, N	A-M	Sp.	•	•				M/H	M
15. OLEA EUROPEA Olive / Olivo	Tree	M, A	N, F	W.	•	•	•	•		H	H
16. CITRUS SINENSIS Orange / Naranjo	Tree	M, A	N, J	Sp.	•	•				M	M
17. PRUNUS PERICA Peach / Melocotonero	Tree	A, M	J-S	W.	•	•	•			M	H
18. PYRUS COMMUNIS Pear / Peral	Tree	M, A	A-O	W.	•	•	•		•	M	H
19. DIESPHROS KAKI Persimmon / Kaki	Tree	A, M	S-M	W.	•	•	•			M	H
20. PRUNUS SATIVA Plum / Ciruelo	Tree	M, A	J-J	W.	•	•	•	•	•	M	H
21. PUNICA GRANATUM Pomegranate / Granado	Bush	May	O-F	W.	•	•	•			M	H
22. CYDONIA OBLONGA Quince / Membrillo	Tree	M, A	S-O	W.	•	•	•			M	H
23. RUBUS IDEAS Raspberry / Frambuesa	Cane	M, N	M, N	W.		•	•	•	•	L	H
24. FRAGARIA ARANASSA Strawberry (Cultivated) / Fresón	Plant *	J, O	JA-A ***	W.	•	•	•	•		M	H

COLUMN CODES:
TBT = Typical blossom time (months): **THT** = Typical harvest time (months):
TPT = Typical pruning time(season): **DR** = Drought resistance (once established): **H** = High: M= Medium: **LOW** = Low.
 * Actually grown from runners from mature plants.
 ** The 'lunar' and 'cuatro estaciones' varieties are perpetual flowering and fruiting.
*** Early fruit if forced under plastic cloches

13. Nectarine
14. Níspero
15. Olive
16. Orange
17. Peach
18. Pear
19. Persimmon
20. Plum
21. Pomegrante
22. Quince
23. Strawberry

4.9 EVERGREEN TREES

NAMES Botanical English - Spanish	Height and Spread	Suitability for small and large gardens & rockeries			WHERE	BY SEA	CONTAINERS	HEDGES	SLOW GROW	DR	FR
		Small	Large	Rockeries & smaller beds (dwarf types)							
1. ABIES Fir / Abito	H H		•		S	•			•	M	H
2. ARAUCARIA HETEROPHYLLA Norfolk island pine / Araucaria heterophylla	H H	•	•		S	•	•		•	M	H
3. CEDRUS Cedar / Cedro	H H		•		S	•			•	M	H
4. CEDRUS LEBANI Lebonon ceder / Cedro lebaní	H H		•		S	•			•	M	H
5. CHAMAECYPARIS LAWSONIANA Lawson Cypress/ Ciprés lawsoniana	H H	•	•	•	S	•	•	•		M	H
6. CUPRESSOCYPARIS LEYLANDII Leyland ciprés / Ciprés leylandii	M M	•	•		S	•		•		M	H
7. CUPRESSUS Cipres / Ciprés	M M	•	•		S	•		•		M	H
8. CUPRESSUS SEMPERVIRENS Funeral trees / Cupressus sempervirens	H M		•		S	•			•	M	H
9. EUCALYPTUS GUNNII Cider gum / Eucalipto gunnii	H H		•		S	•				M	H
10. FICUS ELASTICA Indian rubber tree / Ficus elastica	H H	•	•		S SS	•	•		•	M	L
11. JUNIPERUS Juniper / Enebro	M M	•	•	•	S	•	•	•	•	M	H
12. PICEA Spruce / Picea	H H	•	•	•	S	•			•	M	H
13. PINUS HALEPENSIS Aleppo pine / Pinus halepensis	H H		•		S	•			•	M	H

1. Abies
2. Araucaria
3. Cedrus
6. Cupresocyparis
7. Cupressus
10. Ficus Elástica
11. Juniperus
12. Picea
13. Pinus Halepensis
14. Pinus Nigra Maritime

153

4.9 EVERGREEN TREES

NAMES Botanical English - Spanish	Height and Spread	Suitability for small and large gardens & rockeries			WHERE	BY SEA	CONTAINERS	HEDGES	SLOW GROW	DR	FR
		Small	Large	Rockeries & smaller beds (dwarf types)							
14. PINUS NIGRA MARITIME Corsican pine / Pinus nigra maritime	H H	•	•		S	•			•	H	H
15. PINUS PINEA Pine nut pine / Pinus pinea	H H		•		S	•			•	H	H
16. TAXUS Yew / Tejo	H H	•	•	•	S	•	•	•	•	M	H
17. THUJA Thuja / Tuja	M H		•		S	•	•	•		M	H
18. TSUGA Hemlock / Tsuga	H H	•	•	•	S	•			•	M	H
19. QUERUS ILEX Holm oak / Encina ilex	M M	•	•		S	•			•	H	H
20. QUERUS SUBER Cork oak / Encina suber	H H		•		S	•			•	M	H

COLUMN CODES:
HT = Height: **L** = Low (less than 2m); **M** = Medium (2 – 10m); **H** = High (over 10m). **SP** = Spread: **L** = Little (less than 2m); **M** = Moderate (2- 5m); **H** = Spreading wide. **SUITABLE FOR GARDENS: Small** = up to 1,000 square metres; **Large** = over a 1,000 square metres.
For rockeries and containers there are slow growing ornamental dwarf varieties.
DR = Drought resistance: **L** = Low; **M** = Moderate; **H** = High. **FR** = Frost resistance: **L** = Low; **M** = Moderate; **H** = High.

15. Pinus Pinea
16. Taxus
17. Thuja
19. Querus Ilex
20. Querus Suber

155

4.10 PALMS, YUCCAS, CORDYLINES & MUSAS

NAMES Botanical English / Spanish	Height and Spread	Format of Trunk	Typical Colours of a. flowers b. fruit	When Flowering S S A W	WHERE	BY SEA	POTS	DR	FR
A. FEATHER PALMS									
1. ARCHONTOPHOENIX Archontophoenix / Archontophoenix (fronds fall off naturally leaving smooth ringed trunk)	H H	Single, slender. Smooth ringed	a. Cream b. Red	•	S SS	•		L	L
2. ARESCASTRUM Coco palm / Coco	H M	Single, slender. Smooth ringed	a. Cream b. Brown/red	•	S SS	•		M	L
3. HOWEA BELMOREANA (Kentia) Sentry palm / Howea belmoreana	L*/M L*/M *in pots	Single, slender. Smooth ringed	a. Small green b. Brown/red	•	SS	•	•	L	L
4. PHOENIX CANARIENSIS Canary Island date palm/ Phoenix canariensis	H H	Single up to 1m wide. Rough rippled	a. Small green b. Yellow inedi- ble dates	•	S	•		M	M
5. PHOENIX DACTYLIFERA Date palm / Phoenix dactylifera	H H	Single medium. Rough rippled	a. Cream b. Yellow edible dates	• •	S	•		M	M
6. PHOENIX RECLINATA Senegal date palm/ Phoenix reclinata	M/H H	Multiple from base	a. Cream b. Red	• •	S	•		M	L
7. PHOENIX ROEBELENII Dwarf date palm/ Phoenix roebelenii	L/M L	Single medium rough	a. Cream b. Small black	•	S	•	•	H	M
8. SYAGRUS Syagrus / Syagrus	M M	Smooth with rings	a. Cream b. Greeny	•	S SS	•		M	L
B. FAN PALMS									
9. BRAHEA ARMATA Hesper palm / Brahea armata	M M	Single with blue/grey stiff fronds	a. Cream b. Yellow	•	S SS	•	•	M	M
10. CHAMAEROPS Mediterranean fan palm / Palmita (Indigenous to Spain grows wild on scrublands.)	M M	Multiple Slender Sha- ggy/fibrous	a. Male-yellow Female-green c. Orange date like	•	S SS	•		H	H
11. LIVISTONIA CHINENSIS Chinese fan palm / Livistonia chinensis	H M M	Single medium rough	a. Cream b. Blue	•	S SS	•	•	H	H
12. TRACHYCARPUS FORTUNEI Windmill palm / Trachycarpus Shallow rooted good pot plant	L	Single medium fibrous	a. Small yellow b. Dark blue berries	•	S	•	•	M	H

1

2

3

6

4

5

7

8

9

10

11

1. Archontophoenix
2. Arescastrum
3. Howea Belmoreana
4. Phoenix Canariensis
5. Phoenix Dactylifera
6. Phoenix Reclinata
7. Phoenix Roebelenii
8. Syagrus
9. Brahea Armata
10. Chamaerops
11. Livistonia Chinensis

157

4.10 PALMS, YUCCAS, CORDYLINES & MUSAS

NAMES — Botanical English / Spanish	Height and Spread	Format of Trunk	Typical Colours of a. flowers b. fruit	S	S	A	W	WHERE	BY SEA	POTS	DR	FR
13. WASHINGTONIA FILIFERA Cotton palm / Washingtonia filifera. Named because of the cotton like thread between the frond segments	H M	Single medium rough	a. Small white b. Black berries			•		S	•		H	M
14. WASHINGTONIA ROBUSTA Mexican fan palm / Washingtonia robusta. Circular fronds less segmented than filifera.	H M	Single narrow tapered rough	a. Cream b. Small brown berries		•			S	•		H	M
15. CYCAS REVOLUTA Japanese sago palm / Cycas revoluta	L M	Single	Cream	•		•		S SS	•		M	L
C. YUCCAS												
16. ALOIFOLIA Spanish dagger / Aloifolia (green and variegated varieties)	M M	Branching	a. Cream b. Brown	•	•			S	•	•	H	M
17. ELEPHANTIPES Spineless giant yucca /Elephantipes	M M	Branching	a. Cream b. Brown	•	•			S	•	•	H	M
D. CORDYLINE												
18. CORDYLINE AUSTRALIS New Zealand Cabbage tree/ Cordyline / Dracena australis	M M	Branching after flowering	a. After 8 years cream b. Insignificant	•				S SS	•	•	M	H
E. MUSA - BANANA FAMILY												
19. PARADISÍACA (fruiting) Banana-plantain / Platanero. Variety 'Lady finger' suitable for smaller gardens	H M	New growth each year	a. Pinkish b. Yellow	•	•			S SS	•	•	L	L
20. ENSETE (ornamental) Ensete / Ensete	M M	As above large wide eliptic leaves	a. Red b. Brownish	•	•			S SS	•	•	L	L

COLUMN CODES
HT = Height; **L** = Low (less than 2 metres); **M** = Medium (2 – 5 metres); **H** = High (over 5 metres)
SP = Spread: **L** = Little (less than 2 metres); **M** = Medium (2 – 5 metres); **H** = Spreading wide.
BY SEA = Good for gardens near sea; **POTS** = Suitable for growing in large pots. **DR** = Drought resistance;
L = Low; **M** = Moderate; **H** = High. **FR** = Frost resistance; **L** = Low; **M** = Moderate; **H** = High.

12. Trachycarpus Fortunei
13. Washingtonia Filifera
14. Washingtonia Robusta
15. Cycas revoluta
16. Aloifolia
17. Elephantipes
18. Cordyline Australis
19. Paradisíaca
20. Ensete

159

4.11 BULBOUS PLANTS

NAMES Botanical English / Spanish	Height and Spread	Typical Flowers Colours	S	S	A	W	WHERE	GIP	PERF	FOL	DR	FR
1. ALLIUM — Ornamental alliums / Allium	M M	Pink, White	●	●	●		S	●	●		M	H
2. AGAPANTHUS — Lily of the Nile / Agapanto	M M	Blue, White	●				S	●			H	H
3. ALSTROEMERIA — Peruvian Lily / Alstroemeria	M H	Many	●	●			SS	●	●		M	L
4. AMARYLLIS — Beladonna Lily / Amarilis	H M	Many	●	●		●	SS SH	●			M	M
5. ANEMONE — Wind flower / Anemona	M L	Many	●				SS	●	●		M	M
6. BEGONIA — Begonia / Begonia	M M	Many	●		●	●	SS	●		●	M	L
7. BERGENIA SCHMIDTII — Bergenia / Bergenia	H H	Pink	●			●	S SS	●		●	L	M
8. CANNA — Canna Lily / Caña de las Indias	H H	Many			●	●	S			●	M	M
9. CLIVIA — Kaffir Lily / Clivia	M M	Orange	●				SS SH			●	M	L
10. CROCOSMIA — Montbretia / Crocosmia	H L	Red, Orange	●				S SS				M	H
11. CROCUS — Crocus / Azafrán	L L	Many	●		●	●	S SS				M	H
12. CYCLAMEN — Cyclamen / Cyclamen	M M	Many	●			●	SS SH	●		●	M	H
13. DAHLIA — Dahlia / Dalia	M M	Many	●				S SS	●			L	M
14. EREMURUS — Foxtail Lily / Eremurus	H M	Pale white, Yellow, Pink	●				S SS				M	H
15. FREESIA — Freesia / Fresia	M M	Many	●			●	S SS	●	●		M	H
16. GLADIOLUS — Gladiolus / Gladiolo	H L	Many	●				S SS				M	H
17. HEMEROCALLIS — Day lily / Hemerocallis	H H	Yellow, Orange	●				S SS	●	●		M	H

2. Agapanthus
3. Alstroemeria
4. Amaryllis
5. Anemone
6. Begonia
7. Bergenia
8. Canna
9. Clivia
12. Cyclamen
14. Eremurus
15. Freesia

4.11 BULBOUS PLANTS

NAMES Botanical English / Spanish	Height and Spread	Typical Flowers Colours	When Flowering S S A W	WHERE	GIP	PERF	FOL	DR	FR
18. HYMENOCALLIS FESTALIS Spider Lily/Hymenocallis festalis	H L	White	•	S SS	•	•		L	M
19. HYACINTHUS Hyacinth / Jacinto	M L	Many	• •	SS	•	•		M	M
IRIS Iris/Iris									
20. IRIS GERMANICA - hybrids Common flag / Iris germánica	H L	Many/single and double	•	S SS				M	H
21. IRIS XIPHIUM Spanish iris / Iris xiphium	H L	Blue, mauve, white, yellow	• •	S SS				M	H
22. IRIS XIPHIUM - tingitana Dutch iris / Iris tingitana	H L	Blue, mauve	• •	S SS			•	M	H
LILIUM / LILY / LIRIO (Nᵒˢ 23-25)									
23. LILIUM CANDIDUM Madonna lily / Lirio candidum	H L	White	•	S	•	•		M	H
24. LILIUM LANCIFOLIUM Tigre lily / Lirio lancifolium	H M	Orange	•	S		•		M	H
25. LILIUM ASIATIC - hybrids Asiatic lily / Lirio Asiatic	H M	Many	•	S	•	•		M	H
26. MIRABILIS JALAPA Flower of the night/ San Diego de noche	H H	Many	• •	S SS				M	M
27. MUSCARI Grape hyacinth/ Jacinto de panacho	L L	Blue, white	•	S SS		•		M	H
28. RANUNCULUS Buttercup / Ranunculo	M M	Many	• •	S SS	•			M	H
29. TULBAGHIA Society garlic / Tulbaghia	M M	Mauve	• •	S	•	•		M	H

We have left tulips and daffodils out the chart as they are well known. However they are best grown in higher wooded areas as in dry areas they tend to be eaten by slugs and other insects searching for moisture.

COLUMN CODES:
HT = Height: **L** = Low (less than 10 cm); **M** = Medium (10 – 20 cm); **H** = High (over 20cm). **SP** = Spread: **L** = Little (less than 10 cm); **M** = Moderate (10 – 20 cm); H = spreading wide. **WHEN FLOWERING: S** = Spring; **S** = Summer; **A** = Autumn; **W** = Winter. **WHERE: S** = Likes full sun; **SS** = Likes semi shade; **SH** = Likes full shade. **GIP** = Good in pots. **PERF** = Plant has pleasant perfume. **FOL** = Plant has an attractive foliage. **DR** = Drought resistance: **L** = Low; **M** = Moderate; **H** = High. **FR** = Frost resistance: **L** = Low; **M** = Moderate; **H** = High.

16. Gladiolus
17. Hemerocallis
18. Hymenocallis
19. Hyacinthus
21. Iris Xiphium
22. Iris Tingitana
23. Lilium Candidum
24. Lilium Lancifolium
25. Lilium Asiatic
26. Mirabilis Jalapa
29. Tulbaghia

163

4.12 SUCCULENTS

NAMES Botanical English / Spanish	Height and Spread	Typical Flowers Colours	S	S	A	W	Leaf Colour	WHERE	GIP	PERF	FOL	DR	FR
1. AEONIUM Aeonium / Aeonium	H M	Yellow	•			•	Pale green, burgundy	S	•		•	H	L
2. CARPOBROTUS Giant pig face / Carpobrotus	L H	Purple, pink, yellow	•	•	•		Green	S	•	•		H	M
3. CHEIRIDOPSIS Lobster claws / Cheiridopsis	L L	White, yellow, pink		•	•		Green	S			•	H	L
4. COTYLEDON Cotyledon / Cotyledon	M M	Orange, red, yellow	•				Green	S			•	H	L
5. CRASSULA Crassula / Crassula	M M	Many	•	•			Green	S	•		•	H	L
6. DUDLEYA Live for ever bluff lettuce / Dudleya	L L	Red, white, yellow		•	•		Green/grey	S			•	H	L
7. ECHEVERIA Echeveria / Echeveria	M M	Yellow, orange	•	•		•	Brown/green	S	•		•	H	M
8. EUPHORBIA Milkweed Spurge / Euforbia	M M	Many	•	•	•	•	Green	S	•		•	H	L
9. GIBBAEUM Gibbaeum / Gibbaeum	L L	White, pink, red			•		Green	S			•	H	L
10. GRAPTOPETALUM Graptopetalum (Echeveria family) /Graptope-talum	M M	Pale pink, white	•	•			Bluish grey	S	•		•	H	L
11. JOVIBARBA Jovibarba / Jovibarba	L M	Yellow	•	•			Green with brown tips	SS			•	H	H
12. KALANCHOA - (cultivated) Flaming Katy / Kalanchoa	M M	Many	•	•		•	Green	SS			•	M	L
13. KALANCHOA TOMENTOSA Pussy ears / Kalanchoa tomentosa	M M	Rarely flowers					Grey/green velvety edged, brown	S			•	H	L

0. Group of Succulents
1. Aeonium
2. Carpobrotus
3. Cheiridopsis
4. Cotyledon
5. Crassula
7. Echeveria
8. Euphorbia

165

4.12 SUCCULENTS

NAMES Botanical English / Spanish	Height and Spread	Typical Flowers Colours	When Flowering				Leaf Colour	WHERE	GIP	PERF	FOL	DR	FR
			S	S	A	W							
MESSEMBRYANTHEMUM FAMILY (Nº 14-17)													
14. APTENIA (photo p.125) Aptenia / Aptenia	L H	Red	•	•			Shiney pale green	S	•	•	•	M	M
15. DELOSPERMA Mesem / Mesem	L H	Many	•	•			Green fleshy in pairs	S	•	•	•	M	M
16. DROSANTHEMUM CANDENS (photo p.125) Rosea ice plant / Drosanthemum candens	L/M H	Many (open in sun)	•	•			Tiny pale green	S	•	•	•	M	M
17. LAMPRANTHUS Ice plant / Lampranthus (More shrubby variety shorter lived)	L H	Red, pink, orange, yellow	•	•			Narrow fleshy leaves	S	•	•	•	M	M
18. SEDUM SPECTABILE Ice plant / Sedum spectabile	M M	Pink			•	•	Green	S SS	•			H	H
19. SEMPERVIVUM Sempervivum / Semprevivas	L M	Pink, white, yellow		•			Green/ browny/red	S		•	•	H	L
20. SENECIO ARTICULATUS Candle sticks / Senecio articulatus	H H	White/yellow		•			Blue, Green	S			•	H	M

COLUMN CODES:
HT = Height: **L** = Low (less than 20cm); **M** = Medium (20 – 40cm); **H** = High (over 40cm). **SP** = Spread: **L** = Little (less than 10cm); **M** = Moderate (10 – 20cm); **H** = spreading wide. **WHEN FLOWERING: S** = Spring; **S** = Summer; **A** = Autumn; **W** = Winter. Where: **S** = Likes full sun; **SS** = Likes semi shade; **SH** = Likes full shade.
BY SEA = Very tolerant of sea spray. **GR/COVER** = Plants suitable for ground cover. **GIP/W** = Good in pots and window boxes. **DR** = Drought resistance: **L** = Low; **M** = Moderate; **H** = High. **FR** = Frost resistance: **L** = Low; **M** = Moderate; **H** = High.

10. Graptopetalum
12. Kalanchoa
13. Kalanchoa Tomentosa
15. Delosperma
17. Lampranthus
18. Sedum Spectabile
19. Sempervivum
20. Senecio Articulatus

167

4.13 CACTI, AGAVES AND ALOES

NAMES — Botanical English / Spanish	Height and Spread	Format	Typical Flower Colours	S	S	A	W	WHERE	BY SEA	GHB	POTS&WB	DR	FR
CACTI													
1. ASTROPHYTUM MYRIOSTIGMA Bishop's cap / Astrophytum myriostigma	H M	Spineless, ribbed	Yellow	•				S	•		•	H	M
2. CARNEGIEA GIGANTEAN Giant saguaro / Carnegiea gigantean	H M	Columnar	Red	•				S	•			H	L
3. CEREUS Cereus / Cereus	H M	Columnar	White, cream	•				S	•			H	L
4. CHAMAECEREUS SILVESTRII Peanut cacti / Chamaecereus Silvestrii	L L	Clustering/ floppy	Orange, red	•				S	•		•	H	L
5. ECHINOCACTUS Golden barrel cactus / Echinocactus	H H	Round	Yellow, red, pink	•				S	•		•	H	M
6. ECHINOCEREUS Hedgehog cacti / Echinocereus	M M	Globe	Many	•				S	•		•	H	M
7. ECHIOPSIS Sea urchin cacti / Echiopsis	M M	Columnar, round	Many	•				S	•		•	H	L
8. EPIPHYLLUM OXYPETALUM Orchid cactus / Epiphyllum	M M	Pendular perfumed	White (nocturnal)	•	•			S		•	•	H	L
9. FEROCACTUS Barrel cactus	M M	Barrel	Orange, yellow	•	•			S			•	H	M
10. GYMNOCALYCIUM Chin cacti / Gymnocalycium	M M	Round	Yellow, pink	•				S	•		•	H	L
11. HAAGEOCEREUS Haageocereus / Haageocereus	H M	Columnar	White (nocturnal)	•				S	•			H	L
12. MAMMILLARIA Pincushion cacti / Mammillaria	M M	Round & columnar clump forming	Many	•				S	•		•	H	L
13. OPUNTIA FICUS INDICA Prickly pear / Opuntia	H H	Branched joints	Yellow flowers. red fruit		•	•		S	•			H	M
14. OPUNTIA MICRODASYS Bunny ears / Opuntia microdasys	M M	Branched joints	Yellow			•		S	•			H	M

0. A general Cacti garden
1. Astrophytum Myriostigma
3. Cereus
4. Chamaecereus Silvestrii
5. Echinocactus
9. Ferocactus
10. Gymnocalycium
12. Mammillaria
13. Opuntia Indica

4.13 CACTI, AGAVES AND ALOES

NAMES — Botanical English / Spanish	Height and Spread	Format	Typical Flower Colours	When Flowering S	S	A	W	WHERE	BY SEA	GHB	POTS&WB	DR	FR
15. OPUNTIA SUBULATA Pole cactus / Opuntia subulata	H M	Columnar joints	Orange	•				S	•			H	M
16. OREOCEREUS Oreocereus / Oreocereus	H M	Hairy columnar	Red, pink	•				S	•			H	L
17. PARODIA Ball cactus / Parodia	H H	Round	Many	•				S	•		•	H	M
18. REBUTIA Crown cactus / Rebutia	L L	Erect, round & cluster forming	Many	•				S	•		•	H	L
19. SCHLUMBERGERA Christmas cactus / Cactus de Navidad	M M	Drooping flat leaved jointed branches. Indoor or terrace plant	Many	•				SS	•		•	M	L
AGAVES													
20. AGAVE AMERICANA Century plant / Agave Americana	H H	Stiff leaves with sharp edges & tip (variegated)	After 10 years 6m high spike with yellow flowers	•				S	•		•	H	M
21. AGAVE ATTENUATA Agave attenuata / Agave attenuata	H H	Green	3m arching flower spike yellow flowers when mature	•	•			S	•			H	M
ALOES													
22. ALOE VERA Medicinal aloe / Aloe vera	M M	Low candelabra	Yellow	•				SS	•		•	M	L
23. ALOE ARBORESENS Candelabra / Red hot poker / Aloe arboresens	H H	Tall candelabra	Red	•				S SS	•			M	M
24. ALOE MELANOCANTHA Aloe melanocantha / Aloe melanocantha	M H	Clustering	Red, orange	•	•			S SS	•			M	M
25. ALOE SAPONARIA Soap aloe / Aloe de jabón	M H	Clustering	Orange	•				S SS	•			H	M

COLUMN CODES:
HT = Height: **L** = Low (less than 10cm); **M** = Medium (10 – 20cm); **H** = High (over 20cm). **SP** = Spread: **L** = Little (less than 10cm); **M** = Moderate (10 – 20cm); **H** = Spreading wide. **WHEN FLOWERING: S** = Spring; **S** = Summer; **A** = Autumn; **W** = Winter. **WHERE: S** = Likes full sun; **SS** = Likes semi shade; **SH** = Likes full shade. **GHB** = Good in hanging baskets. **GIP/WB** = Good in pots and window boxes. **DR** = Drought resistance: **L** = Low; **M** = Moderate; **H** = High. **FR** = Frost resistance: **L** = Low; **M** = Moderate; **H** = High.

14. Opuntia Microdasys
15. Opuntia Subulata
17. Parodia
19. Schlumbergera
20. Agave Americana
21. Agave Attenuata
22. Aloe Vera
23. Aloe Arboresens
24. Aloe Melanocantha
25. Aloe Saponaria

171

4.14 GRASSES AND BAMBOOS

NAMES Botanical English / Spanish	Height and Spread	SCREEN	VIG	Typical Colours (Plumes for grasses & leaf for bamboos)	When Flowering S	S	A	W	WHERE	BY SEA	GR/COVER	FOLIAGE	DR	FR
A. GRASSES														
1. CORTADERIA Pampas grass / Plumero	H H		•	Cream, pink		•			S	•		•	L	H
2. DASYLIRION Bear grass / Dasylirion	H H			When mature- creamy/white	•				S SS	•		•	H	M
3. FESTUCA Fescue / Festuca	M M			White	•				S SS	•	•	•	H	H
4. MISCANTHUS Ornamental grass / Miscanthus	M M			Many	•	•			S	•		•	M	H
5. PENNISETUM Fountain grass / Pennisetum	H H			Many	•	•			S	•		•	M	H
6. STIPA Feather grass / Stipa	H			Cream		•			S	•	•	•	M	H
B. BAMBOOS														
7. PLEIOBLASTUS AURICOMUS Kamuro / Zasa / Pleioblastus	M M			Variegated	•				S SS	•		•	L	H
8. PLEIOBLASTUS PYGMAEUS Dwarf bamboo/ Pleioblastus pygmaeus	L H			Variegated	•				S SS	•	•	•	L	H
9. PHYLLOSTACHYS AUREA Fishpole bamboo/ Phyllostachys aurea	H H	•	•	Green	•				S	•		•	M	H
10. PSEUDOSASA JAPONICA Metake / Pseudosasa japonica	H H	•	•	Green	•				S SS	•		•	M	H
11. FARGESIA NITIDA Fountain bamboo / Fargesia nitida	H H	•		Green	•				S SS	•		•	L	M

COLUMN CODES:
HT = Height: **L** = Low (less than 50cm); **M** = Medium (50 – 100cm); **H** = high (over 100cm). **SP** = Spread: **L** = Little (less than 50cm); **M** = Moderate (50-100cm); **H** = Spreading wide. **SCREEN** = Suitable for screening and wind breaks. **VIG** = Vigorous and can become evasive. **WHEN FLOWERING: S** = Spring; **S** = Summer; **A** = Autumn; **W** = Winter. **WHERE: S** = Likes full sun; **SS** = Likes semi shade; **SH** = Likes full shade. **BY SEA** = Plants suitable for gardens near the sea. **GR COVER** = Good ground cover. **FOLIAGE** = indicates that the plant has an unusual and attractive foliage. **DR** = Drought resistance: **L** = Low; **M** = Moderate; **H** = High. **FR** = Frost resistance: **L** = Low; **M** = Moderate; **H** = High.

1. Cortaderia
2. Dasylirion
3. Festuca
4. Miscanthus
5. Pennisetum
6. Stipa
8. Pleioblastus Pygmaeus
9. Phyllostachys Aurea
10. Pseudosasa japónica
11. Bamboos for sale

173

4.15 POND PLANTS

NAMES Botanical English - Spanish	Height and Spread	Typical Flower Colours	When Flowering				Deph in Water	F R
			S	S	A	W		
A. MARGINAL PLANTS								
1. ALISMA PLANTAGO AQUATICA Common water plantains/Alisma aquatica	H M	White	•				0 - 20cm	M
2. CYPERUS INVOLUCRATUS Umbrella sedge / Cipero	H H	Cream	•				10 - 20cm	M
3. IRIS PSEUDACORUS Yellow flag / Iris pseudacorus	H H	Yellow	•				0 - 20cm	H
4. IRIS VERISCOLOR Blue flag / Iris veriscolor	H H	Blue	•	•			0 - 20cm	H
5. MENTHA AQUATICA Marsh mint / Mentha aquatica	M H	Lilac		•	•		0 - 20cm	H
6. PONTEDERIA CORDATA Pickerel bus / Pick libelua	H H	Dark blue		•			20 - 40cm	H
7. RANUNCULUS AQUATILIS Water buttercup/ Ranunculus aquatilis	L H	Yellow	•	•			10 - 20cm	H
8. SCHOENOPLECTUS Zebra rush / Scripus	H H	Red brown		•			10 - 20cm	M
9. TYPHA ANGUSTIFOLIA Lesser bulrush / Anea	H M	Brown		•			10 - 20cm	H
10. ZANTEDESCHIA AETHIOPICA Water arum lily/ Zantedeschia aethiopica	H H	White	•	•			10 - 20cm	H
B. SUBMERGED PLANTS								
11. ELODEA CANADENSIS Oxygenating pond weed/ Elodea Canadensis	L H						20 - 100cm	H
12. MYRIOPHYLLUM AQUATICUM (Feathery) Milfoil/ Myriophyllum aquaticum	H H	White		•			20 - 100cm	H

2. Cyperus Involucratus
3. Iris Pseudacorus
5. Mentha Aquatica
6. Pontederia Cordata
7. Ranunculus Aquatilis
8. Schoenoplectus

175

4.15 POND PLANTS

NAMES Botanical English / Spanish	Height and Spread	Typical Flower Colours	When Flowering S S A W	Deph in Water	F R
C. FLOATING PLANTS					
13. NYMPHAEA Water lily / Nenufar	H H	Many	• • •	20 - 100cm	H
14. EICHHORNIA CRASSIPES Water Hyacinth/ Eichhornia crassipes	M H	Pale blue/ mauve	• •	Floating	L
15. PISTIA STRATIOTES Water lettuce/ Pistia stratiotes	L L			Floating	L
16. NELIMBO NUCIFERA Lotus / Nelimbo nucifera	H H	Pink and white	• • •	60-100cm	M

COLUMN CODES:
HT = Height: **L** = Low (less than 10cm); **M** = Medium (10 – 20cm); **H** = High (over 20cm).
SP = Spread: **L** = Little (less than 10cm); **M** = Moderate (10-20cm); **H** = Spreading wide.
When Flowering: S = Spring; **S** = Summer; **A** = Autumn; **W** = Winter.
FR = Frost resistance: **L** = Low; **M** = moderate; **H** = High.

10. Zantedeschia Aethiopica
11. Elodea
12. Myriophyllum Aquaticum
13. Nymphaea
14. Eichhornia Crassipes
15. Pistia Stratiotes

4.16 HEDGES

NAMES Botanical English / Spanish	Height and Spread	Growth Fast, Med, Slow	Typical Flower Colours	S	S	A	W	EVG	FOLIAGE	PERFUMED	BY SEA	INTERNAL	BOUNDARY	DR	FR
1. BERBERIS Barberry / Berberis	M M	M	Yellow, orange	•	•		•	•	Purple, Green			•	•	H	H
2. BOUGANVILLEA GLABRA Bouganvillea glabra / Buganvilla glabra	H M	S	Purple	•	•	•	•	S	Green	•	•	•	•	H	M
3. BUXUS Common box / Boj común	M L	S	White	•			•	•	Green	•	•	•	•	M	H
4. CALLISTEMON (also 137) Bottlebrush / Callistemon	M M	M	Red	•			•	•	Green		•	•	•	H	H
5. CHAMAECYPARIS LAWSONIANA False Cypress / Ciprés falso	H H	M						•	Green, yellow			•	•	M	H
6. CITRUS AURANTIUM Orange bitter / Naranja Sevilla	H M	M	Creamy white	•					Green	•	•	•	•	L	L/M
7. CUPRESSOCYPARIS LEYLANDII Leyland cypress / Ciprés leylandii	H M	M						•	Green, golden			•	•	M	H
8. EUONYMUS JAPONICUS Spindle tree / Evonimo	L M	S		•	•	•		•	Green variegated			•	•	M	M
9. EUPHORBIA MILII Crown of thorns / Euphorbia milii	L L	S	Yellow in red bracts	•	•	•	•	•	Green			•		H	L
10. HIBISCUS SINENSIS Chinese Hibiscus / Hibisco Sinensis	M H	M	Many	•	•	•		SM	Green				•	M	L
11. LAURUS NOBILIS (also 137) Bay-laurel / Laurus	M M	M	White	•				•	Green			•	•	H	H
12. LANTANA CAMARA (also 137) Lantana / Lantana	M M	F	Many	•	•	•			Green			•	•	M	H
13. LAVANDA Lavender / Lavanda	L L	F	Pink, purple	•	•			•	Green, grey	•	•	•	•	H	H
14. LIGUSTRUM Privet / Aligustre	H H	M	White	•	•			•	Green		•	•	•	H	H
15. MYPORUM LACTUM Good-for-nothing / Gandula	H H	F	White followed by white berries	•	•			•	Green			•	•	M	H

3. Buxus
5. Chamaecyparis
7. Cupresscyparis
8. Euonymus Japonicus
10. Hibiscus Sinensis
11. Laurus Nobilis

4.16 HEDGES

NAMES Botanical English / Spanish	Height and Spread	Growth Fast, Med, Slow	Typical Flower Colours	When Flowering				EVG	FOLIAGE	PERFUMED	BY SEA	INTERNAL	BOUNDARY	DR	FR
				S	S	A	W								
16. NERIUM Oleander / Adelfa	H H	F	Many	•	•	•	•	•	Green variegated	•			•	M	H
17. PITTOSPORUM TOBIRA Japanese mock orange / Pittosporum	M M	M	Cream	•	•		•		Green	•	•	•	•	M	H
18. PYRACANTHA Firethorn / Espino de fuego	M M	S	Red, orange berries		•	•	•		Green		•		•	M	H
19. ROSMARINUS Rosemary / Romero	L M	S	Blue	•	•		•		Green	•	•	•		H	H
20. SPIRAEA CANTONIENSIS Spiraea / Spiraea	M M	M	White	•	•		•		Green		•	•	•	M	M
21. TEUCRIUM FRUTICANS Bush germander / Teucrium	M M	M	Blue	•	•		•		Silver, grey		•	•		M	H
22. THUJA OCCIDENTALIS Cedar / Cedro	H H	S					•		Green, yellow		•		•	M	H
23. VIBURNUM Viburnum / Viburnum	M M	M	White	•	•	•			Green		•		•	M	H

Agaves Americana (page 170) and Optunia/prickly pear cactus (page 168) also make good hedges, especially to keep animals out and as fire breaks.

COLUMN CODES:
HT = Height: **L** = Low (less than 50cm); **M** = Medium (50 – 100cm); **H** = High (over 100cm).
DEP = Depth: **L** = Little (less than 50cm); **M** = Moderate (50 – 100cm); **H** = spreading wide.
WHEN FLOWERING: **S** = Spring; **S** = Summer; **A** = Autumn; **W** = Winter. **PERF** = Plant has pleasant perfume.
BY SEA = Plants suitable for gardens near the sea. **INTERNAL** = Suitable for internal hedging.
BOUNDARY = Suitable for boundary hedging. **DR** = Drought resistance: **L** = Low; **M** = Moderate;
H = High. **FR** = Frost resistance: **L** = Low; **M** = Moderate; **H** = High.

12. Lantana
13. Lavanda
14. Ligustrum
15. Myporum
16. Nerium
17. Pittosporum Tobira
19. Rosmarinus
21. Teucrium Fruticans
2. Bougainvillea Glabra

181

4.17 NAYA PLANTS

NAMES Botanical English / Spanish	Height and Spread	Typical Flower Colours	S	S	A	W	FOL	WHERE	GHB	Watering Needs	DR	FR
1. AECHMEA (bromeliad family) Aechmea / Aechmea	M M	Many	•		•		•	SS		Moderate. Water down through centre of plant	M	L
2. AESCHYNANTHUS Aeschynanthus / Esquinantus - Columea	M M	Orange	•		•		•	SS SH	•	Keep damp	L	L
3. ANTHURIUM Flamingo flower / Anturio	H M	Red & others		•	•		•	SS		Keep damp and spray regularly	L	L
4. ASPIDISTRA Aspidistra / Aspidistra	H H	Tiny white	•				•	SS SH		Keep damp	L	L
5. AZALEA Azalea / Azalea	H H	Many	•			•	•	SS SH		Water well from base when flowering. Less when dormant	L	H
6. BEGONIA REX Begonia Rex / Begonia Rex	M H	Pink	•				•	SS SH	•	When it dries out	M	L
7. CALADIUM Elephant's ears / Caladium	M M	Greeny/white	•				•	SS		Keep damp	L	L
8. CALATHEA Calathea / Calathea	M M	White	•	•			•	SH		Moderate	L	L
9. CATTLEYA Orchid / Orquídea	H M	Many	•	•			•	SS SH		Damp plus mist spray	L	L
10. CODIAEUM Codiaeum / Croton	M M	Yellow	•				•	S SS		Water well in summer. Less in winter	L	L
11. DIEFFENBACHIA Dieffenbachia / Diefenbaquia	H H	Greeny/white	•	•			•	SH		Let soil dry out between watering to avoid rot	M	L
12. DRACAENA FRAGRANS Dracaena fragrans/ Dracena fragrans	H L	Cream	•				•	SS SH		Moderate. Keep leaves clean	M	L
13. EUPHORBIA PULCHERRIMA Poinsettia / Poinsettia	M M	Many			•	•	•	SH		Keep moist	L	M
14. FICUS BENJAMINA Ficus Benjamina/ Ficus Benjamina	H H	Unlikely					•	SS SH		Moderate. Keep leaves clean	M	L

1. Aechmea
2. Aeschynanthus
3. Anthurium
4. Aspidistra
5. Azalea
6. Begonia Rex
7. Caladium
8. Calathea
9. Cattleya
10. Codiaeum
11. Dieffenbachia
12. Dracaena
13. Poinsettia
14. Ficus Benjamina

183

4.17 NAYA PLANTS

NAMES Botanical English / Spanish	Height and Spread	Typical Flower Colours	When Flowering				FOL	WHERE	GHB	Watering Needs	DR	FR
			S	S	A	W						
15. FUCHSIA THALIA Fuchsia thalia / Fuchsia thalia	M M	Orange	•	•	•		•	SS		Keep moist	L	M
16. HOSTA Hosta / Hosta	H M	Pale pink	•		•	•	•	SH	•	Moderate	M	L
17. MARANTA LEUCONEURA Prayer plant / La Maranta	M M	White		•	•		•	S SH		Moderate	M	L
18. NEPHROLEPIS Fern / Helecho	H H	None					•	SH	•	Keep moist	L	L
19. PHILODENDRON Bread plant / Filodendro	H H	Yellow	•				•	SH		Moderate. Less in cooler months	M	L
20. PLECTRANTHUS Money plant / Planta de dinero	M M	Lilac, white		•	•		•	SS SH	•	Keep moist	L	L
21. POTHOS AUREUS Pothos / Potos	H H	Insignificant					•	SS SH	•	Moderate	M	L
22. SANSEVIERIA Snake plant / Lenguas de tigre	H L	Greeny/ white	•				•	SS SH		Do not overwater	M	L
23. SPATHIPHYLLUM Spathiphyllus / Espatifilo	M M	White	•	•			•	SS SH		Keep moist	L	L
24. STREPTOCARPUS Streptocarpus / Estreptocarpo	M M	Many		•	•		•	SS		Water when dry	L	L
25. STROMANTHE Stromanthe / Stronmanthe	H H	White, pink, mauve	•	•			•	SS		Moderate	L	L

Notes:
1. These plants can also be grown in the shade of porches and under trees.
2. A number of other good naya plants are included in other sections e.g., Spider plant (4.4), Clivia (4.12), Ficus elastica (4.10), Howea (4.11), Hydrangea (4.5) and Succulents (4.3).
3. A single or collection of Bonsais can be attractive on a naya, but need specialist daily care. Orchids are included in the list in view of the number now sold but they also need more care than most others if you are to keep them over winter.

COLUMN CODES:
HT = Height: L = Low (less than 10cm); M = Medium (10 – 20cm); H = High (over 20cm). SP = Spread:
L = Little (less than 10cm); M = Moderate (10 – 20cm); H = Spreading wide. WHEN FLOWERING: S = Spring;
S = Summer; A = Autumn; W = Winter. WHERE: S = Likes full sun; SS = Likes semi shade; SH = Likes full shade.
FOL = Plant has an attractive foliage. GHB = Good in hanging baskets. Watering = Guidelines for watering.
DR = Drought resistance: L = Low; M = Moderate; H = High. FR = Frost resistance: L = Low; M = Moderate;
H = High.

15. Fuchsia Thalia
17. Hosta
18. Nephrolepis
19. Philodendron
20. Plectranthus
21. Pothos Aureus
22. Sansevieria
23. Spathiphyllum
24. Streptocarpus
25. Stromanthe

4.18 VEGETABLES

This is a selection of the more that a hundred vegetables including in the sister book 'Growing healthy vegetables in Spain' which provides full information for their selection, planting, growing, watering, feeding and harvesting etc.

VEGETABLE NAME Botanical English / Spanish	Grow in: Og RB C	Manure Needs	Water Needs	Frost Resistance	Plants Seeds				Plant Plantlets				Harvest Vegetables			
					A	W	S	S	A	W	S	S	A	W	S	S
1. ARTICHOKES / Alcachofas	OG/RB	H	H	H	0	/	/	/	0	0	/	/	/	/	0	0
2. AUBERGINE / Berejenas	All	H	H	L	/	/	0	/	/	/	0	/	0	/	/	0
3. BEANS-dwarf / Climbing	All	H	H	L	/	/	0	/	/	/	0	/	0	/	/	/
4. BEETROOT / Remolacha	All	L	M	H	0	0	0	/	0	0	0	/	0	0	0	0
5. BROAD BEANS / Habas	All	L/M	M	H	0	0	/	/	0	0	/	/	/	/	0	/
6. CABBAGE / Col	OG/RB	M	M	H	/	/	/	0	0	/	/	/	/	0	0	/
7. CARROTS / Zanahorias	All	L	M	H	0	0	0	/	/	/	/	/	0	0	0	0
8. CAULIFLOWER / Col de flor	OG/RB	M	M	H	/	/	/	0	0	/	/	/	/	0	0	/
9. CHIVES / Cebollinos	All	L	M	H	0	/	0	/	0	/	0	/	0	/	0	0
10. COURGETTES** CALABACINES	All	H	M	L	/	/	0	/	/	/	0	/	0	/	/	0
11. CUCUMBERS / Pepinos	All	H	H	L	/	/	0	/	/	/	0	/	/	/	/	0
12. FENNEL / Hinojo	OG/RB	H	H	H	0	/	0	/	0	/	0	/	0	0	0	0
13. GARLIC / Ajo	All	L	M	H	0	/	/	/	0	0	/	/	/	/	0	/
14. JERUSALEM ARTICHOKE TUPINAMBO	All	M	M	H	0	/	/	/	0	/	/	/	0	/	/	/
15. LEEKS / Puerros	All	L	L	H	0	0	0	/	0	0	0	/	0	0	0	0
16. LETTUCE / Lechuga	All	M	H	H	0	0	0	0	0	0	0	0	0	0	0	0
17. ONIONS / Cebollas	All	M	M	H	0	0	0	/	0	0	0	/	0	0	0	0
18. PARSNIPS / Chirivias	OG/RB	L	M	H	0	0	/	/	0	0	0	/	0	0	0	0
19. PEANUTS / Cacahuetes	All	M	M	L	0	/	0	/	/	/	/	/	/	0	0	0
20. PEAS / Guisantes**	All*	L/M	H	M	/	/	0	/	/	/	/	/	0	/	/	/

VEGETABLE NAME Botanical English / Spanish	Grow in: Og RB C	Manure Needs	Water Needs	Frost Resistance	Plants Seeds				Plant Plantlets				Harvest Vegetables			
					A	W	S	S	A	W	S	S	A	W	S	S
21. PEPPERS / Pimientos	All	H	H	L	/	/	0	/	/	/	0	/	0	/	/	0
22. POTATOES / Patatas*	OG/RB	H	M	L	0	0	0	/	/	/	/	/	/	0	0	0
23. RADISHES / Rábanos	All	M	H	H	0	0	0	0	/	/	/	/	0	0	0	0
24. ROCKET / Oruga	All	M	H	H	0	/	/	0	0	0	/	0	/	0	0	0
25. SPROUTING BROCCOLI** / Brecol	All*	M	H	H	0	/	/	0	0	0	/	/	/	0	0	0
26. SQUASHES / Calabazas	OG/RB	H	H	L	/	/	0	/	/	/	0	/	0	/	/	0
27. SWEET POTATOES / Boniatos	All	M	M	L	/	/	0	/	/	/	0	/	0	/	/	/
28. SWEET CORN / Maíz	OG/RB	H	H	L	/	/	0	/	/	/	0	/	/	/	/	0
29. SWISS CHARD / Acelgas	All	M	M	H	0	0	0	0	0	0	0	/	0	0	0	0
30. TOMATOES / Tomates	All	H	H	L	/	0	0	/	/	/	0	/	0	/	/	0

COLUMN CODES:
OG = Open ground; **RB** = Raised bed ; **C** = Containers.
* = Best to sow miniature varieties in containers.
(1)' Growing healthy vegetables in Spain' includes full instructions for growing over a hundred different vegetables on a mini scale in less than one square metre as well as larger raised beds and large vegetable plots.

PART FIVE

GARDENS FOR DIFFERENT SITUATIONS

Whether your property is on the coast or inland mountain valleys it is possible to develop attractive and productive gardens even on apartment terraces and penthouse roofs.

5.0 GARDENS FOR DIFFERENT SITUATIONS

Over the last 30 years, several hundred thousands of northern Europeans have purchased properties for permanent or holiday homes in Spain in a wide range of situations – some hot and totally sheltered and suitable for the full range of subtropical and tropical plants grown in Spain, and others in more exposed, higher and more northerly places too cold during the winter for such plants.

More and more properties are being purchased and gardens laid out in inland valleys and even on mountainsides, as stretches of the coastal plain become overbuilt and overcrowded.

Recognising this migration, we consider here the design of gardens in a wide range of very different situations, from coastal apartments to inland mini estates.

At first, some of the situations may seem very hostile, but over the past 30 years amazing gardens have been created from the southern tip of the Gran Canarias to the foothills of the Pyrenees – in situations where before there was nothing other than windswept sand dunes or solid rock..

All that was needed was a regular supply of water and new settlers with creativity, patience and perseverance, the last quality being very important as gardens take some years to mature and be at their best.

When you visit botanical gardens, remember that most of them were laid out 100 years ago by plant collectors who travelled the world looking for interesting species. Luckily, we can now take advantage of their early endeavours, as nurseries and garden centres are fully stocked with the species and varieties they brought back – and many more.

The table next page provides a summary of the general practicality of the plants included in the previous section describing 350 popular plants – as well as the 14 different kinds of situations covered in this section.

PRACTICALITY OF DIFFERENT TYPES OF PLANTS

Situation of Garden	General practicality of types of plants included in previous section														
	A	P	H	GC	FS	CS	FT	ET	Pa	B	S	C	G/C	PP	H	N
1. COASTAL PLAIN																
a. small	*	*	*	*	*	*	R	R	R	*	*	*	*	*	*	*
b. large	*	*	*	*	*	*	*	*	*	*	*	*	*	*	*	*
2. PATIOS	*	*	*	R	R	R	R	R	R	*	R	R	R	R	R	*
3. NAYAS	*	*	R	--	R	R	--	--	R	*	*	R	--	--	--	*
4. APARTMENTS	*	R	*	*	*	R	*	R	*	*	*	R	--	R	--	*
5. PENTHOUSE	*	R	*	R	R	R	--	R	R	*	*	R	R	*	R	R
6. MOBILE HOME	*	*	*	*	*	*	R	R	R	*	*	R	R	*	*	--
7. WOODLANDS	R	R	*	R	R	*	*	*	R	*	R	R	*	--	R	*
8. GIANT TREE	*	R	R	R	R	R	--	--	--	*	R	R	R	*	--	*
9. INLAND VALLEY	*	*	*	*	R	R	R	*	R	*	*	*	*	R	*	R
10. MOUNTAIN SIDE	*	*	*	*	R	R	R	*	R	*	R	R	*	R	*	R
11. CENTRAL PLAIN	*	R	R	R	R	R	*	*	R	*	R	R	*	*	*	R
12. SALINE/BARREN SOILS	*	*	*	R	R	R	R	R	*	*	*	*	*	--	R	*
13. WINDOW BOXES	*	*	*	R	--	--	--	R	--	R	R	R	--		--	R

COLUMN CODES:
A = Annuals: **P** = Perennials: **H** = Herbs: **GC** = Ground cover: **FS** = Flowering shrubs: **CS** = Climbing shrubs:
FT = Flowering and fruiting trees: **E** = Evergreen trees: **PA** = Palms: **B** = Bulbs: **S** = Succulents: **C** = Cacti:
G/C = Grasses and canes: **PP** = Pond plants: **H** = Hedges: **N** = Naya plants.
* means most plants in group appropriate. Any restrictions are related to the amount of shelter that can be given to the more delicate varieties.
-- means generally not practical: **R** means choice restricted by:
a. Size in situations 1 to 6 and 3. **b.** Lack of shade in situations 7 and 8. **c.** Salinity in situation 9, 11 and 12. **d.** Frost in situations 9 to 11. This also applies ato winter vegetables.

5.1 HOMES ALONG THE MEDITERRANEAN AND SEMI - TROPICAL COASTS

Many expatriates buy properties along the Mediterranean coastline of mainland Spain and on the Balearic and Canary Islands, mostly in areas with an enviable climate throughout the year, where homeowners can create wonderful gardens.

In the warmer south and more-sheltered northerly areas it is possible to grow a wide assortment of the most delicate subtropical and even tropical plants, provided the soil is enriched and well watered.

From the tip of the Gran Canarias and the tropical gardens of Orotava in Tenerife to sheltered areas in Blanes and Lloret de Mar on the Costa Brava, there are exceptional gardens with amazing collections of plants thriving in their microclimates. We refer to them as being on "semi-tropical" coasts because their climates are not truly sub-tropical.

They do not have the true climatic conditions, especially the pattern of rainfall or constant humidity of the sub-tropics, but provided your garden has south-facing, totally sheltered pockets, you will be able to grow the following plants:

- Tropical plants such as frangipani, bananas, papayas, pineapples and poinsettias.
- The more delicate of sub-tropical plants such as white and yellow bougainvilleas and euphorbias in the sun and jungle bromeliads and orchids in the shade.
- Provided you have shade, the plants used as house plants in northern Europe, or naya plants in more exposed situations. These include ficus, pothos, philodendrons, aspidistras, anthuriums, fatsia and staghorn ferns, which can grow to impressive sizes in gardens.

Not all situations along the coastlines or in the centre of the islands are suitable for such plantings, including:

- Gardens perched on low coastal cliffs that have no tall hedges and are exposed to gales and salt spray.
- Gardens further away from the sea that do not have high hedges to totally shelter the garden and provide a balance between sun and shade (some of the special plants prefer shaded jungle conditions).
- North facing hillsides that lose the sun early, especially in the winter, and have the occasional frosts.
- Windy ridges exposed regularly to strong winds – the type of situation that will be vulnerable to the next generation of wind generators.
- Very dry, arid areas where the hot drying winds, perhaps even sand storms, make it difficult to maintain a sufficiently humid microclimate within the garden for the tropical and sub-tropical plants.
- Situations with an unreliable water supply, especially during the spring and summer months, for watering and spraying plants to maintain the humidity around their leaves.

THE SUCCESS FACTORS

Against the above background, the following conditions are essential for the successful and relatively easy growing of tropical and sub-tropical plants:

- Rich loamy water-retaining but well- draining soil, achieved by improving the soil you inherit. See section 6.1.
- A sheltered south-facing garden with particularly well sheltered niches.
- A property surrounded by high hedges, walls or banks of trees, depending on the size of the property, to protect it from all strong winds, especially from the north.
- A garden that is not exposed to sea spray or frost.
- A constantly good water supply for watering the roots of plants and spraying them to raise the humidity around their leaves.

Major constraints that can hold you back from success include the following:
• The size of your garden, which can range from 100 square metres belonging to a small townhouse to 20,000 square metres on a rural finca.
• The time you are able and willing to put into the development and maintenance of the garden.
• The extent of your creativity in making the best of the garden area you have.
• Whether you are able and willing to employ a gardener for some hours in a small garden or fulltime in a larger estate.
• The extent of your budget for construction work, equipment, soil, plants and water.
• Your own creativity.

Following are some creative ideas for gardens of various sizes, keeping in mind that even if your garden is not totally sheltered, most of the other plants in Part Four will be suitable.

SMALLER GARDENS

Although garden areas may be small, they still provide you with the opportunity to create a number of different styles of interesting gardens. In sheltered but sunny spots, some of the most tender plants can be grown in the ground or in large pots. Following are some practical suggestions:

A small front garden:
• **A basic design** – A low hedge, a monkey-puzzle tree or cordyline (as they are both slow growing), a bougainvillea up the wall, and a round bed of annuals in the centre

193

of a square of stone chippings. garden appear bigger by covering the whole area from the house to pavement with a wooden pergola. Cover the walls and pergola with climbing plants. Have wrought iron railings that are not totally enclosed to avoid making the area claustrophobic. Pave the short path to the front door with a bright attractive finish. If the path is in the centre with two small square areas on either side, brighten up one side with a small fountain or an interesting group of pots, and the other side with a small wrought iron round table and chairs.

A small back garden:
- **A basic design** – Lay crazy paving from wall to wall. Install a blind for shade, an oblong table and chairs, and a collection of potted plants.
- **A more creative design** – Cover half the area with a colourful canvas or open weave cooling awnings and the other half with a metal or wooden pergola. To save space, build two bench seats in a corner along the boundary wall or fence, and a table and chairs for the other side. Grow climbers in narrow, deep-raised beds and restrict the number of potted plants on the limited floor space, but be courageous in your choice. If the area is half shady and half sunny, create a mini subtropical garden. In the far corner from the table, construct a pond or fountain or install a mini Jacuzzi. White walls will make the area look larger and feel cool. Brighten unplanted walls or fences with coloured plates, murals or artefacts. Add style by tiling the terrace with large light-coloured terracotta tiles. (Read section 5.2 on patios and 5.3 on nayas for more detailed ideas.

Four-metre-wide side passageways:
- **A basic design** – Use as thoroughfares with perhaps a few potted plants. Stack chairs and bikes and cover with plastic.
- **A more creative design** – Design one passageway as a narrow, sheltered and cosy eating area, leaving more room in the back garden for perhaps a mini table tennis table. Roof over half with a pergola and arbour for climbing plants, or a canvas-roofed gazebo. Leave the other half open to the sky so that the table can be moved into the sun in the winter. There will be little room for potted plants, so decorate the space with petunias in wall pots. Design the second passageway as a work and storage area with a covered walk-through shed for tools, beach things, folded garden furniture, etc.

A single four-metre-wide passageway:
- **A basic design** – Decorate with a few potted plants. If there is no garage, build a place to store tools and folding furniture.
- **A more creative design** – Create either an eating or stage area or a combination of the two, if there is no garage.

A roof terrace:
- **A basic design** – create an area for sunbathing and drying washing.
- **A more creative design** – Add a collection of succulents or cacti and a table and chairs for moonlit dining.
A first floor terrace:
- **A basic design** – Fit an awning or blind for shade, and have a collection of ivy-leafed geraniums in pots.

- **A more creative design** – Install a metal pergola and cover with climbers grown in large pots. If you are an avid gardener, develop a colourful mini/garden with plants in pots and hanging baskets.

400 TO 1000 METRE PLOTS

One way to approach this size of garden is to surround three sides with three/metre/wide, cantilevered, wrought iron pergolas, with their posts concreted in around the boundary.

The pergolas, when covered with a variety of climbing shrubs and vines, would create a continuous, covered walkway some 30 metres long around three sides of the garden. When mature and in flower, it will create a very dramatic effect, with shade for terraces and shade loving plants.

Other suggestions include:

- **A basic design** – A boundary hedge, large terrace and pool, areas of stone chippings, a couple of palms and a few pots of geraniums, annuals and succulents. A barbecue beside the pool terrace, and umbrellas for shade.
- **A more creative design** – A boundary of colourful climbers and trees, some of the latter to give fruit and others to give spring flowers and shade. Create different styles of garden, a few fruit trees on each side of the house – for instance, a courtyard/patio at the front, a pool garden on one side, a garden shed and work area on another side, and the main flower garden with perhaps a central pond and fountain in front of the main terrace or naya.

It could be a tight squeeze perhaps with only 500 square metres, but with double that size you could even fit in a small vegetable garden, a greenhouse, garden frame and an area for poultry and rabbits – creating the complete small garden, interlaced with a meandering network of paths and terraces, and with a number of choices as to where to eat, entertain or take a siesta.

1000 TO 3000 METRE PLOTS

- **A basic design** – This is often a blown up version of the 400 to 1000 metre plot, with an added lawn, larger pool, second terrace, carport and a more dedicated orchard.
- **A more creative design** – An expansion of the basic design, perhaps with herb, cacti and water gardens as well as a succulent-based rockery garden, separated from the perennial and shrub garden by internal hedges or patches of taller shrubs. Mature trees, including palms, could provide cool and cosy corners in the summer and, as there is now more space, you could allow some shrubs to grow to their full mature height. There is also enough room for a larger vegetable plot and soft fruit garden.

LARGER PROPERTIES

- **A basic design** could be a wire and post enclosure with the house in the centre surrounded by an inner circle of lawn, terrace, pool and garden totalling 4000 square metres. The rest is left wild, with a few trees and perhaps a copse, unless it is agricultural land still being worked or rented out.
- **A more creative design** could include the following:
  1. An inner series of flower gardens. The wide choice includes a cool garden, hot garden, herb garden, perfumed garden, textured garden, cactus garden, rockery, palm garden and water garden. Create a special area in the garden for the most tender and spectacular of the tropical and subtropical plants. Restrict the whole area to 1,500 square metres and surround it with a 25-30 metre-deep wood of a wide variety of deciduous and evergreen trees. The more evergreen and non-fruiting trees there are, the easier the annual cleanup will be.
  2. Banks of plants such as spreading purple lantana, pelargonium graveolens, artotis, osteospermums, marigolds and lantanas camara. With luck, some of them will self seed, and you will have the space to allow them to grow wild.
  3. Full size shrubs and trees. The big advantage of your large garden is that you will be able to allow shrubs and trees to grow to their mature height without the major winter cutback essential in smaller gardens to keep them under control.
  4. Maturing natural woodlands. Consider the ideas included in section 5.7 (In the Shade of Trees) or section 5.8 (Under the Umbrella of a Giant Tree).
  5. A sizeable, organic vegetable garden.
  6. An adjacent and comprehensive orchard and soft fruit garden.
  7. A pool area including a Jacuzzi and sauna hut.
  8. A lawn for games (putting green, croquet, petanc court) and guard-bird peacocks.
  9. A hard-surface games area for basketball, table tennis, etc.
  10. An area for animals and poultry.
  11. Paddocks for grazing, surrounded by trees for protection against winds.
  12. A large natural and wilderness area.
The possibilities are endless but, as with all sizes of garden, maintenance is in direct

proportion to the size and complexity of the garden. A basic 1000 metre plot probably needs a gardener for two hours a week, while a fairly complex layout on a 10,000 metre plot could require a fulltime gardener once the garden is established.

5.2 PATIOS AND COURTYARDS

Patios have been popular in Spain for over a thousand years, since the Moors incorporated an open-air inner courtyard into the design of their townhouses, fortified farms and palaces. Originally the townhouses would have had no other garden space, so the patio was of major importance to their lifestyle. The best patios were beautiful gardens, attractively furnished for outdoor living and maximising the benefit of deep shade in the summer and any touch of sun in the winter, though some in deep wells received no sun.

The concept continues and the best features of the original and the new can be incorporated into a wide range of homes, including:

a. The small inner courtyard of traditional townhouses.

b. The larger courtyard of country cortijos (farms).

c. The rear-walled corral of a terraced village house originally used for the mule and chickens.

d. The small rear-walled back garden of new terraced townhouses.

The concept is now also applied to any terrace surrounded by three walls, fences or trellis.

In this chapter we concentrate on the original inner courtyard concept. The key features can be readily adapted to other situations as appropriate to your lifestyle.

DESIGNING A PATIO GARDEN

When designing your patio garden, keep the following points in mind:

1. Decide on what sort of patio you want.

2. Design and maintain it as an important place in which to relax, eat and entertain.

3. Combine all the skills of gardening and interior design.

4. Use the limited space available to the maximum. Think three- dimensional. If the patio is ten metres square it has a floor area of only 100 square metres, but if you add in the surface of four walls seven metres high you have another 280 square metres to work with.

It is amazing what you can do if you make the most of the space available. Some people achieve more in a small patio than others achieve in a large garden. If you are tempted to go the patio route, consider the following before going into action:

1. To what extent will the patio be important to your daily lifestyle?

2. What will be the maximum and minimum annual temperatures? The warm walls of the patio may raise the temperatures just those few degrees required to prevent winter frost damage but in the summer the south facing wall could become hot and turn the courtyard into a furnace.

3. Where is the natural shade? Recognize that the larger the courtyard the lower percentage of shade and the greater the exposure to the sun in the summer and swirling cold winds in the winter. Naturaally awnings can be used.

4. Where can the rainwater from the roof and floor run to? Decide whether it can be harnessed by fitting gutters and a cistern. The water can then be used for plants and topping up the water features.

The best patios all have certain key features that are indispensable to the full enjoyment of patio living. They include:

1. SHADE – provided by trees in the centre or one or more corners of the patio. Popular choices are olive, orange, palm, ficus, fig, jacaranda, judas tree, *galan de noche* and cordylines. Remember that leaves, flowers or fruit need to be swept up.

2. PLEASANT SOUNDS – the soothing and cooling sound of water cascading from a wall fountain or from one crowning a miniature pond in the centre of the patio or a mini water feature. Perhaps also a caged bird.

3. COLOURFUL AND PERFUMED WALLS – achieved with window boxes and wall pots trailing pelargoniums/geraniums, petunias, fuchsias, carnations, vincas and nasturtiums; and with climbers such as bougainvilleas and the less rampant bignonias, wisterias, jasmine, roses, honeysuckle, passion flower, clematis, stephanotis and plumbago.

4. COOL EVERGREEN PLANTS – placed in the shady parts of the patio, the choices including ferns, aspidistras, spider plants, pothos, philodendrons, succulents, mother-in-law's tongue, cacti, bamboos and bonsais of various types.

5. FLOWERING PLANTS IN POTS – such as kalanchoa, fuchsias, begonias, pansies, busy lizzies, azaleas, hydrangeas, some bulbs such as clivias, cyclamens, freesias, irises, lilies and agapanthus – and groups of herbs for their texture, perfume and culinary/medicinal uses.

6. COMFORTABLE AND COMPATIBLE FURNITURE – sufficient for relaxing or dining alone or with company. For comfort, why not a canopied swing chair and perhaps trellised screens to create quiet corners and covered pergolas for shade when the sun reaches down into the well of the patio? Remember it may rain, so choose furniture that won't spoil easily.

7. FLOOR COVERING – large stone slabs or terracotta tiles are amongst the best. Artificial turf can also be used.

5.3 COLOURFUL NAYAS

The nayas – or arched covered terraces – of old country homesteads and barns were originally built for drying and storing crops and agricultural equipment. Many are now popular features of converted properties and newly built houses – and for good reason.

As gardeners we see the naya as the first part of the garden rather than the last part of the house. If its design includes a display of colourful flowering plants along the shaded inner wall and the east and west ends, and there are uninterrupted views of the garden through the open arches, the naya can literally catapult one into the garden.

Unfortunately, if all the plants are along the outer edge across the arches or there are heavy balastrades, the effect can be the opposite. One can then feel hemmed in towards the house.

Nayas provide an ideal microclimate for a wide range of semi shade and shade loving plants. They retain moisture longer, therefore needing less frequent watering than those in the full sun. Some of our favourites are as follows:

a. If south facing – fuchsia thalia, begonia rex, streptocarpus, aechemea, succulents, amaryllis, lilies, dicliptera, ivy leafed geraniums, petunias and stephanotis.

b. If north facing – hydrangea, cyclamen, azalea, authurium, aeschynanthus, clivia, streptocarpus, philodendron, calathea, pothos, ferns, kalanchoa and minature palms.

Whether a naya has one, two, three or even six arches, it provides an interesting outlook not only to the garden but also to the landscape beyond. Most nayas face south because they were designed for drying crops. Nowadays, they are ideal as an outdoor room and can be regarded as patios for design and living purposes. The low arch keeps out the high sun in summer and lets in the low, warming sun in winter. Open-ended nayas are even more attractive as the low morning sun can shine in at the eastern end and you can enjoy the evening sunsets through the western arch.

If the ends are glazed in, nayas become more sheltered from the wind during the winter without losing the morning and evening sun, but the impact and essence of a naya can be lost if it is totally glazed in.

For the gardener, the naya continues to be an ideal place for drying flowers, herbs, garlic, onions, red chilli peppers, tomatoes and raisins – as well as a convenient place for starting off winter seed trays.

They are the natural home for many geckos that do a good job of nightly reducing the population of mosquitoes and other flying insects. Geckos love hiding behind one or two large bunches of herbs hung in the top shady corners.

If you are an absentee gardener, the naya can be first place to brighten up with temporary plants during your visits. Using the garden before you have created some shade and a terrace or two could be difficult during June, July and August. Potted plants in nayas dry out more slowly than they do in the full sun, however, they do need to be kept just damp.

5.4 APARTMENT TERRACES

One can soon gain an impression of what can be done to create an interesting and colour-ful apartment terrace by looking up at a number of apartment blocks or, better still, look-ing down from a top apartment or terrace onto the terraces below. The best stand out very clearly, but are few and far between.

There are ten main ingredients for creating an interesting and colourful terrace:

1. The owners see the terrace, however small, as extra living space and as an elevated covered patio. They provide for its maximum pleasurable use.

2. Keen gardeners have no problem in continuing their hobby on a small scale. They overcome the limited floor space by training plants up walls and trellis, and along the ceiling.

3. Colourful flowering plants and evergreens are used to provide a year-round impres-sion of being in a garden environment and are planted in attractive pots and contain-ers – square and oblong rather than round being used for economy of space.

4. The plants used are appropriate to the direction the terrace faces.

5. Plants are planted in a combination of window boxes attached to the terrace walls or railings, in pots on top of end sideboard cupboards, hanging baskets and wall pots as well as in floor pots, especially for climbers trained up the wall on hooks or attrac-tive trellis.

6. The owners are resident and enjoy plants. The watering of plants is their first priority in the early morning and late evening. In the summer, south-facing pots may need watering twice a day as well as deadheading most days. Dead flower heads will be more evident in a small space than in a large garden.

7. Blinds are fitted to protect the display of plants from the hottest sun as well as creating shade for an afternoon siesta or other activities on the terrace.

8. On north-side terraces, outer trellises are used to support plants to give some protection from the chillier breezes.

9. Plants are supplemented by tasteful ornaments and artefacts displayed on the walls. A mini self-contained water feature may add the magic of trickling water – or a painted or tiled wall mural may brighten up a wall between windows.

10. The terrace area is small and furniture is selected for its aesthetic appearance, colour, comfort and, most importantly, compactness. A matching table and chairs, rocking chairs and end cupboard units for storage and to provide waist high surfaces for a major display of potted plants is sufficient to enjoy a garden terrace to the full.

If you are a resident apartment owner, consider such a transformation. If you are an absentee owner living in the apartment for only a few weeks or months a year, consider buying colourful plants for the terrace as the equivalent of buying cut flowers for the house at home. Buy them on the first day of each visit and remove them when you leave, unless a friendly neighbour or porter will water them for you during your absences. We recommend removing them when you leave as dying plants soon give a forlorn appearance and advertise the fact that you are not in residence.

If you are a frustrated ex-allotment owner, why not grow a few vegetables and herbs in pots and containers on the terrace? Try tomatoes, peppers and the herbs you use for cooking or infusions as starters. The sister book 'Growing healthy vegetables in Spain' tells you how.

The table opposite gives you a number of planting options, but whatever you do, plant well, water regularly and watch out for and combat bugs and diseases.

5.5 WINDY PENTHOUSES

Penthouse gardens are at the top of the gardening world. Large terraces with 360 degree views await the creativity and care of a keen gardener. Some interesting and restful rooftop gardens undoubtedly exist – but so do some disasters.

Recently we visited friends who have lived for some years in a penthouse with a large terrace on three sides of the house with vistas of mountains, valley and sea. We walked through panoramic sliding doors onto the terrace. The wind blew hard. Dried out plastic pots of herbs bounced across the terrace, although only watered a few hours earlier. The original boundary beds had been converted to seats some years earlier as water had seeped through into a downstairs flat. Seaward geraniums showed signs of salt burn and in only one sheltered shady corner did some succulents and annuals survive well.

Across on another block we could see a verdant rooftop garden with container palms, bougainvilleas, oleanders and conifers, etc., – but the owner had problems with windbreaks attached to the outer railings that broke community regulations.

The two gardens highlighted the special challenge faced by rooftop gardeners, which can include the following problems:

1. The intensity of the direct and reflected rays of the sun that cause normal plant pots and even larger containers to dry out very quickly.

2. The danger of wind-blown salt burn if the property is on the sea front.

SOME PLANTS SUGGESTIONS FOR APARTMENT TERRACES

FACING DIRECTION	PRACTICAL PLANTS
EAST (*)	Petunias, portulacas, bizzy lizzies, pansies, herbs, geraniums, orchids, fuchsias, aloes, bulbs, bougainvilleas, plumbago, potos, kalanchoas, succulents and carnations.
SOUTH (*)	Geraniums, pansies, petunias, portulacas, succulents, cacti, aloes, freesias, herbs, bulbs, plumbago, bougainvilleas, and carnations.
WEST	Petunias, pansies, herbs, aloes, begonias, geraniums, bizzy lizzies, tronco de brasil, bulbs, fuchsias, spider plants, potos agapanthus, and miniature conifers.
NORTH	Azaleas, cyclamen, herbs, clivias, bizzy lizzies, pansies, geraniums, bulbs, aloes, herbs, miniature heathers, dwarf conifers, small palms, a collection of bonsais and traditional house plants such as kalanchoe, asparagus ferns, aspidistras, hostas, capisicum, veronica, skimmia, cinerias, bromeliads, ivies, money plant, potos and succulents.

(*) Blinds on the east and south sides will help to protect plants from the hottest low suns.

3. Winds from all directions, often constant and stronger than at street level, blow anything light around or over.

4. Thermal uplifts similar to those that rise up the faces of mountainsides and cliffs (but a cliff top house has a cliff on only one side).

5. The danger of moisture, even running water, seeping through the terrace into the ceilings of the flats below.

6. The regulations of community associations and town hall planning departments, particularly in respect of high screens around the perimeters.

7. The transporting of plants, ornaments, pots and materials to the top floor by lift or crane.

8. The limited weight bearing properties of wide terraces that overhang the building line of flats below which may restrict the installation of a Jacuzzi, swimming-pool, pond or large earth-filled containers.

9. Many owners are non-resident, only visiting for holidays.

As with all gardens, you should first review your life style needs and ask some very pertinent questions. If you could provide more shelter from the sun and wind, would you sit, eat, exercise and siesta on a more regular basis on the roof terrace? Or do you prefer to look at your panoramic views through the windows of your panoramic, air-conditioned lounge – cool in summer and warm in winter. And ask yourselves these questions:

• Would we enjoy the sound of a fountain to compete with the whistling wind?

• Would an electric raclette or hot stone cooker make more sense than a barbecue or paella ring in the windy conditions?

• Would a modern lightweight Jacuzzi be used regularly?

• Do we want to spend time preparing and tending for plants in pots and containers, or would we be best with a minimalist garden?

Be creative in your design. Consider the following:

• **For protection** – strengthened glass windbreaks around the windiest sides and surrounding the cosiest corners.

• **For shade** – A gazebo with a canvas or open weave cooling roof, awnings or a large umbrella on a heavy base with safety guy lines. A euonymus, pittosporum, thuja, bougainvillea or bottle brush hedge planted in a line of large pots.

• **For comfort** – comfortable dining chairs, rocking chairs and sun loungers. Why not a colourful Brazilian hammock hung on a wooden or metal stand or a traditional swing seat with a sun canopy?

• **For interest** – Metal trellises around the outside walls and as internal dividers, partially covered with climbing plants. Groups of interestingly shaped, textured and coloured ceramic or terracotta pots and ornaments. A mini rockery in a large container; ceramic murals, modern or traditional sculptures, statues, a collection of coloured tiles or plates on the walls.

• **For relaxation** – the sound of water from a mini water feature, fountain or cascade between two small ponds.

• **For colour** – plants. Walls painted in interesting colours, Astroturf over the terrace tiles (or painted in an attractive colour with industrial grade polyurethane concrete floor paint), attractive cushions on seats and benches, and coloured pots.

• **For romance** – interesting lighting effects. A cosy corner with a good night view sheltered by a perfumed climbing shrub.

If you decide to have plants:

• Plant them in plastic pots with a diameter of twice what you would normally use at ground level. This will increase the moisture holding capacity of the soil around plants four fold.

• Place the plastic pots inside larger earthenware pots. This will stop pots from rolling in the wind and shade the inner pots from direct and reflected solar heat. Select a range of pots that will look good individually or in groups with compatible sizes and designs. Ensure pots have wide and deep watering trays.

• As an alternative, plant plants in earthenware pots that have been pre-sealed on the inside to prevent speedy drying out by evaporation. Unsealed pots dry out very quickly.

• Use a good water-retaining potting mix but not one that becomes water logged, causing root rot. It is a good idea to include vermiculite, lava lumps, pieces of water absorbent foam plastic and a little of a proprietary absorbing gel in the soil.

• Mulch the surface of the soil in all pots with a centimetre or two of small stone chippings, grit or lava balls.

• Instead of a group of pots, consider plastic or sealed earthenware troughs, 1-2m long and 30 to 50cm wide and deep. The best come with excellent deep watering trays.

• If your new or existing pent house terrace has built-in raised flower-beds, perhaps as part of the outside barrier of the terrace, ensure that they are waterproof before you plant and water. Empty the beds, which may be sizeable and   deep, of all soil and builders rubble. Then clean the inside thoroughly. Fit a line of drainage tubes along the base to run off excess water from rain or watering. Paint 3 or 4 times with a high quality bitumen paint or swimming-pool paint, designed to give a secure waterproof layer. Then fill the beds with 10cms of rock chippings for drainage, topped with a good potting mix.

Plant the pots and troughs with plants that will withstand high temperatures, winds and wind-blown rain and they will provide greenery and flowers for most if not all of the year. For example:

- Flowering succulents and cacti.
- Zonal and ivy-leaved pelargoniums/geraniums in the sun.
- In the shady corners clivias, lilies, ficus, aspidistras and other naya plants.
- Herbs for perfume, flowers, leaf effects and cuisine.
- Controllable climbers such as bougainvilleas of various colours, plumbago and jasmines. Plumbago grows well in a large pot when pruned as a shrub.
- Lantanas kept pruned to shape when flowers die off or grown as standards. Yellow varieties stay more compact.
- Soft leafed yuccas, cordylines and small palms for their architectural form, height or shade.
- Slow growing evergreen shrubs such as bottlebrush, pittosporum and variegated euonymus.
- Include annuals only if you are happy to water twice daily in the summer.

There are plenty of plants to choose from to create controlled or kaleidoscopic colour schemes. It is important to water and feed plants regularly, and keep the following points in mind.

- To ensure that water gets down to the roots of shrubs and small trees, plant lengths of 2 or 3cm plastic tubing adjacent to plants and water through the tube.
- If you are likely to be away, install a timer-controlled watering system. Set the system at the lowest setting just to keep plants damp. Thoroughly test the system to ensure that excess water does not run out of drainage holes during or after watering, as it could drip down onto lower properties. It is better to water for 3 minutes twice a day than 5 minutes once a day.
- Remember that plants will need more dead heading and pruning than in the garden. The more you plant the more work you will create, and untidy plants look worse on terraces than in the open garden.

If you have a suspect terrace surface you have two possibilities:

- Take up all the tiles, reseal the roof and then retile.
- Thoroughly seal the suspect tiles and cover with Astroturf to provide a non-slip, protective layer.
- Cover part of the terrace with wood slat paving.

By using some of the above ideas you could lay out the rooftop as two or three mini gardens, separated by metal or wooden trellis work with planters in front and perhaps connected via tunnel pergolas.

5.6 MOBILE HOME SITES

More and more mobile home parks are being opened as less expensive alternatives to town houses or small villas. Some parks are a mass of greenery and colour. On others, only the sites of enthusiastic small-scale gardeners stand out.

The challenge is obviously to create a small complete garden that provides year-round colour, perfume and a degree of privacy. The main obstacles to achieving this are as follows:

1. The restricted size of the plot.

2. Site restrictions on what can and cannot be done, especially where the park owners plant hedges between plots and trees for shade.

3. Often the sites are on bedrock with shallow soil or a substantial thickness of hardcore to create a stable level site resistant to the effects of heavy rainfalls.

4. The need for a separate watering system to the general system put in by the park management.

5. The need on some basic sites to do everything from scratch as no framework of hedges around plots and trees are provided.

6. The problems created by neglected adjacent gardens owned by absentee owners. For instance, geraniums attacked by the geranium moth being left untreated, resulting in other plots becoming infested.

Possible solutions include:

1. Provide privacy by (a) planting a hedge around the site, keeping it trimmed to keep it tidy and narrow so that it takes up the minimum of space, (b) construct a white or green-painted, open panelled or trellis wooden fence if you don't want to be totally enclosed and the park regulations do not allow a hedge, or (c) construct a green wire mesh fence and grow a climber on it.

2. Plant a lawn if you have good soil, or terrace the area leaving space for a flowerbed in front of the hedge or fence.

3. If there are no pre-planted trees, plant a tree in each front corner of the site to provide summer shade in addition to the front awning of the mobile home. As trees and climbers grow, check that they are securely supported.

4. Decide whether you want to plant plants in a flowerbed around the site or in a number of large pots or containers. The latter is the better solution on a rocky site. Even trees can be planted in large deep containers as long as they are regularly watered.

5. As your space is limited, plant plants that are not too vigorous.

6. Decide whether you want a permanent display of flowers or a seasonal display to give variety.

7. Invest in good potting compost for flowerbeds and pots/containers.

8. Install a battery controlled watering system to avoid having to water daily during the hot dry periods of the year.

9. Deadhead and prune regularly to keep everything in order.

10. Spray weekly against the geranium moth and also spray plants on adjacent plots if the owners are absent.

5.7 WOODLAND SITES

Many traditional Spanish houses were built amongst trees, especially summer homes where the cool shade was once considered essential from June to September for both people and many plants. Most Spaniards continue the tradition, but it seems many expatriates are happy to fell the trees to build a larger swimming-pool and terrace, and to avoid having to sweep up falling leaves and fruit. They seem to prefer air-conditioning to the natural coolness of shade trees.

Depending on where you live in Spain, the woodlands may be oak (perhaps even cork with the wonderful orange of their stripped trunks brightening up the garden), chestnuts and walnuts in the south, beech in the north, and pine – the last being the most prolific, especially along the coast.

The following are four possible woodland sites:

1. A well-kept woodland garden. Maintain it well for a year to see what plants appear and flower season by season before considering changes or making additional plantings.

2. An unkempt garden previously used only in the summer. Give it an early winter clean up to see what is underneath the layers of pine needles or leaves. If   reasonably attractive proceed as above. If it turns out to be a disaster, start a new garden from scratch.

3. No garden at all because either you have a new house or the previous owners preferred the natural woodlands to a manmade garden. If you prefer the latter, gradually enhance the site.

4. Woods exist, but some of the trees are diseased and dangerous. Hire a qualified tree surgeon to fell and prune as necessary and then plant in the glades.

Above all, if the trees are attractive and safe, preserve the shade and design your garden accordingly. There is often sufficient light coming through the trees to have a good lawn. You may have to rake up fallen leaves but the grass will be sheltered from the burning sun.

If you do no more than plant a good hedge around the property, add a lawn and some pink hydrangeas, you would have a pleasing garden. A few cycas and containers of colourful begonias, busy lizzies, vincas and aganpathus in the centre of the lawn and on the terrace around the house would add interest and colour and still be easily maintained.

If you want to do more, first check on the depth and quality of soil. Woodlands often grow in an amazingly thin layer of topsoil, over a stony or rocky subsoil. When a tree falls in a storm, the root ball may be six metres across but less than half a metre deep.

If the woodlands are old you may be lucky that there is a good depth of peaty soil rich in humus but perhaps on the acid side. You can take advantage of the acidity by planting plants that have an affinity for such soils, such as camellias, hydrangeas, aspidistras, rosemary, lavender, thyme, sage and rockroses. Roses also seem to do well. If the woodlands are new, the soil may be very shallow and you will need to import soil to fill large planting holes and raised beds, or provide the base for a rockery.

In woodland glades, both original glades and those created by cutting down one or two trees, plant a mixture of woodland plants and bulbs that thrive in the semi shade with occasional sun. The mixture could include:

a. Herbs such as rosemary, lavender, thyme and sage.

b. Smaller trees that add interest such as bay, ginko biloba, strawberry tree, jacaranda, magnolia, small palms, fig, and small decorative conifers, thuja and horizontal junipers.

c. Shrubs such as oleander, hydrangea, pittosporum, lantana, broom, echium, viburnum, soft leaved yuccas and rock roses.

d. Climbing shrubs such as ivies, bignonias, clematis, honeysuckles, jasmine, wisteria, passion flower and roses where the sun shines on trunks.

e. Perennials such as leonotis, argyranthemum, senecio and euryops.

f. Patches of irises, lilies, agapanthus and grape hyacinths.

If there is a rocky outcrop or gully, consider creating a rockery with succulents, aloes or cacti. And don't forget forest fruits. In a dappled shaded area, try planting alpine strawberries, raspberries and blackberries. Dig in plenty of well-rotted manure and compost before planting.

When walking in the autumn, we often meet Spaniards out collecting setas (wild mushrooms). If you like this delicacy, try and obtain some spawn to seed an area of the woods.

No woodland is complete without a natural pool. One can be easily constructed with a plastic liner. Add natural reeds, bulrushes, bog irises and other marsh loving plants and you will soon have an interesting feature, hopefully full of frogs and toads.

If you long for home grown organic vegetables, prepare a raised bed in a clearing or on the edge of the woods. New potatoes can easily be grown in a damp pile of pine needles or leaves as well as in raised beds.

Woodland sites do have their problems. Mature trees are thirsty and might leave little moisture for other plants, so you will need to install an irrigation system until new plants are established. Pine needles and leaves can suffocate low-growing plants, so you will need to clean up regularly.

Large trees can become unstable in gale force winds. Check for any movement of root balls when you wander through the woods – and, at the same time, look for any signs of disease from wood-boring beetles or fungi.

Woods, especially pinewoods, can be fire hazards. Put up "no smoking" signs, have a hose that reaches the edge of the property and locate fire brooms at various visible points in the woods. Cut off branches to three metres above the ground and keep dry, wild under-growth under control. And never have a bonfire!

5.8 UNDER THE UMBRELLA OF A GIANT TREE

Some gardens are dominated by a giant tree – a monster that has grown amazingly fast in a damp spot or is centuries old with a gnarled trunk and branches. Some olives were even planted by the Romans two millenniums ago and are now sold at extravagant prices as the centrepieces of large courtyards or terraces.

Olives, carobs and evergreen oaks provide heavy shade throughout the year. Others, such as fig, mulberry, plain and weeping willow, being deciduous, drop their leaves in the winter but create welcome deep solid shade in the summer. Pine trees are continuously dropping needles and cones. Often, old trees have been trained when young to create an abnormally wide umbrella of leaf, by pruning and hanging weights on the branches to make them grow horizontally rather than upwards. All of them provide maximum shade – that vital ingredient for a truly enjoyable Spanish summer – yet are often forgotten in today's rush towards a pool, terrace and air conditioning.

If you are lucky enough to inherit an old tree, how ever big, think twice before lopping or felling it. It is worth more than the value of its logs.

Start by deciding how best to use the shade while at the same time recognising the risks.

A big tree gives you the chance to create a cool place for siestas and fiestas. You can hang a hammock or sky chair from a heavy bough and install a weighty wooden table and chairs for outdoor dining and partying. You could even build a circular seat around the trunk.

There are risks such as falling figs, acorns, olives,staining mulberries, carob pods and pollinating bees but these inconvenients only last for a few weeks.

The area under any tree can be brightened up with pots of flowering plants or a flower-bed around the drip line – as well as deep-shade-loving evergreen house plants in a bed around the trunk or in hanging baskets from the boughs.

Unfortunately, few plants will flower successfully in full shade, but there is a solution to this problem -- the colourful jacaranda, especially in warm coastal situations where it does not lose all its leaves in the winter and so provides dappled shade all year round.

The jacaranda can grow to 20 metres with a spread of 25 or more metres.

So how can we best use its special shade once its wonderful early summer display of enormous blue bunches of flowers has faded?

First see the shade as having three distinct zones, each one worthy of special treatment to create an overall integrated, magical mini garden:

• **The deepest shade around the trunk** – the place for plants in pots, as the root system will prevent satisfactory plantings. Many plants, including aspidistras, ferns, and ficus benjamina would be suitable, but you can also train a jungle climber, such as a pink dipladenia, up the trunk to create a central colourful heart, and tie bromeliads to some of the branches. Run a narrow stepping stone path a few metres from the trunk and brighten up the spaces between the evergreen plants with raised pots of colourful orchids and trailing fuchsias.

• **The inner circle of dappled shade** – plant shade loving plants in the soil and infill with a wide assortment of colourful plants in pots with a meandering path running through. There are many plants to chose from for this semi-shade, humid microclimate: shrubs such as camellias, hydrangeas, azaleas and datura; perennials such as orchids, fuchsias and succulents; bulbous plants such as clivias, lilies and agapanthus; annuals such as trailing petunias, busy lizzies, salvias and nasturtium. Create humidity by the natural heat and the moisture of an extensive drip irrigation system and, in summer, a mist spray several times a week. This type of garden is not for the faint hearted or the absentee gardener, as it will require a watering system with several hundred individual drip heads.

• **The outer circle** – plant shrubs such as the devils tongue, lantanas, hibiscus, dwarf salmon flowered oleander, datura, cassia/senna and bottlebrush; perennials such as argyranthemums, leonotis, lavandar and heliopsis for summer colour and echiums, euryops and rock roses for spring colour; and patches of freesias, irises, lilies and agapanthus.

Overall, this is an amazing mix of semi-jungle-loving plants as a stand alone garden or a set piece in a broader landscape.

Such a garden could obviously not be created in a windswept situation.

It would need to be surrounded by high boundary walls, fences or hedges for shelter from both summer and winter winds, the former preferably covered with brightly flowering climbers such as bougainvilleas, bignonias and wisterias, and the latter perhaps with a mixed-coloured oleander hedge. In a larger property it could be a mini garden – the jacaranda garden – enclosed within high hedges or walls.

If, like most of us, you are not lucky enough to inherit a large jacaranda tree, you could move towards the same effect under a group of maturing palm trees or a group of young jacaranda or albizia trees.

5.9 IN AN INLAND VALLEY

Developing a garden in an inland valley presents some special opportunities as well as some particular problems.

SOME SPECIAL OPPORTUNITIES

Besides the obvious one of having good views along or across the valley, other special opportunities a garden in an inland valley can offer you include:

1. Old terraces that can be used to create a garden on several levels.

Each terrace wall can be developed into a feature. For instance, plant the face as a rockery with plants growing between the rocks or plant ground cover plants on the top to cascade down the wall.

2. The depth of soil behind walls. Terraces were generally built and then in-filled behind to grow crops such as grapes, olives, almonds, cherries and vegetables as well as apples and pears in cooler areas of the country.

3. Good deep soil on the valley floor, especially if a river runs through it.

4. Sheltered south and east-facing valleys can provide opportunities to create microclimates where semi tropical and tropical plants, including fruits, can be grown – provided the valleys are below the general frost line or your garden is facing south and is 50 to 100 metres above the valley floor.

5. Valleys at 200 metres or more above sea level are generally a few degrees cooler than the coastal plain, experience more morning dew and have cool summer breezes.

6. Many north slopes have springs. You may be lucky enough to inherit one in an old garden.

7. Established pines, oaks, carobs, olives, almonds and chestnuts will provide shade.

8. Fruit trees, bushes and vegetables often grow well if the soil is improved.

9. Terraces or a slope of wild herbs, rock roses and bulbs may exist if the land has not been bulldozed clean.

10. Perennials thrive in the cooler, damper climate.

11. Rocky hillsides can be perfect for natural terraced gardens.

12. Annual rainfall will probably be higher than on the coast.

SOME POSSIBLE PROBLEMS

Early loss of sun on north facing slopes, especially in the winter, is one obvious problem. Others include:

1. Frost, most often on the valley floor and north facing slopes.

2. The chance of snow above 600 metres.

3. North facing slopes can be damp in the winter.

4. Low sheltered valleys can be hotter than the coast in summer.

5. Soil on mountainsides and over large rocks can be shallow.

6. Flash floods can occur after storms, especially where terraces have been bulldozed away, woodland felled or old waterways filled in.

7. Natural plant cover on a rocky plot on a south-facing slope can wither in the summer.

8. Soil is often heavy reddy orange clay that needs stabilising if bulldozed by builders and if the terraces have gone.

9. Topsoil could have been removed or buried when site was levelled.

SOME SUGGESTIONS

Retain all natural features such as stone terraces, well heads, large rocks and mature trees, and design your garden to make best use of them. Other suggestions include:

1. Maximise the planting of frost hardy plants. If you are above 400 metres on the mainland or in the Balearic Islands, try growing banks of daffodils, peonies and Christmas roses.

2. Give special attention to creating warm sheltered spots for sitting in the winter sun and planting some of the less hardy shrubs.

3. Retain as many established healthy trees as possible for shelter and shade and plant a thick hedge.

4. Don't plant delicate plants until you have established sheltered areas that are protected from the wind.

5. Build a spectacular rockery.

6. Build a series of ponds with waterfalls between to attract the valley wildlife.

7. Site a number of terraces with tables and chairs at different levels for interest.

8. Frame the best vistas so that they can be enjoyed from the places where you are most likely to sit.

9. Plant fruit trees and grow a terrace of vegetables.

10. Build a garden frame and greenhouse for growing early plants and over wintering delicate plants.

11. Check when you lose the winter sun and whether you get frosts before considering whether to plant sub tropical plants.

12. Protect tender shrubs in the winter from possible night frosts.

13. Take advantage of the slope to channel rainwater to where it is most needed.

14. Don't build paths and terraces right up to the boundary. Leave space for planting a hedge to provide privacy and to act as a windbreak.

5.10 HIGH UP ON AN INLAND MOUNTAINSIDE

As the coastline becomes overbuilt, more and more people are moving inland, seeking existing houses or building sites on the slopes of mountains – a challenge to even the most dedicated and determined gardener. Good gardens can, however, be developed if you recognize and respond to the following positive and negative aspects of such locations from day one.

ALL HILLSIDES

The positive factors for home sites on all hillsides are good vistas, cooling breezes, naturally growing plants, peace and quiet, and perhaps a spring, fed by higher-up melting snows. The negative factors can be full-sun parched areas in summer, possible frost or snow in winter, hot and cold drying winds, possible steep slopes, and erosion by wind and rain.

NORTH FACING HILLSIDES

The additional positive factors of hillsides facing north are more early morning mist and dew, more chances of natural springs, cooler temperatures in summer, higher rainfalls and less need to water, losing the sun earlier.

The negative factors can be many days of frost, colder temperatures in winter, a shorter growing season, and non-survival of tender plants.

TEN BASIC GUIDELINES

Here are some tips to improve the chances of your hillside garden being a success:

1. Retain as many existing natural herbs and shrubs as possible. They obviously enjoy the microclimate and have probably taken years to establish themselves. Clear unwanted vegetation from around them, mulching with stones and trimming lightly to shape.

2. Decide how to best incorporate existing plants into your future garden.

If you are lucky enough to inherit an intact hillside with a good mix of native herbs, bulbs and shrubs, do nothing except for a few carefully considered enhancements, such as pathways and terraces in natural stone.

If your hillside is not totally covered with native plants, use what there is as the main framework for an interesting and colourful garden. Even a few pockets of existing plants may be worth keeping as special features.

3. Decide on a budget for developing the garden. The main costs will be buying plants and building materials for constructing walls and terraces as well as importing good soil, compost and manure if on a dry, rocky hillside.

4. Decide whether trees are advisable to provide a windbreak and shade or as specimens to provide focal points in shaping the garden. Look around the area and check what trees grow naturally or are being imported successfully by neighbours at your height on the mountainside. Check out from what size the latter were grown (50cm high saplings or mature specimen trees). Also check what depth of soil your neighbours have compared with your own.

5. Decide on what plants will give shape, colour and perfume. The choices include brooms, rockroses, santolina, rosemary, sage, thyme, rue, lavender etc. Many perennials can be grown successfully, especially if planted below a wall or bank. Aloes can survive high up and grow into spectacular plants.

6. Select planting places carefully. First try and map where you have:

- Solid rock, less than a metre below soil level.
- Deep soil between outcrops of rocks.
- Holes or hollows that could be filled with good soil.
- Areas of fine sedimentary soil washed down by of years of rain.
- Areas of rock that could be cleared down to soil level, keeping the rocks for a rockery or mulching.
- Places where you could sink a plastic barrel to fill with soil for planting a conifer or large shrub. The purple flowering bougainvillea can grow even in exposed situations if protected in the winter.
- Natural rain waterways.
- Consider terracing part of the garden with dry stone or concreted rock-faced walls in-filled with local or imported soil.

7. Decide whether to have a small vegetable and soft fruit garden. Raspberries grow well in the Alpujarras in Andalucía at up to 1,800 metres.

8. Provide extra colour by planting pots and window boxes. There are plants appropriate for both the summer and the winter.

9. Plant subtropical plants in pots for their summer splendour, but ensure that you take them inside to a well-lit window during the winter months. There they can provide an interesting winter display.

5.11 EXPOSED ON THE CENTRAL PLAIN

The wide-open plains of La Mancha and Aragon can be hostile places to live but, increasingly, more and more newcomers are settling there. The plains can be hot and dusty in summer, erosion dust storms sometimes blocking out the landscapes, and in the winter, winds can be cold and wet with many areas experiencing frost and snow. These are the high plains of Spain – around 1200 metres above sea level – surrounded by higher mountains where ski resorts are open most winters.

Properties on the plains are either isolated farmhouses and cottages – many of them abandoned since their inhabitants moved away to villages and cities – or houses in lonely villages, such as those in La Mancha that Don Quijote passed through in his travels.

Summer gardening in these parts is not that different from elsewhere, but in winter plants will need to be more frost resistant, and temperate trees such as planes, mulberries, oaks, conifers, weeping willows, laburnum, philadelphus and walnuts are more usual than chorisias and jacarandas. Vines are more normal than lemons; spring peonies and hellebores more in evidence than echiums and acacias. Garden soils are often good, having served as the yards for sheep and goats for centuries, and vegetables should grow well in the sheltered village gardens.

Out in the open it will be a different story. With no mutual protection from other houses, windbreaks will be the number one priority. If you have struck lucky, your house will have a walled yard waiting to be turned into a combined flower and vegetable garden, and an outhouse or two that can be used as a workshop, storeroom or a place to keep a few hens and rabbits.

If your property is just a cottage, we suggest you first build a high-walled area around both the front and back of the house, if the plot and local regulations allow. If there is space, you could build a high wall around the whole property in which to develop a walled garden. Winds can hop over walls, so plant some trees as a windbreak either within the embryo walled garden or just outside the wall if you can. Check around the surrounding 50 kilometres or so to see what trees survive and where you can buy some sizeable saplings. Choose trees that will grow fast with the help of some animal manure and regular watering.

Make a feature of any wellhead, trough or washbasin you inherit – and an old farm cart if you can find one. Consider adding a sheltered terrace, if planning regulations allow, and build a frame and greenhouse in order to grow plantlets for planting out as soon as the frosts are past.

It's now the time to consider what sort of garden you want, bearing mind that your lifestyle will probably be rather different than on the Costas, at least in the winter. Aim to have a mixed garden because, being isolated, it makes sense to be as self sufficient as possible.

Grow vegetables in the spring, summer and autumn (the winters will probably be too cold) and plant fruit trees and bushes. Nuts, apples, pears, plum, raspberries and peaches should be possible crops – but a lemon tree will need to be well protected in winter if it is to have any chance of survival. Within the garden a herb area would make sense, as well as frost resistant perennials and shrubs. Train a grapevine over a traditional iron arbour in front of the most south-facing doorway.

Brighten up the summer garden with pots and window boxes of bright coloured annuals. Develop a rose garden and grow climbing roses up walls and over pergolas rather than the bougainvilleas and bignonias of the coast. Grow delicate shrubs in large pots and take them inside for the winter as one would in Madrid, which has a similar climate.

MADRID

The climate in Madrid will be very hot in summer and cold in winter, as on the open plains, although high and dense building gives protection from winds. Sheltered gardens will be like an oven in the summer, so a wide variety of plants can be grown (including sub tropical plants) if watered well and maximum use is made of any shade.

Anything that is not frost resistant needs to be planted in pots and taken into the house or apartment during the winter and placed in front of a south-facing window. Remember what you used in northern Europe to give winter colour – even if it was only varied shades of green. Maximise the planting of temperate evergreen shrubs, trees, roses, herbs and bulbs, and brighten up spring, summer and early autumn gardens with colourful window boxes, pots and hanging baskets.

5.12 ON SALINE AND BARREN SOILS

Fewer and fewer new houses are built on good soil. Increasingly, saline or barren land is being used for building, as it is of no use for agriculture, fruit growing or vines. Sometimes land is classified as tierra de secano – to be left as dry, non-irrigated land to go wild. Many such areas are rural and have enviable views, but initially there are two problems that need to be overcome.

First it is important to understand why your land is said to be saline or barren. There are four main causes of salinity:

a. Seawater entering the water table along the coastal strip during a period of several years of drought.

b. A rising water table over salty sub strata as a result of the felling of trees and therefore less extraction of water by plant roots, especially where native trees grew previously on the slopes of a valley.

c. The over use or deepening of a well.

d. The irrigation of soil with salty water over a number of years which. eventually kills fruit trees and vines.

There are four main causes why very little or nothing will grow in certain situations. They are:

a. Builders have stripped all the topsoil off your plot and all you have left is very infertile sub-soil.

b. Serious salinity.

c. Years of very little rain resulting in desert land, although in reality the desert-like soil may be rich in nutrients.

d. Pollution of the land by factory effluent and the inclusion of industrial waste tips.

What can be done to improve the soil? Obviously you need to reduce the salinity in the soil, and you can do this by:

a. Stopping the use of saline water immediately.

b. Having the extent and type of salinity checked and then searching out a suitable and economic desalination unit.

c. Washing through over a number of years by watering with collected rainwater or imported tankers of spring water.

d. Enriching the soil where you will be planting flower-beds and trees by mixing in large quantities of well rotted manure and compost.

e. Replanting/planting salt resisting trees such as pines.

f. Installing a magnetising water improvement unit to treat well or piped water.

g. Installing a mini reverse osmosis or evaporation desalination unit.

To improve barren soil, you need to do the same as in 'b' above and irrigate well, import loads of good soil and grow plants in raised beds in enriched new soil rather than directly in the ground.

Other steps you can take are to design the garden with large terraced and paved areas to minimise the areas to be planted, situate shrub beds under the eaves so that they catch all the rainwater; slope the surrounding terrace towards the bed to increase the amount of fresh water; and plant things that are reasonably tolerant to low levels of salinity.

What can be planted in saline situations? If you walk along many beach areas, you will often find:

a. palms and tamarix being grown on the beach,

b. yuccas, cordylines, pittosporum, aloe, arboresens (red hot poker), agaves, prickly pear cacti and succulents such as aeoniums and messembryanthemums growing at the edge of the beach,

c. ground covers such as carpobrotus, aptenia, morning glory, asteriscus maritime covering sand dunes,

d. bamboo thickets in damper areas,

e. pines that adapt to the salty situation.

The best thing is to start with the planting list above before mass planting other shrubs. Plant a few and see how well they grow for a year.

5.13 WINDOW BOXES AND LINES OF POTS

Window boxes or lines of pots planted with colourful or evergreen plants make attractive mini gardens on the window sills and front edge of the balconies of houses, apartments and penthouses. Some can be planted up with vegetables. Sadly, window sills and balconies are under utilised in this way, even though garden centres stock a much better selection of suitable containers these days – and an example has been set by many inland villages.

When they are planted well and cared for, plants in window boxes or lines of pots can do the following:

1. Brighten up the outlook from windows and the doors onto balconies and terraces.

2. Provide a screen from prying eyes.

3. Brighten up the overall appearance of a building from the outside, from both the garden and the street.

4. Be colourful all the year round with either permanent or seasonal plantings. Tiers of window boxes on four storey village houses or even taller apartment blocks can create an amazing Hanging Gardens of Babylon effect, even during the winter months when house fronts can otherwise look drab and communal gardens are not at their best. See section 2,14.

PART SIX

CARING FOR PLANTS

There are probably several hundred plants that could do well in the microclimate of your garden provided you nuture them from the day you buy them in the garden centre or start to grow from seeds or cuttings. The sections that follow tell you how.

6.1 PREPARING THE SOIL

Like the family cat, plants have nine lives, each one of them easily lost and largely irrecoverable. The more lives lost, the less chance of having strong, healthy and colourful plants in your garden. The nine lives are:

1. The quality of the seed or cutting used to propagate the plant.

2. The ambient conditions in which the seedlings are grown into plants in nurseries for sale to the public or, if home grown, for planting out.

3. The ambient conditions during the transfer of plants from the grower to the garden centre – increasingly by trans-European pantechnicons and international airlines.

4. The pre-sale care of plants in the garden centres, especially during the winter and summer months, and the quality of advice given regarding the planting and ongoing care of those you buy.

5. The selection and purchasing of plants.

6. The acclimatisation of plants before planting in their final positions.

7. The selection of their planting positions.

8. The planting and aftercare.

9. The quality of the soil in which your plants are planted.

The quality of the soil is the most fundamental issue and often ignored until too late. Many plants in Spain are in a permanent state of survival due to a combination of poor soil and watering.

Numerous surveys we have carried out on the problems of expatriate gardeners in Spain have destroyed the myth that all Spanish gardens have good soil. Response to surveys by people living between Valencia and Cadiz classified their soils as follows: excellent 5%, good 30%, poor 50% and very poor 15%.

Many of those claiming excellent and good soils did so because they or their predecessors had improved the soil. Soils were poor for the following reasons:

1. Clay soil, heavy to work when wet and impossible to work when dry and baked. It is often rich in minerals but they are not easily extracted by roots of plants. It dries out quickly in the sun and roots can be compressed by the drying clay.

2. Sandy soil that drains quickly and can be acidic. It is light in nutrients as millions of years of rain have dissolved and washed away many of the minerals to the subsoil or water table.

3. Shallow soil, sometimes just two or three centimetres over bedrock. Some gardeners use a Kango hammer to create planting holes, while others resort to raised beds.

4. Soil full of stones or rocks, sometimes even large flat rock slabs within 30cm of the surface.

5. Soil full of builder's rubble.

6. Topsoil removed by builder and not replaced.

7. Topsoil bulldozed under subsoil.

8. Barren soil due to over use or no rainfall.

9. Soils that have become saline by over use of wells or felling of forests.

10. Acid soil low in nutrients.

Plants may survive in poor soil but they will not be at their best. They will only remain alive with regular watering and feeding, so check your soil and improve it, whatever its current condition. But first what is a good soil? For most plants the ideal soil is one that is:

a. Crumbly and friable, high in humus (decomposing vegetable matter) and allows roots to spread and go down deeply in search of moisture and nutrients.

b. Water retaining, due to the humus content but sufficiently gritty and open to allow excess water to drain away.

c. Attractive to and retains earthworms that process humus and improve the draining and oxygen penetration of the soil.

d. Rich in micro organisms and minerals required for the healthy growth of plants.

NUTRIENTS REQUIRED BY PLANTS

1. Carbon dioxide taken in through the leaves at night to create chlorophyll.

2. Moisture taken in by roots and leaves. Together with micro- organisms, water extracts nutrients from the soil and causes plant cells to swell to provide rigidity and strength in stems, branches and leaves.

3. Nitrogen (N), required for the development of green plant structures (stems, branches and leaves) and for root growth.

4. Phosphorus (P), often known as phosphate, essential for the development of strong root structures.

5. Potassium (K), often known as potash, essential for the development of flower buds, flowers, seed heads and fruit – and to enhance the drought and disease resistance of plants.

6. Minerals and trace elements that maintain health and vitality. The most important are as follows.

  a. Magnesium, which prevents yellowing of leaves between veins.

  b. Calcium, essential for cell growth and resistance to diseases.

  c. Sulphur, which promotes general plant health when in the soil and increases soil acidity to enhance the extraction of minerals. Fed on the surface of the leaves, sulphur also prevents mildew and fungal diseases.

  d. Iron, which helps create chlorophyll and prevents bleaching of leaves between veins.

  e. Zinc, which prevents leaves from developing yellow spots.

  f. Manganese, which prevents yellowing of leaves between veins.

  g. Boron, copper and molybdenum, which contribute to the development of cell structures and natural disease control.

All are found in Spanish soils although not always in the right balance, so they need to be supplemented by the addition of manures, compost, seaweed, comfrey and nettle feeds, and proprietary organic and inorganic fertilisers.

Get to know your soil. To improve it, try the following:

1. Dig holes in several places in the garden and check the depth of the darker topsoil before you get down to a lighter-coloured subsoil or rocks.

2. Water a few square metres of soil for two minutes, wait until the surface water has drained away and the surface is firming up, then dig down to find out how far the water has penetrated. Repeat this until you get water down to 30cm.

3. Leave the area to dry out for two days and then dig down to find how far it has dried out. Repeat every two days for a week.

4. If the top soil is less than 20cm and the water drains away or dries out quickly, deepen the soil with earth from other parts of the garden or brought in and work in plenty of compost and manures to improve its fertility, water absorbing properties and openness.

5. If the water does not soak away and the soil becomes waterlogged in the top 10 or 20cm, loosen the soil down to a depth of 50 to 60cm and mix sharp sand or grit into the soil at the same time you add the compost and manures.

6. Another way to test the composition of the soil before and after making manure/ compost additions is to put a handful of earth in a tall thin glass, fill it with water, place your hand over the top and shake. Then leave to settle. The solid matter will settle in layers – the heavier larger stone particles at the bottom, the smaller stones and grit in the middle and a dark layer of fine particles and light organic humus on top. You should notice a big difference in your soil after you have enriched it.

7. If you are taking over an existing garden and the earth is poor, you have four options.

   • Mulch the surface of the soil around plants with well-rotted compost/manure and work it into the surface of the soil with a hoe and harrow after rain.
   • Clear each bed in turn and enrich the soil before replanting with the plants you took out or with new plants.
   • Make new, perhaps raised, flowerbeds in another area and, if feasible, transfer existing plants to the new bed. Use the original area for a terrace or special feature such as a pond or rockery.
   • Reduce the areas of the garden used for flowerbeds by clearing the least attractive ones or those in the wrong position.

8. The preparation of the soil alongside walls needs special attention. Often you will find a large quantity of builder's rubble buried there. This causes two problems. Firstly the soil drains instantly and secondly the buried mortar makes the soil too alkaline for favourite wall plants such as bougainvilleas and bignonias. So dig deep alongside walls and remove most of the rubble before changing or enriching the soil.

9. If you have good soil, or improve poor soils, most permanent flowering plants in the garden will rarely need extra feeding. Annuals will, however, as well as potted plants, vegetables and fruit trees.

10. Some plants, such as camellias, blue hydrangeas, irises and rock roses, like acid soil, as found on wooded or cleared sites, especially in pine woods.

11. If you are planting acid-loving plants in normal soil, either plant in large buried pots full of acid potting compost, the compost from under pine trees, or develop a special acid mix for a bed that is preferably in the semi shade.

12. If you have a small garden you may want to restrict the growth of some plants while encouraging others to grow rapidly. For instance, you may want a cactus/aloes bed, but not with huge mature plants. In this case plant them in poor soil but add sand/grit to ensure that it is free draining. Just enrich the beds for your prize shrubs and other plants.

CHECK YOUR SOIL ACIDITY

Most Spanish garden plants will grow well at acidities on the pH scale of 6 to 7.5, with an optimum of around 6.5. Acid-loving plants will be happier at a pH of 4 to 5. The pH scale runs from a high acidity of1 to a high alkalinity of 14, with 7 regarded as neutral. The difference between two numbers on the scale indicates a tenfold difference in acidity.

If interested, buy an inexpensive soil testing kit or ph meter from a garden centre or a roll of litmus paper (pH papel) from a chemist. Using litmus paper is easy. Put an inch of soil in a jar, half fill with water and shake. Let it settle for a few minutes and then stick one end of a strip of litmus paper into the water. Leave for a minute and then check the colour against the colour chart provided. Just one precaution: check the pH of the water you use before doing the tests as this could distort the results.

The issue of soil fertility and acidity is most important in the growing of vegetables and fruit.

6.2 GUIDELINES FOR BUYING PLANTS

Whether you purchase plants or propagate your own, only plant out strong healthy plants. The following are guidelines for buying plants:

    1. Select plants that match your local microclimate and the style of garden you have decided to develop. Most plants sold are suitable for planting along the Costas, but there can be big differences in the winter microclimate between coastal gardens at sea level, five kilometres inland, inland valleys, north facing slopes and mountainsides. Temperatures often vary by one degree centigrade per 100 metres of height on normal days, but this can rise to two or three degrees per 100 metres during wintry weather. Two hours of frost every three years can make the planting of tropical and the more tender subtropical plants very disheartening. Also recognise that some plants love acid soil such as found on plots near to pine trees.

    2. Select and purchase strong healthy plants that have:

223

- No sign of disease or infestations,
- A good shape with strong joins between the branches and trunk,
- A good root ball in relation to the size of the growth above the soil. If a plant is top heavy, the small root structure may struggle to extract sufficient moisture and nutrients from the soil to support the super structure when planted in the harsher conditions of the average garden compared to those in a propagating house. We often prefer to buy a smaller, balanced plant and bring it on at a realistic rate in the garden.
- Plenty of new, unopened flower buds. Purchase a plant with just one or two open flowers in order to check the colour, with many buds that will open later in the garden, unless you need instant colour as in-fills for a special occasion. If you buy a plant in full flower with few oncoming buds, it will soon finish flowering, as the plant's priority when first placed in the garden will be to put down roots. Yes, many garden centres do market plants in full flower and some now charge more for budded but un-flowered plants.
- Good supporting canes and ties which have not started to rub or cut into the bark. This is especially important when selecting tall shrubs and trees.

3. Do not buy plants that show signs of being:
   - Wind or frost burnt, especially when purchasing during the winter or early spring.
   - Seriously root bound. However, if bu-ying a tree, there is an advantage if strong roots have grown through the bottom of the container into the soil beneath.
   - Very recent propagations, as yet without good root structures. This is especially important with climbers sold in very small pots.
   - Stressed by heat or having been allowed to dry out.
   - Waterlogged, and therefore perhaps susceptible to fungal diseases.

4. Don't buy very early annuals and vegetable plantlets unless you have a very sheltered garden or a cold frame in which plants can be hardened off.

5. When buying something unusual, check that the garden centre can tell you how to care for the plant. If not, ask them to find out before you buy.

6. If the garden centre does not have the variety or colour of flower you want, ask if they can order it for you.

7. When purchasing very large plants such as palms or old olive trees, check that the garden centre is able to deliver and plant for you at a reasonable cost.

8. Search widely for good and unusual plants. Recognise that there is a wide range of sources as illustrated in the "Some Useful Sources of Plants" table opposite.

9. If plants seem expensive, check at a number of other places. Prices can vary widely.

10. Recognise that unlike most other purchases, no warranty normally comes with plants. Few outlets will readily replace plants that die. It is up to you to manage the transfer of plants from where you buy them to your garden – avoid transferring them in a hot car in mid July/August – and plant them well and nurture them into the best specimens in the neighbourhood.

11. When your garden is fully planted, ensure that the unplanned, impromptu purchase of a special/unusual plant that catches your eye can be fitted in by replacing an existing plant, re-planning part of the garden or adding yet another pot to a mounting collection. Remember that they all need to be cared for.

SOME USEFUL SOURCES OF PLANTS

1. Nurseries that propagate most of the plants they sell.
2. Garden centres and supermarkets that buy in all their plants, often imported.
3. Weekly markets, rastros and garden club stalls where enthusiastic amateurs sell some of their own propagated plants.
4. Agricultural cooperatives – especially for fruit trees and vegetable plants.
5. Swaps with friends or gifts.
6. Self-seeded plants on the roadside or in the garden.
7. Neighbours about to either replant a garden or add a swimming pool.
8. Jobbing gardeners who propagate to produce in fills in the gardens they maintain.
9. Mail order catalogues – especially for roses, bulbs, speciality shrubs and vegetables.
10. You own propagation from seeds or cuttings.
11. Stalls at gardening clubs.

6.3 PLANTING EFFECTIVELY

New plants should be planted in as near an ideal position as possible using the best available soil. Under those circumstances each plant has the best chance of speedily developing the deepening and spreading root system necessary to extract the nutrients and moisture essential to achieve the strong, healthy, and continuous growth.

POSITION

Select planting sites appropriate to each plant. For instance:
- In the sun, semi shade or shade.
- In sandy, chalky, stony or rich-in-humus soil.
- In swampy or free draining soil.
- In acid, neutral or alkaline soil.

When deciding where to plant, recognise that situations such as alongside a drive, terrace, path or stone chipping area will provide roots with a natural damp shelter, once they grow sideways and downwards, searching for moisture and dissolved nutrients.

TIME

Plant at the optimum time of the year, preferably after a period of rain and, if sunny, late in the afternoon. If you garden according to the lunar calendar, take note of the special planting days for flowering and evergreen leaf plants.

Although most plants are now sold in pots with a well developed root system and not dry rooted (although the latter still occurs), the best time of year to plant perennials, shrubs and trees is during the cooler months of October through March. However, if your garden is in a frost belt, delay the planting of any delicate plants until after the last frosts.

PREPARATION OF THE SOIL

Prepare flowerbeds and areas for trees and vegetables as outlined in first chapter of this section 6.1 entitled "Preparing the Soil".

PREPARATION OF PLANTS

Water all plants the evening before planting so that the compost around the root ball stays as firm as a ball when you remove the pot.

PREPARATION OF PLANTING HOLES

Prepare planting holes carefully. If you are lucky enough to have a garden with a light, good draining loamy soil it will normally be sufficient to dig a hole slightly larger than the size of the root ball. Fill the hole with water and let it drain away. Carefully transfer the root ball from the pot to the hole, working some compost into any air holes left.

If you are unable to fully prepare beds in this way, dig a hole twice as wide and deep as the pot containing the plant. Fill with water and let it drain away. Then line the hole with a 50:50 mix of soil and well-rotted compost or a water-retaining planting compost from a garden centre. If the planting hole drains away quickly or your soil normally dries out very quickly, add a teaspoon of a water-absorbing gel such as TerraCottem - into the compost at the bottom of the hole. Firm the compost at the bottom of the hole and add more until the depth of the hole is equal to the depth of soil in the pot containing the plant.

PLANTING

Remove the plant from the pot, taking care not to disturb the root ball, and place in the planting hole. If the plant was root bound in the pot, loosen some roots before putting in the hole.

Infill the hole around the root ball with the 50:50 planting mix mentioned above. Firm each five centimetre layer until you reach the level of the surrounding soil. Then mulch with two centimetres of loose, well- rotted garden compost or purchased compost. If you are planting acid loving plants such as camellias, hydrangeas, rock roses and conifers, use acid planting composts.

If strong roots were coming through the bottom of the pot, or the soil in the pot was very loose or fibrous, cut off the pot rather than try to pull the plant out of the pot. After planting give the soil around the plant a good watering.

When planting vegetables plantlets dig holes deep enough for the root balls and firm soil around them. It's of benefit to add a little water retaining gel to each hole in dry areas.

STAKING AND PROTECTION

If the plant needs a supporting cane or post, knock this firmly into the ground before planting and tie up the plant as soon as planted. Likewise, fix screw eyes into a wall if the plant is to be tied against it. Ensure that plant ties leave plenty of room for the stem and branches of the plant to expand and that they do not chaff or rub. See section 6.4.

If you are planting in a sunny position, cover the surrounding area with woven plastic sheeting and mulch with stones, chippings or wood bark to keep the soil cool and moist and to make it difficult for weeds to establish themselves.

If planting in a windy position, protect plants with a woven plastic screen until they are established.

WATERING NEW PLANTS

If you have an irrigation system, fix a drip feed for each new plant. Check the soil regularly to see that it is moist and that you can push a finger down into the soil. Recognise that a plant can die from the bottom upwards just as easily as from the top downwards, so a deep watering down to the base of the roots will be better than a shallow watering three times a week. It helps to push in a 20cm length of 5cm diameter plastic tubing beside the plant, and then water down it to get water to the roots.

Be especially careful to water sufficiently during the first summer. By the second and third year most shrubs and trees will have their roots well down towards the water table, so you should be able to reduce the watering progressively.

FEEDING

If you enriched the flowerbeds and planting holes, plants should find sufficient nutrients in the soil to sustain their continuous growth. However, if plants are yellowing or become stunted even though you are watering properly, give the plants a boost with a liquid comfrey/nettle natural feed or an organic general fertilizer for flowering plants or evergreens as appropriate. If using the latter, we recommend using half the indicated strength and applying it twice as frequently. From then onwards, give your plants a light slow release granular feedeach spring. Water in well if it doesn't rain within a day.

EARLY CARE

As the plants grow, keep a wary eye out for pests and diseases and treat promptly. Prune plants lightly during the first year to achieve an attractive balanced shape.

PLANTING BULBS

Plant bulbs according to their recommended depths. Typical planting depths in Spain are as follows:
- Small bulbs and corms such as crocuses, anemones and grape hyacinths 3 or 4 centimetres.
- Shallow rhizomes such as miniature irises, 2 or 3 centimetres.
- Medium sized bulbs and rhizomes such as daffodils, tulips, San Pedro and gladioli, 8 to 10 centimetres.
- Large bulbs such as lilies and dahlias, 10 to 12 centimetres.
- Large rhizomes such as flag irises and canna lilies, 3 or 4 centimetres.

6.4 USE EFFECTIVE TIES AND SUPPORTS

Many plants need to be tied to walls, fences and trellises or to supporting canes or stakes. Trunks and branches can be strangled or severely chaffed if tied or supported poorly and branches may be lost or plants, including maturing trees, die. To prevent this, we recommend you take the following actions:

1. Recognise that the diameters of the main stems and side branches of climbers planted against the wall of the house, boundary walls or fences or mid garden terrace soon expand, especially after the first year. For instance, a bougainvillea planted with a thin one-centimetre stem may have a thick five-centimetre diameter trunk within five years and double that in ten.

Unless ties are loosened or replaced as the plant grows, strangulation soon starts, with tie wires being absorbed into the new flesh and eventually killing off the branch or entire plant. It is all too easy to fix a few metal eyes into a wall, tie plants tightly to them with small-gauge round or flat garden wire and, at the same time, wind wire around branches to train them straight – and then assume that all is well.

Go into your garden now and examine all your climbers. You may be surprised at how many wires are already cutting in, even being totally enclosed by new woody growth. Remove all immediately, pulling out any sealed wires if possible.

Replace all such ties with a length of garden wire passed through an appropriate length of the 5, 10 or 15mm diameter black plastic tubing as used for drip irrigation systems. Use the narrower tubing for small plants and the wider for thicker trunked and branched shrubs and trees.

Note that the flat garden ties, even if plastic covered, can be worse than round ties as they act as saws on windy days. This problem is very critical for absentee gardeners who may only see plants in full flower and leaf and not when bare in the winter after leaf fall or the winter cut back.

2. The supporting canes and tight ties on plants in the garden centres are designed to ensure that plants are not damaged in transport to or from the garden centre. Rarely are they intended as a long-term support for the plants when planted out in your garden.

If you purchase a plant with one or two plastic strips held firmly to a cane by metal staples, remove both the cane and strips as soon as planted. If necessary, especially with climbers, get someone to hold the plant firmly while you insert a more appropriate support stake and tie.

Very often the cane supplied by the garden centre is too thin to stay firmly in the ground in high winds. Replace it with a thicker and taller cane so that you can push the cane into the ground for 30 centimetres and not just the few centimetres in the original plant pot.

3. If you have plants, including young citrus trees, planted in the garden still with the original canes and ties, examine them carefully. In many cases you will find that the tie has started to chaff the bark, especially if the metal staple is touching the trunk.

4. When planting larger trees, obtain thick canes or poles to support them, long enough to be able to knock into the ground for 30 to 50 centimetres. If the trunk is thin, support it at several places.

Fix each tie first to the support post, and then loosely around the trunk to avoid cutting into the bark and to allow the trunk to recognise that it needs to build up its girth to support the tree in the wind.

Yes, you can purchase proprietary plastic tree ties, but wire and rubber tubing is less expensive and you can size each tie to match the diameter of each tree. When making the ties, allow enough spare wire to be able to let out the ties as the girth of the trunk increases.

5. Lastly, but most importantly, check all ties once or twice a year. Adjust or replace as appropriate and add more ties to climbers as they grow.

6.5 ECONOMICAL WATERING

Watering is required to replace moisture lost by evaporation, to cool the earth and support the cellular growth of strong healthy plants. Water needs not only to reach shallow roots seeking nutrients in the surface soil but, more importantly, to the larger and deeper tap roots. Many plants will survive drought for a time but they will rarely become the best specimens in the garden.

Watering can be both time consuming and expensive, and water prices are forecast to rise in many areas of Spain in the future. It therefore makes sense to follow the xeriscaping and waterless gardening practices below to save time and money:

REDUCE REQUIREMENTS

1. Plant plants that require the least water.
2. Plant deep-rooted rather than shallow rooted-plants.
3. Make major new plantings in the autumn and not later than March.
4. Minimise the planting of annuals.
5. Keep plants in pots and containers in semi shade rather than full sun.
6. Increase the percentage of the garden that is covered by paths and terraces.
7. Water at the drip line of trees rather than around the trunk, to stimulate spreading root balls.
8. Plant on the north side of the house, especially if you are an absentee gardener.
9. Stop watering for awhile after rain.
10. Water non flowering plants to just keep them alive in August. Three times the amount of water won't bring them back into flower until temperatures drop in September and October.
11. Don't water mature plants unnecessarily (to help, insert 20cm lengths of 5cm plastic tubing alongside deep rooted shrubs and trees when planting and water through the tube).
12. Sweep rather than washing down terraces.
13. Install an automatic time-controlled watering system with an adjustable drip feed to each plant needing water

14. Turn off or remove redundant drips.
15. Check watering system every week to make sure there are no leaks and losses of water.
16. Reduce the size of the lawn, or better, don't have one.
17. Plant alongside paths and around terraces so that roots can travel under-neath to seek water and retain shade.
18. Use perforated tube irrigation systems along lines of vegetables.
19. Design a minimalist garden with a few or no plants.
20. Don't leave hoses running unnecessarily.
21. Mix a little TerraCottem (www.terravida.com) soil enhancing gel into the composts for containers, and in the garden into planting holes and seed drills.

IMPROVE THE QUALITY OF WATER

1. Install a fine filter before the start of your irrigation system to ensure that small particles do not block the watering jets.
2. There are a number of water improvement technologies that are as useful to the amateur gardener as the professional.
   a. If you have a saline water supply or well a small scale reverse osmosis unit is the easiest way of enabling you to use the water to irrigate the garden.
   b. If you have dead or mildly polluted water a Grosse GIE unit <www.lumenssal udnatural.com>that improves the quality of water by using vortex and magnetic technologies can be of benefit.
   c. Unfortunately both of the above are relatively expensive for the average gardener. However there is a less expensive technology for improving the qua-lity of piped water supplies. That is a hand held or fixed inline Vi-Aqua unit (www.viaqua.com) which changes the properties of water via low frequency radio wave electromagnetic technology. The energised water produced has enhanced wetability and makes it easier for roots to extract nutrients from the soil. The main benefits are reduced fertilizer and water needs and stronger root and plant growth. The stronger root growth being particularly important in Spain.
3. Many gardeners are wanting to use the grey water from the shower, washing up or washing machine during periods of water shortage or irrigation bans. Our experience is that provided you use soft biodegradable washing gels/solutions this is unlikely to harm most plants.
4. If you need to use the swimming pool water to save your garden during periods of severe drought and water restrictions get the Ph level down to 7 or lower and the residual chlorine level to zero before using.

IMPROVE THE RETENTION OF WATER

1. Enrich the soil with compost and manure before planting.
2. Add water-retaining gel to the bottom of planting holes and compost in pots.
3. Build at least a low wall around the entire garden to prevent water loss over the boundary.
4. Build a secure retaining bank around vegetable plots that are watered by flooding.

HOW TO CONSTRUCT A DRIP IRRIGATION SYSTEM

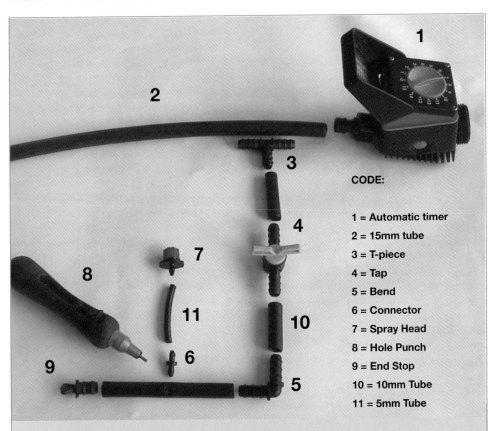

CODE:

1 = Automatic timer
2 = 15mm tube
3 = T-piece
4 = Tap
5 = Bend
6 = Connector
7 = Spray Head
8 = Hole Punch
9 = End Stop
10 = 10mm Tube
11 = 5mm Tube

The main features of this basic design illustrated above are:
a. Adjustable drip heads (red) to each plant.
b. 5mm diameter tubing to feed heads from main pipe.
c. 1.5mm diameter tubing for a main distribution pipe.
d. Joiners to go round corners.
e. A whole range of different sized tubing, connectors, stoppers, drips, etc., to suit your needs.
f. In a larger garden, the 1.5mm tubing will need to be joined to a 3cm mains to get the necessary pressure of water.
g. A battery operated timer or a more complex mains electricity computerized timer for a multi zone system in a large garden.
h. A filter on the watermain in addition to the filter built into the timer will help prevent the blocking of drip heads.

Alternatives to mains water are a pump feed from a cistern or a gravity feed from a header tank at the highest point of the garden.

REDUCE EVAPORATION

1. Water in the late evening rather than in the morning or midday.

2. Plant trees for shade or semi shade.

3. Plant closer together and use ground-cover plants to reduce the areas of bare soil exposed to the sun.

4. Plant through holes in plastic sheeting and cover with a mulch.

5. Keep potted plants in the semi shade to reduce evaporation.

6. Paint or varnish the inside of pots and containers to stop evaporation through the sides.

7. Mulch window boxes with a thick layer of moss, grit or stone chippings.

8. Underlay stone chipping areas of the garden with plastic sheeting.

9. Leave fallen leaves under shrubs and hedges as a natural mulch.

10. Mulch vegetables and soft fruit.

11. Soak newspapers in a thin water/ flour paste and lay as a blanket around established shrubs, then cover with earth.

12. Water deeply down to the lowest roots. Shallow watering stimulates shallow roots turning back to the surface.

13. Lay woven plastic around shrubs and mulch with stones, pebbles or shredded tree bark.

14. Lay a mulch of crushed volcanic rock around succulents and cacti in rockeries and containers.

15. Lay light coloured terraces rather than dark to reduce the amount of reflected light evaporating water from the leaves.

COLLECT AND REUSE

1. Locate major shrub beds under the eaves of the house.

2. Fit guttering and collect rainwater in a cistern or butt and use for watering the garden.

3. Set up used eight-litre water bottles with the tops cut off to collect rainwater with a drip tube to a recently planted shrub or tree.

4. Channel rainwater from paths and terraces to where it is most needed.

5. Slope the drive so that valuable water is not lost into the road.

6. Use eco detergents and washing up liquid then reuse the cool water for hardy plants and vegetables.

7. Use cooled water from cooking or steaming vegetables for pot plants.

8. If you have a natural spring, collect the water in a large holding pond and distribute to the garden.

9. Create a concrete volcanic landscape with 30cm planting holes for a desert like mature cacti and aloe bed. Tint the concrete with a sand colouring and texture the surface with ripples like a wind blown sand dune (useful in absentee minimalist gardens).

10. Place trays under potted plants.

The use of a few of these ideas should reduce your water bill as well as allow you more time to enjoy the garden.

6.6 SEASONAL FEEDING

Your initial improvement of the soil will have built up the reservoir of nutrients and also made it easier for the roots of plants to access and extract those nutrients at a natural rate, the rate necessary to support healthy and sustained growth, flowering and where appropriate fruiting..

For those plants that stay in the ground year after year – perennials, shrubs and trees – the initial soil enrichment and an annual or biannual topping up with a mulch of well-rotted manure or compost, or a light feed of natural slow release bone meal or other organic fertilizer, should be all that most plants will require to continue growing steadily, flower profusely and fruit without major health problems.

There is no point in overfeeding as it makes plants grow too quickly, resulting in excessive foliage needing frequent trimming, weak growth susceptible to pests and diseases and an earlier maturity than occurs naturally.

Gardeners with smaller gardens will find plants big enough without attempting to grow giant specimens. Gardeners with large gardens can plant larger specimens and let them grow at natural rates for decades.

Anyone who had a total instant garden laid out with mature shrubs and trees with regular heavy watering and an inline system for adding fertilizer will know the amount of over vigorous growth that soon needs to be pruned back to keep the originally pristine mature garden under control.

There are, however, some exceptions. Shrubs that are slow to come into flower or produce very few flowers even after one or two years could benefit from a high in potassium liquid feed to stimulate the reproduction cycle. There are many organic and inorganic products available.

Plants that have been caught by a frost can benefit from a high in nitrogen foliar feed to stimulate new green growth, after first cutting out the damaged foliage. We use a dilute nettle feed.

Annuals need regular feeding to stimulate a long flowering season, for the following reasons:

1. They have relatively shallow and short roots and therefore search for moisture and nutrients in the top 10cm of the soil.

2. They have been able to obtain sufficient nutrients without trying hard in the nursery greenhouse where they have been fed continuously hydroponically.

3. They can probably extract sufficient nutrients from the soil to support one flowering and seeding natural reproductive cycle, but we expect more from annuals. We want large bushy spreading plants that flower continuously for six to nine months, which is quite possible, providing we dead head regularly to avoid any seeds forming, water to keep the plants rigid in hot weather and give the plants a regular fast acting general flower plant fertilizer to stimulate the growth of roots, foliage and new flower buds. We use a comfrey, nettle, compost natural cocktail. Don't use an unbalanced feed, very high in nitrogen, as this will stimulate greenery at the expense of flowers.

The other plants that need ongoing supplementary feeds are:

a. perennials, shrubs and trees in containers as they can only search for nutrients in the relatively small volume of compost in which they are planted. As the plants grow, the initial reservoir of nutrients is soon consumed and the roots get larger and larger to frantically find the last crumbs. In the end, the plant becomes root-bound and starved.

Feed either with an annual spring slow-release general fertilizer or establish a regular feeding cycle – monthly in the winter, fortnightly in the summer and autumn. Use a general fertilizer, except in the spring and summer when a high in potassium feed will stimulate flowering. Naturally give a high-in-nitrogen feed to non-flowering evergreens, but only at diluted strengths to avoid too fast-growing, lush and potentially unhealthy plants.

b. hungry fruit vegetables such as tomatoes, peppers and squash.

Do not under any circumstances give a double-strength feed just because you are going on holiday. The fertilizer could well burn the roots.

Finally, don't only feed pot plants when they become unhealthy. If they are attacked by insects or diseases give them a fast-acting nitrogen foliar feed before treating the plant with insecticides or fungicides.

6.7 DISEASE AND PEST PREVENTION AND CONTROL

Most gardens suffer from only a few pest and disease problems but it would be wise to take the following precautions:

1. Plant only healthy plants, whether from garden centres or your own propagation.

2. Don't force plants by over watering and over feeding them. Fast sappy growth can be susceptible to pest and fungi attacks.

3. Don't let plants dry out and become weak.

4. Be constantly vigilant. Examine plants when you water them.

5. Act as soon as you see any sign of an attack by pests or diseases.

6. Move unhealthy potted plants to a semi-shaded nursery area.

7. Remove any badly affected, dying or dead plants from beds and pots and seal in a plastic bag. Burn on a bonfire if possible.

8. Recognise that roots as well as leaves, flowers, buds, branches or trunks can be attacked.

The ten most common problems and suggested ecological are summarised in the table that follows. The treatments listed include commercially available ecological/biological products such as neem, propolis, dried horsetail and nettles, garlic, geranium oil, potassium soap and sulphur powder, as well as some of our own DIY treatments. If you cannot find neem, dried nettles or propolis locally contact www.trabe.net.

MOST COMMON PESTS AND DISEASES

COMMON SPANISH GARDEN PESTS	MAIN PLANTS AFFECTED	WHAT TO LOOK FOR	CAUSES	SUGGESTED TREATMENTS
ANTS Hormigas	Potted plants. Newly planted grass seed.	Soil being sifted out from base of plant pots. Trails of ants carrying seeds to nests. Ants feeding off aphids on plants, which is beneficial.	Ants looking for moisture and food.	**a.** In pots, drown with heavy watering. **b.** Keep newly sown grass seed continuously wet. Find nests and pour down boiling water. **c.** Sprinkle sulphur powder around problem areas. **d.** As a last resort use ant powder.
APHIDS Pulgones **a. Greenfly**	Oleanders, roses, lady of the night, chrysanthemums, hibiscus.	Countless tiny sticky green flies on stems, leaves and flower buds. Usually ants are feeding off their sticky excretion.	Toolittle water. Too much nitrogen feed.	**a.** Spray twice weekly with a potassium soap, nettle or garlic or neem solution*. **b.** You can add a few drops of Neem. When insects feed on it, it effects their reproduction cycle.
b. Whitefly Mosca blanca	Geraniums, begonias, roses, gardenias, indoor plants.	Tiny white flies on underside of leaves. Leaves wither and die.	High humid temperatures and poor soil.	"
c. Blackfly Mosca negra	Nasturtiums	Masses of small black flies on tips of stems and flower buds.	High humid temperatures and poor soil. Too little water. Too much nitrogen feed.	"
GERANIUM MOTH Mosca africana	Zonal and ivy leafed geraniums.	Small black holes in stems where they lay their eggs. Small insipid brown moths hovering around plants in spring and summer.	Over watering and feeding too much nitrogen produces a weak fleshy plant.	**a.** Don't water plants until they almost dry out. **b.** Don't wet leaves and stems. **c.** Spray twice weekly from March to October with neem, garlic or geranium oil mixed in water*. **d.** Cut out damaged stems and burn.

MOST COMMON PESTS AND DISEASES

COMMON SPANISH GARDEN PESTS	MAIN PLANTS AFFECTED	WHAT TO LOOK FOR	CAUSES	SUGGESTED TREATMENTS
MEALY BUG Cochinilla	Euonymus, stephanotis, citrus, cacti, succulents, indoor plants.	Sticky white bugs on stems and underside of leaves.	Dense foliage and weak plants.	**a.** Clean off with a toothbrush or cotton wool soaked in soapy water. **b.** Spray weekly with solution of horsetail, soapy water or neem*.
PROCESSIONARY CATERPILLARS Oruga procesionaria	Pine trees.	**a.** Winter fluffy white nests hanging out of branches. **b.** Feb/Mar caterpillars file down from nests. **c.** Appear in lines along ground and up walls. (They are blind and follow the leader).	Attracted to pine trees. High humid temperatures and poor soil.	**a.** NEVER allow caterpillars or the green dust left below their nests to touch you or your dog's skin. Can produce serious allergic reactions. **b.** Cut down with care and burn nests within easy reach **c.** Remove from ground and burn. **d.** Wash tools thoroughly. **e.** If trees are badly affected, seek professional advice.
SLUGS Babosas	Young annuals and fleshy plants.	Remains of eaten plants or a missing plant. Slimey slug trail.	Young and juicy plants are very tempting.	**a.** Put down beer traps. **b.** Spray garlic solution around plants. **c.** Encourage birds, toads and frogs into the garden. **d.** Dust neem powder on seedbeds. **e.** Slug pellets as last resort.
SNAILS Caracoles	Bulbs, narcissus, iris, young plants, some succulents.	Bitten leaves and stems and slimy snail trails.	Rain followed by sun.	**a.** Collect at night. **b.** Place bran and cabbage leaves around garden to attract snails and collect. **c.** Use snail traps. **d.** Use snail bait as last resort.
SPIDER MITE Acaro	Roses, privet, oleander, annuals, ficus, indoor plants. Pine trees.	Yellowing leaves and underside of leaves covered in silk-like web and tiny spiders.	High temperatures and too much nitrogen.	**a.** Where possible wipe off. **b.** Spray regularly with potassium soap, nettle or neem solutions*.

MOST COMMON PESTS AND DISEASES

COMMON SPANISH GARDEN PESTS	MAIN PLANTS AFFECTED	WHAT TO LOOK FOR	CAUSES	SUGGESTED TREATMENTS
Fungal diseases Hongos				
BOTRYTIS Botrytis	Petunias, zinnias, dahlias, heliopsis, lilies, annuals, euonymus, roses.	Fluffy grey mould with black blotches.	Damp conditions.	a. Don't over water plants and avoid wetting leaves. b. Clean up affected plants. c. Spray with horsetail, propolis or neem*. d. Plant a garlic clove at the base of rose bushes.
MILDEW Mildiu	Chrysanthemums, heliopsis, annuals, geraniums, dahlias.	Pale yellow blotches on leaves and white powder on leaves.	Damp conditions and high temperatures.	a. Don't wet leaves when watering. b. Don't feed plants too much nitrogen. c. Spray twice weekly with solution of horsetail, propolis or neem*. d. Dust lightly with sulphur.
OIDIO Oidio	Roses, euonymus, dalias, margaritas, cacti, indoor plants.	Leaves curl up and get covered with white mould.	Humid warm temperatures.	a. Don't wet leaves when watering. b. Spray twice weekly with solution of horsetail, propolis or neem*. c. Improve ventilation.
RUST Roya	Regal geraniums, roses.	Orange/brown pustules on leaves.	Damp conditions.	a. Spray in spring with horsetail, tomato leaves, propolis or neem. b. Don't wet leaves when watering.
ROTTING OFF De pudrición	Roses, privet, oleander, annuals, ficus, indoor plants. Succulents.	Discoloured wilting leaves.	Too much moisture with bad drainage.	a. Not much you can do except throw out the plant and start again. b. Always spray young seedlings and plants with horsetail solution.
SCALE AND FUNGAL DISEASES Escama y hongos	Bay, oleander, citrus.	Scales on leaves and black mould on branches and leaves.	Humid conditions. Lack of light.	a. Wipe off with horsetail solution where possible. b. Autumn pruning. c. Twice weekly spray with solution of potassium soap, horsetail propolis, or neem*.
FUNGAL DISEASE IN CONIFERS Hongos	Conifers and hedges.	Browning and dying plants.	Poor drainage and watering too close the base of plants	a. Aerate soil around base. b. Don't wet trunks when watering. c. Spray soil and trees with horsetail, propolis, or neem*.

Note: Potassium soap is often now referred to as insecticidal soap and in Spain is often referred to as jabón negro.

* See following page for making up spray solution.

PREPARATION OF NATURAL SPRAYS

When you are preparing natural sprays, be sure always to use unchlorinated rain or well water in recipes. The following are some recommended natural sprays:

NAME	USES	WHEN TO SPRAY	PREPARATION
GARLIC Ajo	Insect repellent.	Early morning.	Cover 50gr of chopped garlic with boiling water. Leave covered to cool. Filter and add 1 litre of water.
HORSETAIL Cola de caballo	Fungicide and builds resistance to disease.	Evening.	**a.** Simmer 25gr of dried horsetail in 1 litre of water for 30mins. Stand for 24 hours. Strain and use. **b.** Gently boil 100gr of fresh horsetail, without roots, in 3 litres of water for 15mins. Cool, strain and use.
NETTLE Ortigas	Insect repellent and builds resistance to attacks.	Early morning.	**a.** Simmer 25gr of dried nettle in 1 litre of water for 30mins. Stand for 24 hours. Strain and use. **b.** Fill bucket with young leaves and cover with water. Leave one week to ferment. Filter and dilute 15.1 to use.
POTASSIUM SOAP Jabón de potasio	Insecticide	As above	Melt 100gr of potassium soap in 5 litres of hot water. Cool and use. If it thickens add more water.
TOMATO Tomate	Against rust	Evening.	Pour one litre of boiling water over a handful of leaves. Cool, strain and use.
GERANIUM	Insecticide	As above	To 1 litre of water add 2 drops of essential oil of geranium.
NEEM OIL	Insecticide Fungicide.	Early morning or evening.	A couple of drops can be added to any of the above for extra effect or it can be used alone. (Read instructions on bottle).
PROPOLIS	Fungicide.	Evening.	3ml/litre of water.

Neem can be obtained from www.trabe.net and www.niem-handel.de if you have no local stockist.

Propolis and powdered nettle can also be obtained from www.trabe.net.

6.8 DEADHEADING AND PRUNING

The deadheading and pruning of plants are two essential ongoing jobs in the garden.

DEADHEADING

The removal of dead flower heads as they form has several benefits:

- A continuity of flower buds and flowers as the plant attempts to produce seed a second and third time, only to be thwarted each time by your efforts. This is particularly important with plants that are able to produce a continuous display of flowers for some months, such as roses, annuals, perennials, all the daisy flowered varieties, gazanias, carnations, heliopsis, and pelargoniums/geraniums.
- A second flowering a month or two later from some shrubs such as oleander, plumbago and lantanas.
- Tidier plants and a tidier garden once the dead heads and stems have been removed from plants that only flower once a year, such as lavender, rue, and sage.
- Stronger bulbs for the next year by the removal of dead flower heads as they form from bulbous plants. Leave the stem to die back before cutting off, even if a little untidy for a few weeks. This will stimulate the plant to put all its energy into developing a good bulb for next year rather than a ripe seed head that would weaken the bulk (e.g. daffodils, tulips, gladioli, lilies, irises and canna lilies.

If you want to collect seeds for next year, leave some strong and healthy flower heads and allow them to produce seed for you to harvest once dry. Mark the selected stems in case you trim them off a week later. Easy ones for starters are hollyhocks, marigolds, yellow lantanas, nasturtiums and sweet peas.

PRUNING

As well as removing dead flower heads, trim untidy ends of branches and water shoots on an ongoing basis. The benefits are:

- A tidier garden. Just look around weekly and see what is starting to look out of place or getting in the way.
- More naturally shaped plants.
- Control of height and width of plants.
- Special architectural shapes through the trimming and wire shaping of topiary.
- Stopping vigorous plants from swamping smaller, slow-growing plants.
- Stronger plants by cutting out any water shoots that grow from the base of bougainvilleas, jasmine and roses.
- The stimulus of the flowering and fruiting side shoots for the following year.
- A safer garden by removing hazards such as the pointed ends of low-growing branches and yucca leaves, cacti branches and low palm fronds near pathways, terraces and in shrub beds where you need to work.
- To remove branches and twigs damaged by gales, frost or sun- burn.
- The retention of external and internal views.
- Allowing passage on outside pavements. This may mean removing flowering

branches of vigorous hedges such as oleander, honeysuckle, bougainvilleas and bignonias.

• To stimulate larger fruits. If fruit bushes or trees have a very heavy crop, remove some fruits on each branch to stimulate larger fruits.

• To continue to see the fish in the pond. Regularly remove excess aerating weeds and some water lily leaves.

• To maintain neat hedges, such as Conifers, pittosporum and privet.

• To obtain cuttings that can be used to propagate new plants, such as carnations, mock orange, geraniums, messems, oleanders, plumbago, leonotis, hydrangeas and lady of the night.

Use good sharp but safe pruners and saws for the above tasks to reduce the effort required. They are safer than pruning knives. In the summer, prune early morning rather than roasting in the midday sun. Cut ends will seal during the day, preventing the entry of diseases.

6.9 THE ANNUAL CUTBACK AND CLEAN UP

Spanish gardens benefit from a major cutback and clean up each winter rather than in the autumn. For most gardens this is best done during January. There are six reasons for doing it at that time:

1. Shrubs and perennials will have been allowed to continue flowering to give the most colourful Christmas garden possible.

2. Most plants are dormant or at their lowest level of growth. In trees, the sap is down and stable except in early flowering acacias and almonds.

3. Plants allowed to continue flowering beyond December tend to have few flowers and go leggy. If not cutback until March, they will be late to flower in the spring.

4. Plants have a good clean up before starting to bud and grow in earnest when the weather warms up.

5. The soil is cleared of rubbish/weeds and hoed while there is maximum space between plants.

6. The weather tends to be dry and sunny, so you can enjoy the exercise while achieving a tidy garden and an even better one in the coming year.

It is always very tempting not to cut back plants that are still growing strongly and perhaps even flowering, but if you don't do this now, plants will be out of shape and overgrown by the spring and not create the flower and leaf buds necessary for good displays in the spring and summer. So be harsh.

Obviously winter flowering plants such as poinsettias, camellias, acacias, winter jasmine and chrysanthemums are not pruned back at this time as they will be in full flower. They can be pruned as soon as they finish flowering.

MAIN TASKS

The five main tasks involved in cleaning up your garden are:

1. Cut back and prune all perennials, shrubs and trees appropriate to their age, size and format.

2. Divide up and replant large clumps of perennials
3. Clear all weeds and rubbish from the beds.
4. Loosen the surface soil and mulch young plants and plants with shallow roots to prevent weeds from growing, retain moisture and shade roots from the hot sun.
5. Shred all prunings, except thick branches, ready for adding to the compost heap.
The following are guidelines for dealing with a wide range of popular plants.

SHRUBS

The main aim is to cut back to achieve a size and shape appropriate to your garden and to develop strong profusely flowering shrubs.

Bougainvillea – All well established plants benefit from a hard pruning, otherwise they get out of control. When they are in full flower, high winds can tear them away from walls, causing considerable damage. Cut back the side shoots along each of the main branches to stimulate flowering shoots. Cut back the main branches to give shape. Cut out all suckers – these are the paler green straight stems with larger leaves. After pruning, check that the main branches are securely tied. Thread the tying-up wire through an old piece of hose so that it doesn't cut into the stems as they grow. Treat younger plants a little more gently, concentrating on pruning to shape.

Lantanas – One of the most useful plants in a Mediterranean garden. Well pruned, they give colour during most months of the year. Each of the several varieties needs a slightly different treatment:

Low growing – with the purple and white trailing variety, you need to cut back leggy branches by at least half their length and trim to shape. The yellow variety should be pruned lightly to shape.

Medium height – with the yellow, orange/red, pink/yellow, yellow/white varieties you need to cut back all flowering stems to 5 to 10cm from the trunk just above a new budding point. The pruned plants will look very bare but you will stimulate the sprouting of a multitude of new flowering shoots.

Standards – Cut to shape to encourage side shoots and create a round head.

Climbing – The pink/yellow, white, and orange/yellow varieties can be trained to grow up or over walls. Prune side shoots to shape and leave the tallest branches intact.

Hibiscus – Some Spanish gardeners cut these back very hard, but we don't find this necessary. We suggest your shorten the branches by 20 to 50cm, depending on the size of the plant, to produce a good shape.

Plumbago and white flowering jasmine – Shorten branches by half their length and tidy up all side shoots to produce a well-shaped bush. The yellow flowering winter jasmine should be cut back later after it has finished flowering.

Oleanders – To prevent them getting very tall and leggy, prune back very hard every second or third year to stimulate new shoots and side branches. In other years keep them tidy and cut out any suckers. Wear gloves when pruning as the sap and flowers are poisonous.

Bignonia – The large flowered pink variety is the most prolific and needs to be pruned right back leaving woody lateral branches for next year's growth. Just trim other varieties back to shape.

Passion flowers, solandras and solanum – Cut to shape, hard if necessary.

Galan de noche – Cut back hard to a basic fan or standard shape.

Roses – Cut back bushes to two or three buds on each stem and cut out any suckers growing from the base. Cut out the old and weak stems that have few flowering shoots from climbers and ramblers and then shape.

Tall herbs – Lavender, rosemary and sage should be trimmed to shape and cleaned up underneath.

PERENNIALS

Daisy flowering types and rock roses – Cut back leggy growth to produce a more compact and cluster flowering plant.

Gazanias and arctotis – Remove dead leaves and prune untidy side shoots and runners to shape. These can be used to propagate new plants. Pull out any totally dead plants. If they have any life left in them, leave well enough alone as they will normally re-leaf and bud in the spring.

Pelargoniums/geraniums – Clean out all dead leaves and stems. Also look out for signs of geranium moth damage and cut out these stems at a healthy node.

Zonal – Cut back to shape if leggy

Ivy leafed trailing – Trim to shape.

Regal – Cut back hard to shape if very woody and leggy. They will sprout from the old wood.

Graveolens Scented – Cut back hard to shape. Grows rampant.

Leonotis, Rudbekias, Ajania, Valerian and other perennials that flower best on new growth from the base – Cut back to 5cm from ground. Prune chrysanthemums similarly when they have finished flowering in February or March.

Low growing herbs – Remove any dead wood and trim to a shape and size that blends with adjacent plants. Do likewise with herbs in pots.

PALMS

Cut out some lower fronds, taking care to avoid the spikes, and generally tidy up. The heads of taller Canary Island palms should be trimmed to look like giant pineapples.

CORDYLINES

Pull off all dead leaves and cut off dead flower heads.

YUCCAS

Cut off unsightly and dangerous/top heavy branches and dead flower heads. For self preservation and the safety of others, cut off the spiky tips of all leaves within reach and then cut off or pull off the lower leaves on the stems to create a palm like effect.

ALOES

Remove suckers. Cut out dead flower stems and dead plants. Cut off unsightly and dangerous lower leaves.

CACTI

Cut off unsightly and dangerous/top heavy side shoots. Cut out any rotting parts of small cacti. Make sure you clear away any rubbish from within and around the cacti that could cause fungal diseases to set in.

SUCCULENTS

Trim to shape if necessary, using the cuttings for propagation. Leave sappier varieties until after the last frost if in the frost belt. Remove dead flower heads if not done in the autumn.

BULBS

Remove dead leaves and rubbish from around irises and the dead leaves of any autumn flowering bulbs. Carefully clean up the surface of flower beds where you know spring bulbs will be shortly coming up.

HEDGES

All types benefit from a close cut. Cut the top to a height that gives you privacy without being impossible to prune safely. Trim both sides to tidy and reduce the overhang over adjacent shrubs and flowerbeds. A good cut also stimulates flowering shoots on those that flower. If the hedge is getting leggy, cut out some of the hard thick internal branches (privet or oleander), or cut back to the hard internal framework (myporum, bay and hibiscus) to stimulate new and denser growth.

FLOWERING TREES

Many need to be hard pruned to keep them down to manageable size for small and medium sized gardens and to develop pleasing architectural shapes. This will also stimulate new flowering side branches. Always cut out any dead or dying branches as well as any heavy branches that could cause shallow rooted trees to become top heavy or lopsided and therefore liable to being blown over in gales. Leave the winter flowering acacias until they are finished flowering. Be aware that the jacaranda and albizia trees thrive best when left to grow to maturity without pruning. Any pruning of branches tends to stimulate new lower growth and reduce flowering.

EVERGREEN TREES

Trim to shape and size. This is time to start and maintain any topiary shapes. Clean up dead foliage under trees to reduce chance of fungal diseases.

POND PLANTS

Cut back and thin reeds and irises. Also every couple of years lift out the clumps to keep their size under control by splitting and cutting back the root ball. Lift out potted plants such as water lilies and trim off the dead top growth and reduce the size of the protruding root ball. Cut back and remove excess growth of oxygenating weed beds.

PLANTS IN POTS AND CONTAINERS

Remove any dead and untidy growth. Clean the surface of the soil and wash off algae from the outside of pots and the water tray with vinegar and water to maintain a hygienic environment.

PILES OF PRUNINGS AND WEEDS

You can propagate them. Although not an ideal time, try potting up some healthy cuttings and putting them in the greenhouse or garden frame. After all, the cuttings are free so nothing is lost.

You can shred parts of them. Don't bother with fibrous material such as palm fronds or aloes, as they will block the shredder. Shredded material is very useful in the garden as raw material for the compost heap, mixed with leaf mould and manure in preparing raised beds for vegetables and raw as a useful mulch around shrubs – especially where it won't be easily seen – and for creating soft pathways in woodlands and the vegetable garden. So are palm fronds if you first cut off the spiky ends.

You can take them to the local Eco Composting Unit. Some gardeners are lucky enough to be able to sell their prunings and other garden waste to a local composting unit and afterwards leave with bags of inexpensive final compost.

Now take a week's rest from gardening before you start to sow seeds and prepare the vegetable plot for the spring. If you want to enjoy a good garden in the spring, summer and autumn, the winter is a busy time.

6.10 SPRING CLEAN POTTED PLANTS

All pots, window boxes and other planted containers benefit from an annual internal and external spring clean. The spring clean should be thorough and aim to remove anything that might attract diseases or pests, to improve the fertility and moisture retaining properties of the compost within the pots, and improve the appearance of the pots themselves.

We recommend the following ten actions.

1. Thoroughly wash any used pots with washing up liquid in water and then rinse in a dilute disinfectant or vinegar solution to prepare them for reuse.

2. Clean up all potted plants as follows:

    a. Prune all dead leaves and dead or diseased branches.

    b. Prune to shape if out of balance.

    c. Remove all dead leaves, flowers and other rubbish from the surface of the soil.

    d. Scrape out the top 3cm of the compost and replace with new.

    e. Replace any grit or chippings that you had used as a mulch.

    f. Give the drip trays a good wash.

    g. Wash the outside of the pots to remove grime. Algae can be removed from terracotta pots by wiping with a dilute bleach solution or vinegar and water. Protect the plant in a plastic bag while washing. Leave the pots to dry and then wipe lightly with a cloth dampened with olive oil.

3. If potted plants have been in the same compost for several years and you have become unhappy with the plant, re-pot, using new compost. First clean the pot as above or use a slightly larger pot.

4. If you find that the plant or plants are root bound, re-plant in a pot several sizes larger.

5. When re-potting use new compost. Also take the opportunity to incorporate a little water retaining gel into the lower part of the soil. Don't use too much or the gel will push the plant up and out of the compost.

6. Give all plants a spring feed with a weak solution of a general flower plant fertilizer or a comfrey/nettle feed if gardening organically.

7. Clean grimy leaves on evergreen plants by first brushing lightly with a soft paint brush, and then wiping with a solution of milk, beer and liquid nettle fertilizer. If you have no nettles substitute, a few drops of a nitrogen foliar feed

8. Put any plants still covered with spring pine pollen out in the first rain to freshen them up. At the same time, collect spring rainwater in a water butt for summer watering.

9. If there are any signs of an ant nest in a pot, re-pot removing all compost from the root ball and washing the roots before re-potting to remove the last ant. Put some ant powder in the drip tray under the pot to prevent a reinvestation

6.11 PRODUCING GOOD COMPOST

Compost is an invaluable addition to the soil in Spanish gardens. It adds nutrients and useful micro organisms and improves the structure and water- retaining properties of naturally poor or over-worked soil, the sort that many of us have initially.

There is evidence that plants grown in healthy compost-enriched soil are less prone to disease and grow stronger. During the long hot summers, a rich friable loamy soil will lose less moisture through capillary evaporation than a hard-baked poor soil.

Compost can be added to the soil by mixing it into flower and vegetable beds before planting seeds or plants – or as a mulch around plants to help retain moisture and keep the roots cool.

WHAT IS COMPOST?

Compost is the natural decomposition of kitchen and garden waste to achieve a fine, sweet-smelling, crumbly, loamy soil rich in water-retaining humus and plant nutrients, and ready to mix into potting/seed composts, flower beds and vegetable plots.

An ecological recycling of waste, it is less expensive and is of better quality than many commercial brands of compost. It also involves less municipal cost for disposing of household and garden rubbish, and the use of fewer plastic rubbish bags.

Compost is produced by mixing organic waste materials from the kitchen, garden and vegetable plot in a suitable container and then leaving to decompose naturally. All the waste will eventually rot down with the help of heat, moisture, oxygen, micro organisms, insects and worms. Just let nature take its course.

Even so, there are a few tricks to the trade. We list below the factors that contribute to the making of good compost in our generally hot and dry climate:

1. Design of composting bins. Boxes or bins are essential here in Spain, as the open compost heap of a rainy northern Europe would soon dry out in the hot Mediterranean climate. Construct two or three composting boxes at least 1.5m in width, depth and height. It is difficult to build up essential heat at the heart of smaller boxes. Two boxes are better than one because during the process of composting the decomposing material needs to be turned. A third box would allow you to start a   second heap while the first is maturing. A homemade box can be easily constructed by using four posts and wire netting or three old pallets. The front is most easily closed with a wire netting gate or removable wooden slats for ease of access. To increase aeration you could use a fourth pallet as the base, although broken twigs are just as effective. Never place on a concrete base as you need to encourage many small insects, worms and micro organisms from the soil into the heap.

2. Positioning of compost bins. The compost heap needs to retain moisture and build up heat. Ideally it should be situated in a semi-shaded corner of the garden.

3. Line the bin and cover. To retain moisture and internal heat, line your box with cardboard from old boxes or thick layers of newspaper as you build up the waste materials. Don't make air holes as you would have done in northern Europe as this will only result in the rapid drying out of the outer layers. Keep the top covered with a layer of damp newspapers topped with a square of old carpet.

4. Layering the different raw materials. Don't just throw the waste materials into the bin willy-nilly. If you do, the decomposition will be patchy and essential heat will not built up. Build up the heap layer by layer as follows:

- Start with a 15cm layer of coarse twiggy material to create air circulation and help start the aerobic decomposition process.
- 10 – 15cm of manure or half decomposed compost. This will attract worms and essential microorganisms.
- 10 – 15cm of green waste.
- 10 – 15cm of brown waste.
- 4 sheets of wet newspaper laid over the top. Worms love it, but avoid colour printed pages.
- 10 – 15cm of manure.
- A sprinkling of wood ash.
- Repeat the above adding natural accelerators to the layers until the compost bin is full.

5. A good mix of raw materials including:

- **Green waste** – vegetables, fruit (avoid too many orange peelings as they are too acidic), crushed egg shells, weeds, soft green cuttings and prunings, grass cuttings, disease free leaves and stems of vegetables that have finished cropping, dampened and torn-up paper packets, newspapers, cardboard in centre of toilet rolls and kitchen towel rolls. Don't use cooked kitchen waste, cheese, oil or raw meat, fish, etc., as it may attract vermin and flies in the height of summer.

- **Brown waste** – dry fibrous materials such as shredded, hard prunings, branches and cuttings, flower heads, stalks, dry leaves, waste from the vacuum cleaner, animal and human hair. It is preferable not to add cuttings from bay, conifers, acacias and oleanders as their residues can be toxic to other plants.
- **Wood ash –** a little will add valuable potassium and lime.
- **Manures –** horse, sheep, goat, rabbit, chicken and pigeon. Stack the latter two to rot down separately, as they are very strong, and then only use in small proportions.
- **Accelerators –** Seaweed, comfrey, borage, dandelion and nettle in leaf or liquid form are all good accelerators, as well as adding essential nutrients to the heap. The liquid forms can be prepared by steeping leaves in water for two or more weeks. If you don't have access to any of the above, use sulphate of ammonia or a proprietary powder. Diluted human urine is also very effective!
- **Water –** essential to the whole process.

6. **Moisture control.** Dampen each layer where necessary as you build up the heap. This is the best time to add your prepared liquid accelerators. Dilute them 10/1before use. There is no point in leaving material dry because it won't rot down. But don't over-soak as it will then become slimy and smelly. It is just a matter of trial and error.

7. **Temperature control and Decomposition.** It is important to line and cover the heap to build up the temperature necessary for bacterial action. Ideally, it should be at 50 to 60 degrees centigrade to kill off weed seeds, etc. It will still decompose at lower temperatures, but at a slower rate. The fast rate, referred to as "aerobic", requires oxygen. If the heap is well mixed with dampened materials, it will decompose in six to twelve months. The slower rate, referred to as "anaerobic", causes the material in the heap to become smelly, slimy and compacted as a result of being over wet. The solution is to turn the heap, at the same time layering in new dry materials.

The aim is to achieve a totally aerobic process, but even in the best heaps there will be odd corners of anaerobic decomposition taking place.

8. **Turning.** It is advisable to turn your heap after six months to re-aerate it. Prepare your empty bin as for starting a heap. Then fork over the decomposing heap to the empty bin, mixing in any dry materials left on the outer edge or over wet compost in the centre. Remove the lower part if it is ready to use. It should be fine and sweet smelling. At this stage you top up the partially composted material with fresh materials, and then repeat the process in six months time.

9. **Worms.** Worms play an important role in the compost heap. Firstly they eat damp waste material and excrete processed waste, and secondly their burrows aerate the heap. They will be attracted by the heat and dampness, but do add in any you find around the garden and always put back any left in the finished compost. They will leave the compost if it is too dry.

10. **Problems and solutions.**

   Rats – don't include any raw or cooked meat, fish, cheese, oil or salads dressed in oil. **Flies** always top kitchen waste with a layer of dry materials and cover.
   Ants – in a drying heap, ants will look for moisture in the form of retreating worms. Find where their trail is coming from and put sulphur or ant powder.

11. Be patient. One is always short of compost in the garden – but don't try and take a shortcut by using the heap before it is fully decomposed, unless you are using it only for mulching or preparing bean and pumpkin trenches. Our approach to composting in a hot dry climate is based on many years of trial and error. Yes, it does take time, but just think of the end result – all that lovely, inexpensive, fine loam and the fact that you have made the best use of your garden and household rubbish, as well as helping the environment.

6.12 PROPAGATING NEW PLANTS FROM OLD

Propagating new plants from old has several advantages. It is easier than growing them from seed, it is an inexpensive and interesting way to multiply plants in the garden, it is a way of collecting unusual varieties by obtaining cuttings from friends and it can produce stronger, less forced, plants than the ones you buy. You can start cuttings at any time of the year and once potted they take less time to grow than plants grown from seed.

In Spain there is generally no need to use a propagator as the average temperature is higher than northern Europe, but in the hotter months cuttings dry out fast.

Below is a list of different types of plants and information on how to propagate them:

1. **Stem cuttings** from soft wooded plants, e.g., lavender, sage, plumbago, fuchsias, pelargoniums/geraniums, gazanias, margaritas, etc. Pull off a side shoot (preferably

non-flowering) with a heel. Pinch out the growing tip to leave a cutting about 10–15cm long with a leaf node at the top and base. Remove any flowers or buds and all the leaves except four towards the top.

Pelargoniums/geraniums benefit if left to dry out for a day or two before potting up. An alternative way of taking cuttings from trailing geraniums when you are pruning them is to cut off 10cm, keeping at least three nodes from the tip. Pinch out the tip, remove any flowers or buds and leave two leaves.

2. Stem cuttings of more delicate plants. Busy lizzies, fuchsias, pothos, etc., do better if they are placed in water or wet vermiculite and allowed to produce roots before being planted. Break off a piece from the plant and place in a narrow container in a warm place. Fill with non-chlorinated water. Add a small piece of charcoal to keep the water fresh. Top up water regularly. Cuttings will take several weeks to produce roots.

Alternatively, wet some vermiculite and fill a clay pot. Insert your cutting and keep the contents moist. We don't recommend using plastic pots as they don't breathe and the vermiculite often goes mouldy. This method produces stronger root systems.

3. Cuttings from cacti and succulents. The prickly pear and Christmas cacti variety of cacti and all succulents can be easily propagated by breaking off a piece, leaving it to dry for a couple of days and then planting.

4. Stem cuttings from hard-wooded plants, e.g., lantana, bougainvillea, hibiscus, rose, oleander etc. Cut off a woody branch and cut into 10cm lengths. Leave a bud node at the base and top. Cut off any flowers and leave about four leaves. They can be rooted before potting by putting in dark wine or beer bottles to which a drop of fungicide has been added. Leave in semi shade and top up with water when necessary. They can also be started off in slit trenches in the vegetable garden if kept damp.

Rooting can be accelerated by dipping the bottom ends of cuttings into a proprietary rooting powder. It is helpful to follow the Spanish custom of slitting the base of rose cuttings and sliding in a dried sweet corn kernel. The growth hormone in the sweet corn helps stimulate the formation of roots. Try doing the same with other large-diameter, hard- wooded cuttings.

5. Rooted runners. Spider plants, some succulents and aloes produce rooted runners. Detach carefully and plant up in small pots.

6. Babies. Plants such as aloe vera, succulents, cacti etc., produce babies. Remove carefully and pot.

7. Leaf cuttings. Plants such as sedums, echeveria and streptocarpus can be propagated by cutting a healthy leaf and sticking the stem end in damp vermiculite. A new plant will grow from the base.

8. Division of roots. Clump forming perennials such as chrysanthemums, gazanias, agapanthus, coreopsis etc., can be divided in early spring and either planted directly into the ground or potted. Others, such as ground cover purple lantanas, ivies and grey leafed creeping gazanias, put out roots on their spreading branches. Rooted ends can be potted or transplanted.

9. Air Layering. Rubber plants and solandra can be reproduced by sliding a plastic bag with the end cut out over a branch that is getting too long and would otherwise be pruned. Make a cut at a leaf node and with the help of a second person press a damp moss/compost mix around the branch until it is like a 10 to 15cm diameter sausage roll with the branch in the middle and the cut leaf node in the centre. Seal with cello tape at both ends to prevent moisture escaping and leave for a year, allowing a root ball to develop. Then cut off and root.

POTS AND CONTAINERS

Any 8-10cm diameter pot with a drainage hole is suitable for planting single cuttings, and a 12-15cm diameter pot is suitable for planting groups of cuttings. Cut the base of a 1.5 or 5-litre water bottle three quarters of the way up. Keep the lid to create a mini greenhouse. Put some wet gravel in the base and sit your pot on it. Fit the lid over the top to seal.

There are many other containers that can be adapted, for instance milk and fruit cartons with the tops cut off, plastic containers used for packing fruit in the supermarkets, yoghurt cartons, plastic cups and soft drink cans. Just use your imagination.

PLANT IN GOOD COMPOST

When planting a cutting it is important to use good compost, following the guidelines below:

1. For most plants, make a mix of 7 parts light compost, 3 parts peat or peat substitute and 2 parts sharp sand vermiculite or perlite. Dampen evenly in a large container. For succulents, aloes and cacti add a further 3 parts of fine grit.

2. Take a plant pot and put a few pieces of broken pot or polystyrene at the base and fill with compost. Press down lightly.

3. Plant cuttings in prepared pots or bottle containers. If large enough, you can put three or four in each, but if you only put one, they won't need to be divided later.

4. Dip the end of cuttings into hormone rooting powder before potting.

5. Always spray the soil with an ecological fungicide or an infusion of horsetail.

6. Remember to label your cuttings. The vanes of old plastic blinds cut into strips and marked with a waterproof pen create inexpensive labels.

7. Put each pot in a clear plastic bag and prop up the bag with a length of old black watering hose, so that the leaves, especially grey ones, don't touch the plastic. Close with a tie, and cover those in cut-off water containers with the cut-off top half. These methods will create a mini greenhouse that maintains a constant humidity on the leaves and saves you watering the cuttings every day. Also, the enclosed module protects plants started during the autumn and winter.

8. Alternatively, use polystyrene fish boxes – most supermarkets throw them out. Wash well and make holes in the base for drainage and cover with a damp layer of compost/soil mix about 3cm deep. Place potted plants on top or fill the box with potting compost and plant lots of small cuttings. Special plastic module trays can also be used. Fit these into a polystyrene box on top of a 3cm compost base. When using fish boxes, enclose the cuttings and box in a white plastic envelope, secured with clothes pegs to maintain a constantly humid microclimate and the plants won't need watering until they are ready to pot.

9. If you don't use the microclimate method, prepare as in methods 1 and 2. Then line plastic trays or a similar container with 3cm of dampened compost/soil mix. This helps the plants form good roots. Stand prepared pots on soil. Then place in semi shady place or garden frame that is protected from the hot sun. Keep pots and soil underneath damp.

10. Succulents and cacti need a more gritty and free-draining compost than most other plants.

11. If you have a suitable area of bare soil and an automatic drip tube irrigation system, it is possible to propagate a large number of cuttings in full sun as commercial nurseries do. Plant one cutting to a pot. Line the pots up on capillary matting in full sun and place a drip on each pot. Ensure that the compost used is very free-draining to allow the plants to be watered twice a day and at times to be rained on without becoming waterlogged. This method is especially suitable for perennial herbs and shrubs, such as oleanders and plumbago, but not for succulent or cacti varieties.

ONGOING CARE

1. Place in shaded greenhouse or frame. They need light but direct sunlight will broil.

2. Check regularly that cuttings are neither too dry nor too wet.

3. When watering always add a fungicide.

4. Remove any rotting leaves regularly.

5. Do not be too hasty to remove a doubtful cutting. They can appear dormant one day and start sprouting the next.

POTTING ON AND HARDENING OFF

1. If 8-10cm pots are used, you should be able to plant the plants directly into the ground.

2. Once cuttings grown in groups in a pot or a planting tray have rooted well, divide them carefully and pot individually into 8-10cm pots and prick out growing tips. Seal in plastic until they show signs of growing strongly again.

HARDENING OFF

1. If plants are grown in a greenhouse or frame, harden off in the semi shade and the sun before planting out.

2. If grown in the semi shade of a tree or the north side of the house, expose to sun before planting out.

FEEDING

Water with a very dilute plant feed containing potash to stimulate root formation, potassium to stimulate a strong plant structure and flowers and nitrogen to stimulate leaf formation. We generally use a very dilute natural nettle and comfrey feed.

Good cuttings grown annually will expand and thicken your plantings. A 70% success rate will be good, so at all times plant more cuttings than you need. If you achieve more, you can always swap spares with friends or sell them at the local gardening club.

6.13 GROWING PLANTS FROM SEED

Growing plants from seed can be an interesting and rewarding pastime, but it can also be very frustrating when failures occur. Even so, the pleasure and sense of achievement when your own hand-raised plant flowers for the first time makes all the effort worthwhile.

Your own plants can be healthier and stronger specimens than those forced in huge commercial greenhouses. Growing them from seed gives you the possibility of growing popular varieties in larger quantities at lower cost as well as growing unusual plants and building up a rare collection relatively inexpensively.

We recommend that most seeds are first grown in trays and pots for planting out later, especially where spring seedbeds can suffer from wide variations between night and daytime temperatures, drying winds, torrential rain, hail and attacks from snails and slugs.

GROWING PLANTS FOR PLANTING OUT

- **Obtain good seed** - Buy seed from reliable suppliers that have a regular turnover of seeds. Always check the condition of the packet and the "plant by…" date to ensure they are fresh. Also read the plant description carefully to ensure that you are buying what you really want. Plant breeders are continually developing new strains that offer new colours, dwarf or giant plants, bushy and cascading specimens.
It is fun to try some of the new varieties. We buy a combination of Spanish seeds and others through various mail order seed catalogues. You can also save seed from your own and friends' plants. Either collect them as they ripen or cover the seed heads with a paper bag and let them fall. If some are not quite dry, cut off whole seed heads and spread them on a tray in a warm, semi shaded place.
- **Store seed carefully** - Always store seed packets in a dry cool place, never in a greenhouse, tool shed or warm room. Ideally, once opened the packets should be firmly resealed with cello tape, put in an airtight container and stored in the refrigerator. Put your self-dried seeds in brown or kitchen paper and store in the same way. Don't forget to label them clearly.
- **Use a good planting medium** - As with propagating from cuttings, it is important to have a suitable medium for sowing seeds. Seeds need a light, aerated, moisture-retaining, low nutrient compost, preferably soil less. Buy a special seed compost from a garden centre or make your own. We prepare ours with 2 parts sterilized garden compost, 1 part peat substitute to improve moisture retention, 1 part sharp sand to ensure good drainage and 1 part vermiculite to lighten, aerate and prevent the mix from drying out. Vermiculite can also be used alone.
Before mixing the above, sieve the garden compost through a 1cm sieve to remove any lumps, twigs etc., and then sterilize it by putting a layer on your oven tray and bake at 200°C for 30 minutes. Cool and add to your potting mix. Alternatively you can sterilize it in the microwave, using a roasting bag – puncturing the bag before heating up so it doesn't explode.
Wet the peat substitute separately and then add the remaining dry ingredients. Mix in well and add more water if necessary. The mix should be neither too wet nor too dry – a difficult operation and a matter of trial and error. Some people prefer standing the filled pots in water until the compost is damp, but we find the first method better,

especially when we use various types of containers.

• **Use suitable containers -** When choosing the containers in which to sow your seeds, try to economise and be inventive. The choice is vast:

1. Plastic flowerpots.

2. Plastic cups.

3. Juice and milk cartons with the top cut off.

4. Five litre and 1.5 litre water bottles with the tops cut off to leave a 10cm base, keeping the tops to use as lids (in the 5 litre container, we even off the base with some compost and then sit either one flower pot on top or four 6 x 6cm. plastic modules cut from a seed tray).

5. Polystyrene or plastic planting modules with various-sized planting holes.

6. Polystyrene fish boxes filled with compost and planted up with larger seeds such as decorative gourds. You can also put a layer of compost on the base and then sit separate pots on top, which helps retain moisture and encourages stronger roots.

7. Inexpensive newspaper tubes. These are useful for growing a wide range of larger seeds, especially vegetables ready for planting out. Cut out 7cm strips (or the depth of the box you are using) from stacks of four sheets of newspaper. Roll into 3 or 4cm diameter tubes and secure with cello tape. Sit in a fish tray on top of a 3cm layer of compost and put compost in between each one to the top. At the same time, fill the tubes with seed compost. Plant seeds and then cover the tops of the tubes with compost so that the newspaper does not dry out.

You can turn all of the above into a mini greenhouse by putting 1, 2 & 3 into clear plastic bags and closing. With 4, seal as above or slide the cut off closed bottle tops down over the base and seal with cello tape. With 5 & 6, cover with clear plastic and secure with clothes pegs for easy opening. Make a mini, hooped, wire frame under the plastic to allow the air to circulate and to keep the plastic away from the emerging seedlings. Make sure there are no tiny holes where moisture can escape. In the case of larger seeds that don't need light to germinate, cover with cardboard until they emerge, leaving a 2cm air gap.

Before using them, wash all containers in a dilute mix of vinegar and water so that they are thoroughly clean and disease free.

• **Allow sufficient space -** Recognise that if you start off with a packet of zinnia seeds sown in a 15cm diameter seed container and 50% of the seedlings germinate you might need a large fish box for pricking out the seedlings. You could soon fill a small greenhouse, garden frame or cover the terrace table or floor!

• **Temperature control -** Ensure that the seeds are kept within the recommended germination temperature range, which is generally between 20°C and 28°C. Seeds might not germinate, especially in a sub-tropical environment, if day or night temperatures vary widely. A propagator can be helpful if you are trying to grow more exotic plants that need a constant higher heat before late spring.

• **Locating containers -** Containers can be placed almost anywhere:

• **In the semi shade** of a south facing enclosed terrace or a semi shaded window sill. Beware once the weather heats up, as it could be too hot, especially on a south-facing window sill.

• **In a garden frame**, for less delicate seeds.

• **In a greenhouse** with a thermostatically controlled heater for the more delicate seeds when started early in the year. Yes, temperatures do fluctuate in Spain. Nights can drop to 5°C, having been 25°C at lunchtime. The greenhouse and frame need to be shaded once temperatures rise. Without shading, the daytime temperature in the greenhouse could reach 50°C, even in March.

- In an airing cupboard, for seeds that don't need light.
- In a warm, semi shaded corner of the garden.
- Sow at the right time - When to plant seeds depends on:
  - The germination temperature required.
  - The time from germination to first flowering.
  - Whether you want to provide for continuity of flowering by planting out several successive batches of plants.
  - The frost resistance of the seedlings.

Sweet peas, for instance, are best sown in pots or directly in the garden in November for flowering in the spring, while zinnias are best sown in a cool greenhouse in March or directly in the garden in April/May for flowering in the summer.

Naturally, if you have a climate-controlled heated greenhouse you can start seeds much earlier and produce annuals for planting out for Easter. Beware of early spring temperatures that can plummet and of heavy rain storms. In many situations it is best to delay planting out tender young plants until May.

- **Pre-treatment -** Some seeds benefit from special treatment to encourage them to germinate. Very hard coated seeds, such as sweet peas, can be soaked in water for at least 24 hours, or alternatively you can make a small scratch on the seed, being careful not to damage the embryo. This is called scarifying.

Seeds such as peas and beans will benefit from being soaked for a couple of hours. Other seeds, such as special trees, shrubs and alpines, need cold stratification. That means planting, covering and putting them in the fridge for a couple of weeks, then transferring to the greenhouse. The idea is that when you take them out of the fridge they will be shocked out of dormancy and germinate in the warmth.

- **Labelling -** Make labels before starting to sow your seeds. There is nothing worse than not knowing what is in your pot, either because you haven't   labelled it or the markers have faded! You can buy plastic markers and special marker pens, but they can be expensive and fade fast in the hot Spanish sun. After experimenting with various me-thods, we recommend you type a list of seeds on your computer – with the date of planting in bold type. Print it off, cut out each label, seal it in cello tape, push a small length of wire through the label, and attach to a short stick.

- **Sowing -** First of all, fill your chosen containers with dampened compost to about 2.5cm from the top. Press down lightly to avoid air pockets. Then sow your seeds. The number of seeds to each container will vary according to their size and whether you want to plant the seedlings on. We treat larger seeds, such as decorative gourds, the same as we would treat vegetables such as pumpkins, courgettes, melons and beans. These we sow two or three to a pot and, when strong enough, plant directly into their final position.

A simple rule for sowing is to cover the seeds with compost equal to their size. Very fine seeds need light, so either leave uncovered or sprinkle a little vermiculite over the top. Do not sow seeds too thickly.

Most importantly, spray the soil surface with a fungicide after sowing to protect against damping off. Use a fine hand sprayer or a watering can with a very fine rose.

Once seeds are sown, you need to be very vigilant. Check every day that the compost in uncovered containers is still damp. Those sealed in plastic should stay damp, but still check from time to time.

• **Recognise and solve problems quickly -** If seeds don't germinate, check to see if the compost has dried out and compacted, or is too wet. If it is dry, spray with a fine sprayer, always using a dilute mix of fungicide in your sprayer. If the compost is too wet inside the plastic, leave it open for a while to dry out a little and then reseal.

Check to see if the containers are exposed to too much direct sun. If they are, move them to a cooler spot.

Ask yourself if temperatures are fluctuating too much. Perhaps you need more heat in your greenhouse at night and less heat during the day. Make sure you have shading on the greenhouse, and be sure to open the ventilation during the heat of the day. Place a small temperature controlled heater in the greenhouse. Do the tiny seeds have sufficient light? If not, plant another batch on the surface.

If your seedlings become too leggy, they might not have enough light.

Once seeds have appeared, remove the plastic cover or cardboard and place them in good light, but not in the direct sun.

If they are rotting or damping off, the compost could be too wet and you might have forgotten to spray them with a fungicide when sowing the seeds. When seedlings rot off at the base and keel over, it means you have a fungal disease. Quickly remove the rotting seedlings and dry out the compost so that it is just damp to touch. Spray the remaining seedlings and soil lightly with a dilute fungicide mix.

• **Planting on -** Many seedlings will need planting on into larger containers or modules. Make up a planting medium of 7 parts compost, 3 parts substitute peat and 2 parts sharp sand. Dampen as for seed compost but now dampen with a dilute liquid fertiliser. Use a proprietary general fertilizer, liquid seaweed or a nettle/comfrey feed. Prick out the seedlings when they are big enough to handle. This is normally when they have two to four leaves. Always hold them by the leaves, never by the fragile stems. Don't disregard smaller seedlings, as sometimes they grow to be the strongest. Transplant into compost and water very carefully and spray with a dilute mix of fungicide. Don't water again until they are just starting to dry out. At this stage they can rot very easily if over watered. Thereafter, feed once a week feed with a weak solution of liquid fertilizer to encourage strong growth.

To ensure plantlets are not eaten by slugs and snails, always keep several bran or beer traps in the greenhouse and cold frame or, as a last resort, sprinkle some slug pellets around.

• **Hardening off -** Plants grown in the greenhouse or undercover will need to be acclimatised in a sheltered corner of the garden for a couple of days before being planted in their final position. Check that the temperatures are not forecast to drop dramatically before moving them out.

• **Timely planting out -** Finally the time has come to plant out your nurtured plants. Make sure you choose the right situation and soil. For example, annuals could die in one day in a very hot sunny spot, whereas succulents will thrive.

Make sure you work good water-retaining compost into flowerbeds and flower containers. Plant out plants carefully from trays or pots and plant to no more than their previous depth. Firm down the soil around each plant and water gently. Slugs and snails love young plants, so protect them well from the first hour.

• **Sowing seeds directly into the garden** - When sowing seeds directly into the garden, follow the guidelines below:

• Read instructions on seed packets for required temperatures and spacing.

• Prepare beds by digging in plenty of well-rotted moisture retaining compost.

• Make a 4cm trench or hole and fill with seed compost for fine seeds and planting mix for larger seeds. Use the mediums already described above. Firm down lightly.

• Sow seeds thinly to avoid thinning out later. This will be their final position.

• Cover fine seeds with a little vermiculite. Larger seeds are best covered a layer of planting compost equal to their size. Firm down lightly.

• Label and mark your seeds.

• Water well with a fine rose watering can or sprayer.

• Put down some slug protection.

• Don't let your seeds dry out. Water regularly with a fine spray. Heavy watering will quickly damage young stems.

If you are not totally successful in year one, don't give up. The Spanish conditions do take time to get used to.

6.14 BENEFICIAL GREENHOUSES AND GARDEN FRAMES

In spite of the Spanish climate, a greenhouse and garden frame can be invaluable if you grow more than a few plants from cuttings and seeds for the flower or vegetable garden and you have tender plants that need to be moved out of the garden during the winter.

Few Spanish houses have deep inside windowsills that can be used for propagating or over-wintering plants. A south-facing windowsill would be generally too hot.

The difference between day and night time temperatures in the spring, when most seeds are sown, can be 20 degrees. Achieving a constant temperature for good germination can be very difficult.

Tender sub tropical and even tropical plants love the spring and summer temperatures but in many inland areas, especially a high meseta, Madrid and the higher coastal mountains, they would die in the winter if left outside.

For all these reasons it's worth having a greenhouse or garden frame. We all love to try and beat nature by planting newly imported varieties raised in hothouses worldwide, but we can be caught out by just an hour of night frost, even in the south of Spain.

HARDENING OFF

Plants grown in the greenhouse can be hardened off in a cold frame or semi-shaded situation. Plants from the cold frame can be moved to the semi-shade. Place them in the sun for a few days when they are almost ready to plant out.

TYPICAL USES, PROBLEMS AND SOLUTIONS

TYPICAL USES	GARDEN FRAME	GREENHOUSE
Shelter for seed trays	*	*
Late winter sowings		*
Shelter for propagated cuttings	*	*
Housing collection of tender plants, e.g.,cacti, orchids and succulents	* (If temperature never drops below 0°C).	* (If temperature never drops below 0°C).
Early tomatoes and cucumbers	*	*
Winter salad crops	*	
Forcing a grapevine		*
Over wintering potted tropical plants		* (Provided it's heated in colder areas.)

TYPICAL PROBLEMS AND SOLUTIONS

	GARDEN FRAME	GREENHOUSE
Temperature drops below zero	Seal tops and sides. Cover with blanket or blister wrap at night. (ineffective for long cold periods).	Close ventilators. Line with blister wrap. Install thermostat controlled heater.
Temperature can rise above a 100 °C.	• Site in semi shade. • Open top during day.	• Cover with woven plastic or slatted shading. • White wash glazing. • Site on west of house. • Open door and ventilators during daytime.
Slow germination or propagation	• Pre-germinate or root in mini propagator before placing in frame. • Ensure that compost is always just damp. • Place pots and trays with seeds or cuttings in sealed plastic bags to achieve constant temperature and humidity.	• Have propagator in greenhouse (with a mist humidifier in a larger greenhouse). • Ensure compost is always just damp. • Place pots/trays with seeds/cuttings in sealed plastic bags to achieve constant temperature and humidity.
Fungal attacks	• Wash all seed trays and pots in dilute bleach and rinse before use. • Empty, clean out and wash with fungicide once a year. • Don't over-water and include fungicide in water. • Remove any affected plants immediately.	
Slugs and snails	• Put beer traps on floor and shelves amongst the plants. • Ensure there are no entry gaps around the base. • Dust compost surface with neem powder.	

TYPICAL USES, PROBLEMS AND SOLUTIONS (continued)

TYPICAL USES	GARDEN FRAME	GREENHOUSE
Aphids	• Hang proprietary sticky strips. • Place/hang bunches of rosemary. • Take out any affected plants, clean off and spray potassium soap solution.	
Drying out of pots/trays.	• Maintain a daily watering routine. Use drip trays or capilliary trays. • Place seedlings and cuttings in plastic bags until well rooted.	

SITING

Unless you have a very big greenhouse it can get very hot in the full sun. If placed on the east side of the house it will be warmed up by the morning sun, but in the afternoon it will cool down before dusk, especially during the winter months. The west side has the advantage of receiving later sun and will therefore be warmed up for the night. We find it beneficial to have one cold frame in the sun and one in semi-shade.

MINIMUM USEFUL SIZE

A 1sq.m horizontal or vertical frame with four 60x20cm shelves is practical and can produce an amazing number of plants if used throughout the year.

A 1 1/2sq.m base with a height of two metres is probably the smallest practical size for a greenhouse. Naturally, there is no limit to the size, excepting space and budget.

Problems can arise when you install larger units. For instance, where do you fit in all the trays when you prick out seedlings from small cell trays to individual pots? Where do you harden them all off, and where do you plant them all? Remember, considerable time and patience is required to nurse and water hundreds of plants.

TYPES

Both greenhouses and frames can stand alone or be placed against the wall of the house, garden wall or fence. Garden frames can be horizontal with glazed, plastic sides or solid sides (the latter providing better winter and summer insulation).

A large tent cloche made from old wood and plastic sheeting is an ideal frame for raising large seeded vegetables such as pumpkins and melons.

Wooden, metal and plastic covered aluminium frames are all feasible, the latter having the benefit of not rotting or rusting.

Multi-cell, plastic glazing provides better insulation and is safer than glass for both the tops of garden frames and the glazing on greenhouses.

If you have a large vegetable plot, a tunnel greenhouse constructed from heavy grade plastic over a hooped metal tubing frame can be very useful for not only growing plantlets but also for growing early crops of tomatoes, courgettes, beans, melons, etc.

6.15 PHYSICAL PLANT PROTECTION

In all gardens, tender plants need to be protected from the hottest suns and high winds – and from frost in some areas.

There are several practical ways you can protect your plants from the sun. You can protect seedlings and young propagations from cuttings by hardening off in the semi-shade of a tree or purpose-built, woven plastic or cane shade.

Plants that have shallow roots and will dry out fast in the sun should be planted in semi-shaded situations. Don't plant shade-loving plants in full sun. Use the dappled shady areas in the garden to the full when planning areas for flowerbeds and potted plants.

Many new gardens are not protected from hot or cold drying winds or wind-blown rain or hail until boundary hedges, trees and fences are in place.

Protect young hedge plants grown against an open-mesh, wire fence by lining the fence with rolls of woven plastic or cane windbreak material which you can leave or remove when the hedge is mature, depending on what is then on the other side of the fence.

Delay planting delicate shrubs and trees that could be snapped off by strong winds or become burnt by the sun or frost until external and internal hedges and windbreaks are in place. Preferably, plant tender plants against a south-facing wall or in a sunny nook.

If you plan to plant tropical plants, such as the wonderfully perfumed frangipani, ensure that they have the most sheltered position possible. The ideal is against a south-facing wall with large evergreen trees on either side to protect from east and west winds, and with three-metre or more hedges around the garden. If there is any chance of a winter or spring frost, plant in pots and take inside during the risky months.

FROSTS

From time to time we are all tempted to plant one or two of the more delicate of subtropical or tropical plants, knowing that this is a risk – if not during the next winter, then sometime during one of the next five, on average. Early in March 2004, for the first time in more than a decade, a single two-hour night frost decimated delicate plants growing just inland from the coast, from Cataluña to southern Andalusia. The frosts of February and March, 2005 affected even seafront gardens. And of course there can be snow.

This can happen annually in some inland valleys and on mountainsides. If you intend to plant tropical plants, such as bananas and frangipani, or more delicate subtropical plants, such as the white and yellow bougainvillea, be sure to plant them against a protected south-facing wall, wrap them in fleece, woven plastic windbreak material or cover them with a plastic-sheet wigwam.

Keep in them pots and take them inside the house or into a heated greenhouse. In cooler situations, it is best to grow them permanently in a greenhouse.

If you plant out annuals or perennial cuttings early, protect them for a few weeks with cloches made by cutting the bottom 5cm off five or eight litre-water bottles. Stick a cane through the top hole into the ground for stability.

6.16 BE A PLANT DETECTIVE

In general, many of the plants that die in expatriate Spanish gardens do so because they were poorly planted in poor soil, watered insufficiently or drowned, planted in the hottest corners of the garden in midsummer in shallow or hard drying clay soil or were exposed to frosts during the first winter while still tender.

Where a problem exists, it is all too easy to rush to the garden centre for the latest insecticide or fertilizer and give plants overdoses for something they never had. It would be wiser to follow the guidelines below:

Few garden centres offer a warranty on the plants – so be meticulous in choosing the best type of plant for your situation, planting them well in an appropriate soil, and then giving them thorough aftercare.

When a plant looks unhealthy, try and find out why as soon as possible rather than treating the symptoms in an ad hoc fashion. If a plant dies or does not look right there has to be a reason, whether it is just one plant that gives you concern or half the garden. The reason has to be:

- Something you or someone else did or didn't do, perhaps unknowingly.
- Something unusual about how you bought, planted or cared for the plants.
- Something unusual about the source or type of plant.
- Something that is fundamentally wrong with the depth or type of soil – or planting is being done in sun or shade.

For most of us, there are many things that are different when we first come to Spain and we all need to modify or adjust some of our previous gardening practices.

Be aware of the vulnerability of your gardening practices. The next time something goes wrong, analyse the problem carefully. Ask yourself why only this particular plant is affected and not the one nearby or in another corner of the garden. Think through the history of the plant and its location and ask yourself if you have done something unusual and whether a similar thing has happened before? Look around the garden and decide which plants are doing the best and try to think of any reasons why they should be doing so well.

The moment you think you know why a plant is unhealthy or dead, act to stop the problem – stop it from reoccurring and stop it happening elsewhere in the garden.

Fifty possible causes of plant problems are listed below. Read through the list and tick any statements that are at least partly true. Then go back over the list and count how many statements you have ticked. The higher the number the more vulnerable the plants in the garden!

POOR CHOICE OF PLANTS

1. Making a poor choice when buying plants, or being given a present of a plant unsuitable for your soil and microclimate.
2. Buying plants direct from hot houses without them being hardened off.

OVER OPTIMISM

3. Assuming that native Spanish plants require little or no watering when first planted.
4. Delaying watering because a storm is forecast.
5. Assuming that you will never get an air frost.
6. Assuming that all soils are good, including yours.

INADEQUATE WATERING

7. Unclear agreement in the household as to who waters what and when.
8. Failure to remember a special plant in a far away corner of the garden.
9. Watering in full sun, as a busy life prevents watering in the cool of the evening or before the sun is up.
10. Forgetting to water the terrace pots, greenhouse or garden frame.
11. Watering with the hot water lying inside a long hose left in the sun.
12. Watering quickly and shallowly rather than slowly and deeply.
13. No catchment tray under pots.
14. Saline water or highly chlorinated water on tender plants.
15. Watering irregularly rather than using a timer-controlled irrigation system.
16. Letting recently purchased plants dry out before planting in the garden.
17. Not checking the drip irrigation system for leaks or blocked jets.
18. Failure to water annuals daily during the summer months.
19. Allowing the soil to totally dry out when on holiday or when you are an absentee gardener.
20. Failure to improve the humus, water holding property of the soil, so that much water just runs through to the water table.

POOR SPACING OF PLANTS

21. Planting too close so that faster growing plants smother smaller plants.
22. Planting too far apart so that the hot sun bakes the soil between and the shallow roots of plants.

POOR MULCHING

23. Not mulching young plants to keep their roots cool and the soil moist.
24. Mulching deeply with fresh manure and encouraging fungal diseases.

POOR PLANTING IN POTS

25. Using a compost that dries out very quickly.
26. Using thin walled terracotta pots that dry out quickly by surface evaporation.
27. Not mulching the tops of the soil in pots put in the sun with grit or stones.
28. Not re-potting when root bound.
29. Over watering, especially in the winter months.

30. Placing delicate potted plants in full sun rather than semi- shade.
31. Not wrapping up delicate plants in fleece, plastic sheeting or woven cloth.
32. Not taking delicate plants indoors for the coldest months if in a frost or snow belt.
33. Poor windbreaks.
34. Insecure support posts for trees.

POOR PLANT TIES

35. Tight ties strangling or cutting through plants as they grow.
36. Hard or sharp ties acting like saws in the wind and cutting into trunks, stems and branches.

INADEQUATE WEEDING

37. Allowing vigorous weeds to starve plants of moisture and nutrients or smothering weaker plants.
38. Using weed killer near delicate plants.

POOR PRUNING

39. Pruning just before or after frost and not sealing cuts after major surgery on trees.
40. Not cutting out diseased wood.

POOR INSECT/DISEASE CONTROL

41. Failure to act fast when problems are first seen.
42. Failure to take preventive action against snails and slugs at the time you sow seeds or plant out young plants.

ROOT DISTURBANCE

43. Loosening of plants when pulling out weeds.
44. Being washed out of soil by erosion during heavy rainfalls.
45. Being knocked over by strong winds.
46. Digging up or fouling by animals and birds.

BURNING OF FOLIAGE OR ROOTS

47. Watering alkaline-loving plants with the backwash from the swimming pool.
48. Over application of granular general fertilizers in the garden, especially under young fruit trees and on flowerpots.
49. Over-strength foliar feeding, especially when done in full sun and when leaves are very dry.
50. Burning of soft leaved plants by spraying over-strength insecticides and fungi-cides, especially in the middle of a hot day.

CHECK YOUR VULNERABILITY

Go back through the list and count the number of statements that you have ticked.

0 – 10: Doing well. You are obviously getting it right.

11 – 25: Generally a need to be more thorough and attentive.

26 – 50: The garden centres must love you! Perhaps you need a gardener or you should consider creating a courtyard or paved garden with few plants.

6.17 A FLOWER GARDEN CALENDAR

JANUARY

- Do the major annual cut back and clean up.
- Take cuttings of a range of plants and pot up to propagate.
- Process all manageable prunings, cuttings and weeds through the shredder.
- Start a new compost heap, carefully layering soft and harder materials.
- Cut up sawn off branches and trunks for logs for the stove or fire.
- Obtain a licence for a bonfire, if necessary, or take material that cannot be shredded to local eco park. Some now pay for it!
- Divide and replant large clumps of perennials.
- Take cuttings of chrysanthemums for propagation.
- Clean out garden frame and greenhouse.
- Sort through and wash/disinfect all empty plant pots and trays.

FEBRUARY

- Check and adjust all plant ties and posts.
- Prune early flowering acacias after flowering.
- Stake over-wintering sweet peas.
- Plant non-tender perennials, shrubs and trees.
- Sow first annuals in the greenhouse.
- Clean pond and prune back the roots of vigorous pond plants.
- Plant summer flowering bulbs and rhizomes.
- Mix well-rotted compost and manure into flowerbeds. Cut back poinsettias when they lose their leaves.
- Turn last autumn's compost heap and sieve out fine compost for preparing seed and potting compost mixes.

MARCH

- Start to spray geraniums against the geranium moth.
- Start to mow lawn and give it a top dressing of sand, peat and fertilizer.
- Take cuttings of perennial plants such as echium, leonotis, margaritas and succulents: and start to dead head all flowering plants as the flowers die.

- Remove frost protection from delicate plants after last frost.
- Plant hedges and complete the planting of spring and summer flowering and fruiting shrubs and trees.
- Carry out an annual safety check on the garden.
- Plant summer corms such as begonias and gladioli and lily bulbs.
- Divide chrysanthemums after they have finished flowering.
- Take geranium cuttings and pot up.
- Start to plant out hardy summer vegetables.

APRIL

- As weather warms up, commence or increase watering of young plants.
- Plant out the first summer annuals for Easter colour.
- Start to give plants in pots and containers a monthly feed.
- Sow zinnias for cutting in the summer.
- Trim frost damage on succulents.
- Don´t be impatient with plants such as hibiscus, lantana and bougainvilleas that look as if the frost killed them. They often sprout as late as May or even June.
- Give hedges a good spring cut.
- Watch out for processionary caterpillars.
- Make final sowings of annuals such as petunias.
- Ensure that compost heaps are kept damp.

MAY

- When cyclamens start to die back, place in a cool shady corner of the garden until September.
- Start to mow the lawn weekly.
- Cut off any new sharp ends of yuccas, palms and other thorny shrubs and trees.
- Deadhead any spring flowering plants.
- Water and feed sweet peas during flowering season.
- Plant out new perennials and herbs and tender summer vegetables.
- Fill in gaps in the rockery with new herbs, succulents and cacti.
- Start to feed fish in ponds on a regular basis.
- If the weather is dry, set up the irrigation timer to water daily in the evening.

JUNE

- Deadhead and tidy plants weekly.
- Dig out or hoe wind-blown weeds as they come up.
- Increase watering as temperatures start to rise.
- Check watering system regularly for leaks and to ensure that all drip heads work.
- Watch out for pests and diseases that can appear as the heat and humidity rise.
- Go out with a torch to catch active slugs and snails, especially around newly planted plants.

- Ensure you keep up the weekly spraying and health check of geraniums.
- Top up pond and continue to watch levels throughout the summer.
- Hand weed or hoe areas of stone chippings and only if really necessary use weed killer.
- Feed plants in pots and containers.

JULY

- Increase watering if there are no summer storms.
- Cut and dry herbs for culinary, health and decorative purposes.
- Do a deadheading tour twice weekly.
- Keep path and terrace areas swept or vacuumed and clear of leaves and dead flowers.
- Prune unsightly growth on shrubs, especially those that flower on long stems.
- Cut out untidy suckers on bougainvilleas.
- Leave large, selected seed heads to ripen for propagation.
- Cut back excessive growth of pond plants to keep a space clear for the fish to surface and feed.
- Cut back hollyhocks once they have finished flowering and collect the ripe seeds.
- Train and tie in climbers on fences and walls.

AUGUST

- Cut back summer lilies and gladioli.
- Keep cutting annuals such as zinnias to prolong flowering.
- Keep up the dead heading.
- Cut sunflowers and hang to dry.
- Maintain summer level of watering if there are no storms.
- Check that no plants show signs of completely drying out.
- Cut off berried ends on lantanas before they drop and squash on terraces and paths.
- Trim climbers to keep them neat and under control and cut out water shoots on bougainvilleas.
- Keep a wary eye open for pests and diseases.
- Cut dead flowers off lavender to tidy the garden.

SEPTEMBER

- Carry out strategic garden review.
- Decide on projects and changes for the autumn and winter.
- Prune and feed roses to re-stimulate flowering for the autumn and Christmas.
- Turn and dampen compost heaps.
- Start to sweep or vacuum fallen leaves. Mix into compost heap or new raised beds.
- Trim and feed annuals to stimulate the final fling of flowers.
- Remove all dead annuals and put on compost heat.

- Trim back lantanas and other shrubs such as plumbago and solanum that protrude onto terraces and paths.
- Sow hollyhocks, antirrhinums and autumn/winter vegetables..
- Give all pot and container plants a tidy up and feed.

OCTOBER

- Prepare new flower or vegetable beds ready for planting.
- If the rains have come, start to plant perennials, shrubs and trees.
- Take cuttings of succulents and shrubs and propagate.
- Plant Christmas bulbs in pots and place in the dark.
- Bring last year's cyclamens into a north facing porch and start to water and feed.
- Reduce the frequency and extent of irrigation if the weather has cooled down.
- In colder climes, move delicate plants inside or into a greenhouse.
- Prepare and sow new lawns. Start to sow peas and broad beans.
- Clean out summer annuals as they finish and replace with pansies.
- Tidy up plants and take cuttings for propagating in the greenhouse or garden frame.
- Give the garden an autumn tidy up but don't fall into the trap of doing a major UK-style garden clean up at this time. If you do, you will have no colour at Christmas. This is why we recommend the major annual cut back and clean up as the number one job for January.

NOVEMBER

- Plant spring bulbs in the garden.
- Construct a rockery or pond.
- Prune rose bushes to stimulate buds for Christmas flowering
- Start sweet peas in pots or ground.
- Wrap the more delicate plants in plastic or frost fleece in colder areas.
- Collect snails and feed on rosemary to prepare for year-end tapas!
- Check ties on trees and shrubs.
- Do an autumn weed and hoe.
- Purchase just-in-bud flowering pot plants for Christmas.
- Complete the autumn planting of perennials, shrubs and deciduous trees.

DECEMBER

- Make a last planting of spring bulbs.
- Bring on Christmas pot plants to be at their best during the holidays. Obtain next year's seed catalogues and place orders.
- Sweep up last of fallen leaves, dampen, bag up in black plastic bags (with a few air holes) and leave in a corner to rot down to useful leaf mould.
- Do a pre-Christmas weeding and light tidy up. Leave as many buds and flowers as possible.
- Have tops of palm trees pruned and shaped.

• Arrange a display of colourful flowering plants such as cyclamens, poinsettias, azaleas, kalanchoas and bulbs around the front door,
• Start to build new terraces, paths and walls.
• Ensure that Christmas plants are given sufficient light, kept just moist and out of draughts, and are not baked in centrally-heated rooms.

Fruit and vegetable growing calendars are included in the two sister books 'Growing healthy fruit in Spain' and 'Growing healthy vegetables in Spain' respectively. Purchase a copy of the lunar gardening calendar 'Calendario Lunar' published by Artus Porta Manresa. Although in Spanish it is easy to follow and useful in the flower, vegetable and fruit gardens.

PART SEVEN

MANAGING YOUR GARDEN

We look at a number of general issues important to the management of your garden in Spain, issues that could make or break the fun and enjoyment you get from a garden developed by following the ideas and guidance of the earlier sections.

7.1 USING A GARDENER?

A. DO YOU NEED ONE?

This is a very personal question. It needs to be considered objectively against the background of your own situation.

Retirees moving to Spain with plenty of leisure time often have an interest in a variety of activities, including gardening. For some it is their main hobby and for others it is of limited interest. Younger persons who come here to work may have little time for gardening, whether interested or not and there are those of all ages who are physically unable to garden

Every expatriate has genuine ambitions for a new lifestyle in Spain and many will need a gardener, either for a short time to help establish the garden, or on a permanent basis, to maintain it as well.

It is very easy to let your enthusiasm for creating a wonderful garden get out of hand and to assume that every thing can be done in a year. It can, of course, if you take on a landscape gardener to do the whole job for you, but this could be costly.Many will prefer to have the fun and satisfaction of creating a new garden from nothing, or perhaps improving an existing one. In either case, creating a garden that satisfies all their needs will take a good number of years.

It is important to be honest with yourself. Before deciding whether you need a gardener, analyse what you, your partner and close family would like to do in the garden, what you are capable of doing, and how much time you will be able to dedicate to the garden.

The inspiring Alhambra garden Granada

ACTIVITIES REQUIRED TO DESIGN, CONSTRUCT AND MAINTAIN A GARDEN	DO WE REALLY WANT TO DO THIS?			OR SHOULD WE GET A GARDENER?	
	YES	PARTIALLY	NO	PARTIALLY	TOTALLY
• Design of garden					
• Landscaping, including construction of paths, terraces and walls					
• Development of special features					
• Selecting plants					
• Purchasing plants					
• Planting plants					
• Watering and feeding					
• Raising new plants:					
– from seed					
– from cuttings					
• Ongoing maintenance:					
– flower garden					
– fruit garden					
– vegetable garden					
• Care of greenhouse and garden frame					
• Winter cut back					
• Ongoing maintenance:					
– Lawn cutting					
– Flower garden					
– Vegetable garden					
– Fruit garden					
– Pool/jacuzzi maintenance					

Based on this analysis, decide whether you need:
1. No gardener.
2. A gardener to help do an initial cleanup of an existing neglected garden.
3. A gardener to design and develop a garden that you will then maintain.
4. A gardener to design, develop and maintain your garden.

If you are going to be an absentee gardener, decide if you want a gardener to tend the garden 52 weeks a year, whether you are in Spain or not, or whether you want him to do only a major tidy up just before each of your visits and during your stay.

There may be a gardener who goes with the property you have bought. In this case,

271

consider whether he or she has the knowledge, experience, physical fitness, motivation and time to create and maintain the garden you want – or whether you need to find a new gardener. If it is the latter, make the change as early as possible.

If you are lucky enough to inherit a good gardener, make sure you don't lose him or her. In some areas, they are like gold.

B. SELECTING A GARDENER

Now you have to decide what type of gardener you need. There are several choices. It could be a landscaping contractor, an experienced and knowledgeable gardener, a trainee gardener on a local gardening course who has to do six months practical work to gain a final diploma, an enthusiastic amateur new to Spain who needs to make a living, or an odd-job man or girl Friday.

Draw up a short list of possible gardeners, including your inherited gardener, if you have one. Spend a few weeks asking around, reading the services column in the local newspaper or putting an advertisement in the newspaper or on the notice board in your local store.

Don't rush into hiring the first person who puts a leaflet in your post box or the first one you see working down the road. This is an important decision and many of you have never employed a gardener before coming to Spain.

Having drawn up a short list, ask each of them to come for a chat. Then evaluate each in turn, taking into account the following factors:

– **Previous experience:** What gardens do they currently look after and have looked after in the past? What style of garden and size? Have they developed a garden along the lines that you envisage? How long have they been gardeners in Spain?

– **Pride in work:** Do you get the impression that he or she takes pride in their work and could become enthusiastic about your garden?

– **Client satisfaction:** Are current and past clients happy with the gardener's work? Are they willing to let you see their gardens? A visit will tell you a lot.

– **Aesthetics:** Do other gardens suggest that the gardener has an eye for beauty? Are the designs and materials used in keeping with the location, style of garden and most importantly the style and   colour scheme of the house?

– **Knowledge:** Does he or she have a good knowledge of the local nurseries, know what plants are best for your location and style of garden, and how to propagate in order to expand the number of plants in the garden economically? If you want to garden organically, does he or she know about organic fertilizers and insecticides and believe in not using weed killers? Does he or she believe in improving the soil before planting, and know where to obtain organic compost or manures?

– **Contacts:** Does the gardener have good contacts with specialists if he or she is unable to carry out all the work you need doing (e.g., tree surgeons, bricklayers and tilers)?

– **Communication:** Does he or she speak English, Spanish or both? Does he or she have a history of listening and contributing to other house owners? Do you feel that you could establish a good partnership to develop and maintain the garden on an ongoing basis?

– **Reliability:** Do you feel that you can trust the gardener to get on with agreed tasks in your absence and with keys to the property. Have other clients found the gardener reliable in completing jobs on time, tidily and within estimates?

– **Equipment:** Does the gardener have the tools for the job or are you expected to provide them? Are they productive Spanish-style tools suited to hard soils?

– **Availability:** When can he or she start? What hours are possible without creating complaints from other clients? Are the hours sufficient to carry out the work you want carried out in the short and long term? Can the summer maintenance work be fitted in to suit the times that you wish to use the garden privately?

– **Is he or she working legally?:** If a foreigner, is he or she working legally in Spain?

– **Insurance:** Does the gardener have adequate insurance cover.

– **Cost:** What will be charged, and how? Is this realistic and in line with local prices for both initial design and landscaping work and for ongoing maintenance?

Having made your analysis of each gardener available, make an objective choice and negotiate a realistic verbal or written contract.

C. MOTIVATING YOUR GARDENER

The following guidelines are suggested for getting the most out of your gardener:

1. Negotiate a realistic and fair contract and pay on time. in many cases it is preferable to pay the gardener on the basis of:

- A monthly or quarterly retainer rather than on an hourly basis for the ongoing maintenance and minor improvements.

- An agreed budget for the purchase of plants, garden materials, fertilizers and sprays, etc.

- An agreement as to whether the gardener has the right to pick flowers, almonds, olives, other fruit and vegetables for his or her own use.

- Agreed additional payments for the initial landscaping of the garden and major changes in an existing one. You may well use a landscaping company for the latter and then a private individual for the ongoing maintenance work.

– Whether you should increase the rate of pay in line with inflation each year.

2. Share your vision for the garden. Agree realistic milestones for the development of a new garden or changing an existing garden. Tell the gardener what you think and what visitors thought of the results of his or her efforts. Evaluate by results, not hours worked. A good gardener will achieve much in a relatively few hours. The limited results of a poor gardener will soon be obvious.

3. If you plan to work on the garden with the support of a gardener, avoid misunderstandings by:

- Involving the gardener in the planning phase.
- Asking for ideas to supplement your own before making final decisions.
- Agreeing how to share out the work required.
- Agreeing what should be composted and what will go to the refuge tip.
- Visiting garden centres together to choose and purchase plants.

4. If you become dissatisfied with your gardener, be fair before making a change. Make an objective evaluation and then discuss your major misgivings with him. See if you can find out what is causing things to go wrong and try to agree on an improvement plan for the next month or two before making a final decision.

D. EVALUATING YOUR GARDENER

September is probably the best time to evaluate the contribution and performance of your gardener in relation to the creation and maintenance of a garden that suites your site, environment and lifestyle.

You will have just spent, hopefully, a summer in a wonderfully colourful and perfumed garden. Memories and perhaps photographs remind you of the best features of the garden last Christmas and in the spring, and the current state of the garden will give an impression of how it will look during the autumn.

If you have changes and new projects in mind, the autumn and winter are the best times of the year to implement them. September is the most appropriate time for a review to ensure that they will be in knowledgeable, capable, productive and trustworthy hands, especially if you are an absentee owner and are shortly to depart for some months.

Likewise, if you have just returned from spending the summer in cooler climes, take a close look at the garden. Does it look good? Does it look as if you have not been away. And if the property has been rented, have there been any complaints or praise from tenants or the letting agency?

An objective basis for a gardener can be down loaded from www.gardeninginspain.com

E. EFFECTIVE CHANGEOVER OF GARDENERS

Most of us have experienced at some time in our working life a poor handover from the previous incumbent when starting a new job – the inevitable "dropped baton" which is sometimes as disastrous in the working environment as in a relay race.

The same often happens when gardeners are changed, and the result is a lack of continuity in the development and maintenance of a carefully nurtured garden. If you have to make a change, ensure that this takes place with the minimum disruption to the gardening calendar.

The following check list covers the information that needs to be handed over to the new gardener:

1. The extent to which the owner likes to be involved or whether he/she leaves the gardener to do what they think is best.

2. The owner's general vision for the garden and specific likes and dislikes.

3. The current programme for the development/improvement of the garden, e.g., new terraces, flower beds, rockeries etc.

4. Any urgent jobs planned for the next few months.

5. Recently planted plants and any special care they need until established.

6. Provisional planting plans for the next autumn/winter including cuttings required for propagation.

7. The regular programme of watering and feeding plants, trees and lawns.

8. The normal schedule of weeding, hoeing and weed killing (if allowed) and the areas where weeds are normally killed, and with what.

9. The normal frequency and height for cutting the lawn.

10. The range of machinery (mower, strimmer, shredder etc.) and tools provided by the owner, and servicing arrangements.

11. How the watering system works and the normal seasonal settings. Who to contact if there are problems with the electronic controls on a complex system. The owner's attitude to the cost of watering.

12. The normal programme for the winter cleanup in January/February.

13. Facilities for disposal of garden waste, e.g., compost heap, bagging for tip or the ordering of a skip for the winter cleanup.

14. The owner's policy re organic/ecological versus inorganic manufactured fertilizers, insecticides and herbicides.

15. Programme for pruning, watering and feeding fruit trees. Whether the gardener is expected to harvest crops and allowed to take some for his/her own use.

16. Whether the gardener is expected to develop and maintain a productive vegetable garden.

17. Location and types of spring and summer bulbs in flowerbeds to ensure that they are not disturbed or damaged.

18. Owner's desire for displays of annuals in containers or beds.

19. Owner's budget for new plants and any agreed re-plantings.

20. Ownership of hedges and owner's policy re height and depth of hedges.

21. Owner's pet plants and names.

22. Who has the responsibility for maintaining the swing, slide, sand pit etc., in the children's play area.

23. Where tools and chemicals can be stored securely.

24. Who is responsible for repair of steps, paths, terraces, walls, repainting of terrace walls, garden furniture etc. Is there a regular handy man as well as a gardener?

25. What special things need to be done in the week before each of the owner's visits, if the owner is not resident, or if the property is let.

26. Who is responsible, you, the gardener or the cleaner, for sweeping paths and terraces.

27. If the gardener is to maintain the pool, how the pool system works, what pool chemicals are used and where they are purchased and stored.

28. How and when to submit bills for work carried out, and expenditures on behalf of the owner.

29. How and when the owner likes to be contacted.

Clarifying these issues on day one will go a long way to preventing hiccups and demonstrate that you take a great interest in the garden.

7.2 SPANISH GARDENING TOOLS

The soil in most Spanish gardens is initially very unforgiving. Except for a day or two after rain, it can be rock hard, even in the winter. The use of an inappropriate or ergonomically inefficient tool can cause unnecessary hard work and can even lead to injury, especially to backs, shoulders, elbows, wrists and knees.

When we first came to Spain, we soon found that most of the tools we used regularly in the damper climate and the generally more friable soils of northern Europe were no match for traditional Spanish tools.

TRADITIONAL SPANISH TOOLS

Our collection of Spanish tools has been built up over the years by observing how Spaniards work the land and watching out for regional tools as we travelled around.

1. A range of mattocks (azadones).

    a. Small size with a 5 or 6cm wide blade on a short 15cm handle – essential for easy close work such as weeding, hoeing, making seed drills and small planting holes.

    b. Medium double-ended on long handle. We use two types as illustrated. The first has an 8cm flat mattock blade on one side and a U-shape on the other side of the head. The other has a flat mattock blade on one side and a pointed blade on the other. The first is a general-purpose tool used daily. We find it is very useful for taking the strain out of heavy weeding, making medium diameter and deep planting holes. The second is especially useful for weeding between closely planted plants.

    c. Single larger, 10cm wide, light blade on short handle. Very useful for weeding between rows.

    d. Large heavy 12cm head on long handle. Mainly used for digging large planting holes, trenches and clearing irrigation channels, and for removing the tap roots of large rooted weeds, shrubs and trees.

Note that the medium and large sizes often come with handles too short for tall persons. If you have this problem, buy longer handles separately.

2. Heavy ridging rake (bilbadora) with a 28cm wide saw edged head. Comes on a long handle and makes easy work of jobs such as levelling soil, making planting ridges and irrigation channels on the vegetable plot, preparing seed beds, earthing up potatoes and removing bean and pea plants after the last harvesting.

3. Small pruning secateurs (tijeras de podar), used in the fruit orchards. Ergonomic

Our range of mattocks

and very useful for light detailed pruning, cutting flowers for the terrace or house table and deadheading.

4. Long extendable pruners (tijeras de podar extendible), indispensable for cutting back high climbers and thinning out/pruning the highest branches of trees.

5. Short and long handled, straight and curved pruning saws (sierras) with an extendable handle, essential for pruning palms, large cacti, shrubs and trees.

6. Traditional Spanish long-bristle brooms (escobas), light and handy for all sweeping-up jobs, except when paths are heavily encrusted with sand or earth after construction projects, when a shorter tougher bristle head is more effective.

7. Several sizes and shapes of capazos, the plastic buckets used by Spanish builders and gardeners. They are inexpensive, long lasting, easily cleaned and used for a wide variety of tasks such as holding a plastic sack open when weeding and pruning, moving sand, manure and earth, and mixing small quantities of mortar. We use one together with a wheel barrow for heavy loads.

8. Traditional, woven baskets (capazos), good for harvesting and storing vegetables and hard-skinned fruit.

9. A good pair of kitchen scissors (tijeras) for cutting leaves from perpetual salad crops, trimming onion seedlings before planting and cutting raffia, plastic and string ties.

10. A strong cane (caña) to knock down almonds.

11. Various sizes of sprayers (pulverizadores). It's handier to have small and medium-sized hand-held sprayers than a larger twelve-litre backpack version.

MODERN MULTI HEAD TOOLS

Several brands and designs are available, with a long standard handle and a variety of easily attachable tool heads. We use a Wolf Tools handle with the following heads:

1. A double sided hoe, swoe, (azada) with a sharp wavy head, very effective for removing annual weeds in hot weather when the soil is rock hard, both around shrubs and between the rows of vegetables. Also good for loosening the top 2cm of soil when damp to prevent water loss by capillary action.

2. A three-pronged harrow (grada), used to lighten the surface of damp, no-dig beds before planting. It is also used in wet weather to remove weeds when it is more effective than the swoe.

3. Two flexible metal rakes (rastrillos). A narrow, 10cm wide, five pronged version is the best tool for raking around plants in densely planted beds to remove dead leaves and loosen the surface soil. A wider, 35cm pronged head is excellent for raking up leaves, etc.

OUR NORTHERN EUROPEAN TOOLS

We still use some of our northern European tools, but less frequently than before coming to live in Spain. The ones we still use are:

1. Small trowel (desplantador) for digging planting holes for infill small plants and bulbs in densely planted beds and the rockery, but the small mattock is better on the wrists.

2. Small fork (horca), for weeding densely packed beds and the rockery, but, as above, the small mattock is normally more versatile with less effort.

3. Lawn rake (rastrillo) for clearing leaves from areas covered with stone chippings and levelling after periods of major use.

4. Traditional garden fork (horca), for digging up plantlets for transplanting and root vegetables when the soil is too dry to pull up by hand and for turning the compost heaps and loading well-rotted manure into plastic buckets for carrying to where required.

5. Traditional shovel (pala grande), for shovelling sand and stone chippings into the wheel barrow, though a broad mattock is more useful and less strain for mixing mortar or cement.

6. Light-weight wheel barrow (carretilla) with inflatable tyre, for for transporting rocks, stone chippings and soil – and as a cement mixer for smaller quantities when building walls, laying paving slabs, etc.

7. Our old hedging shears (tijeras de jardín), sharpened whenever a traditional afilador passes through the village, for tidying up and shaping evergreen hedges, shrubs and herbs.

8. Ancient pliers (alicates), always useful for cutting, straining and tying wire supports for sweet peas, roses, climbers and raspberries.

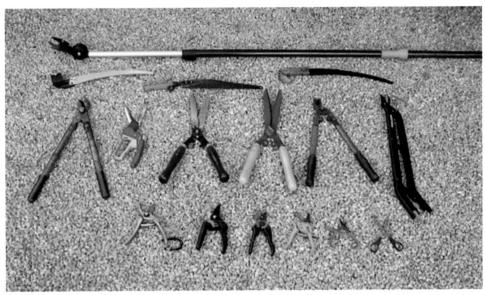

Useful set of pruners and saws.

ELECTRO-MECHANICAL AIDS

We find the most useful machines are:

1. An electric shredder (trituradora), used for the annual winter cutback, when we shred as much as possible to add to the compost heap.

2. An electric strimmer (destrozadora) for trimming the only patch of grass we have – 10 square metres under an almond tree – and rough grass along one side of the vegetable patch, which we cut and dry for hay for the rabbits and guinea pigs.

3. An electric hedge trimmer (cortasetos de cuchilla) to trim the sides of a conifer hedge.

4. A rotovator (moto azada) to clear new areas and lighten consolidated soils.

5. If you have a lawn then you will need a lawnmower (cortacésped).

6. An electric blower/vacuum cleaner (aspiradora), for blowing leaves into piles before sucking them up. Also good for cleaning up stone chipping paths and terraces.

7. If you have a large piece of ground that is rock hard, it may be worth getting someone to work it with a plough (arado).

These are the tools we use. Like many gardeners, we learned the hard way but soon realised that in Spain one follows local tradition or strain the body unnecessarily – definitely not a good thing to do as we get older. If your local nursery or horticultural shops do not stock the tools we describe, search out the nearest agricultural cooperative. Just one warning: be careful when you use mattocks as they have sharp edges.

Buy lightweight tools when possible. They take much of the toil out of gardening and reduce the risk of aching backs, legs and arms. Look after your tools. Dirty handles cause warts and blunt edges double the effort required to use them. Good tools make maintenance work easy and give enjoyable exercise.

7.3 MAKING YOUR GARDEN SAFE

Every year many accidents occur in gardens. Most could be avoided by careful design, construction and safe gardening practices. The following guidelines are based on our own experience and observations:

DESIGN AND CONSTRUCTION

WALLS:

• Ensure that boundary walls are on secure foundations and sufficiently strong to withstand the forces exerted by climbing plants, gale force winds and vibrations of passing lorries.

• Ensure that retaining walls are strong and stable enough to support the infill behind, especially during and after heavy rains.

• Ensure that retaining walls and boundary walls have sufficient and large enough drainage pipes to allow the release of retained water.

• Ensure that dry stonewalls are wide enough and sufficiently well stacked to withstand their own weight and the weight of the retained earth. And be sure the top stones are cemented to make them safe to stand on.

PATHS AND TERRACES:

• Build paths and terraces with none slip surfaces.

• Ensure easy slopes, steps and curves for all ages.

• Regularly clean off the winter build up of slippery algae and moss, especially under trees.

• Repair loose slabs and cracks as soon as they appear that could cause trips.

STEPS:

• Construct with equal rises and treads to reduce the risk of tripping.

• Ensure that the edges of the treads are totally secure. Loose and broken edges can be lethal.

• Use nonslip materials.

• Install handrails alongside.

ELECTRICITY:

• Install a separate trip for the garden circuit.

• Use armoured cables and strong plastic conduits. Sink them a minimum of 20cms deep and cover with slabs of concrete. Mark where they are to avoid hitting them when digging down with a fork, spade, pick axe or mattock.

• Use special waterproof fittings and immediately change anything damaged.

• Use low voltage solar lights and pond pumps.

• Use a qualified electrician.

FENCES:

• Ensure that all fence posts for wire mesh and panelled fences are strong and secure as well as the fixings for the wire and panels. Check them after heavy storms and gales.

    • Keep the weight of accumulated growth of climbers down by an annual thinning out of the undergrowth that often dies back, otherwise fences can become top heavy.

SWIMMING POOLS AND JACUZZIS
    • Ensure that all surrounding terraces are nonslip and have no sharp edges.

    • Check regularly for any loose tiles and sharp edges in the pool.

    • Check that diving boards and slides are firm and that no bolts have worked loose.

    • Only use plastic glasses and tableware in these areas to avoid breakages and slivers of glass falling into the pool or Jacuzzi.

    • Fence in the pool and Jacuzzi to prevent unattended young children from using them or falling in.

    • Clearly mark the depths of both the shallow and deep ends.

    • Store pool chemicals securely.

    • Consider changing to non-chemical cleaning methods.

PONDS:
    • Locate ponds away from main paths and terraces.

    • Fence off or cover when young children are resident or visiting.

    • Ensure that the surrounding terrace and rocks are secure.

    • Store pond chemicals securely.

SAFE GARDEN PRACTICES

PLANTS:
    • Avoid prickly plants or, if you have them, site them back from paths and terraces and keep them under control. Especially cut off the spiky points of yuccas and palms to reduce the chance ofeye and head injuries.

    • Use strong gloves and thick trousers and long sleeved tops when pruning palms, yuccas, cacti, blackberries, etc.

    • Be aware that certain plants are poisonous (e.g,. datura, morning glory and oleander). Either avoid them or locate them away from main paths. Prune them with care and always wear gloves. Warn the family and visitors about the dangers of these plants.

    • Take special care when cutting off and carrying palm fronds. Avoid the spikes at any cost.

    • Fell dying trees and cut off dangerous branches before they fall.

    • Don't touch processionary caterpillars that come down from pine trees in the spring and don't let your pets near them.

AVOID DANGEROUS POINTS:
    • Ensure that the ends of all wire ties are tied in tightly.

    • Prune back low branches on palms, ornamental and fruit trees to the trunk. Don't leave dangerous ends at head height.

    • Ensure that the ends of canes and supporting posts are blunt or covered over with tape to avoid eye injuries when leaning over plants.

AVOID GLASS:
- Use plastic rather than glass for cloches, garden frames and greenhouses.
- Don't use glass jars or jugs in the garden.

PROTECTIVE CLOTHING:
- Wear appropriate protective clothing when handling fertilisers, insecticides, pesticides and herbicides, and especially when spraying with chemicals.
- Purchase a good quality protective hat, goggles, face mask, gloves and gardening shoes. Keep them clean and wash after handling chemicals. Disposable gloves and masks are a good idea when spraying.
- Always use tough topped shoes when digging, raking, hoeing and cutting grass.
- Wear thick gloves when pruning prickly and spiky plants.
- Wear a protective mask and clothing when using a strimmer and goggles and gloves when using a shredder.

CHEMICAL STORAGE:
- Store all garden chemicals in a secure place on high shelving or in secure bins away from pets and children.
- Ensure that all chemical containers are sound with secure tops, no leakages and clear labels.
- Dispose of out-of-date chemicals in the appropriate container at a local eco park.

USE ECOLOGICAL SOLUTIONS:
- Change from manufactured chemicals to less hazardous natural/organic/ecological solutions.
- Start to grow and use beneficial plants, especially in the vegetable garden, such as:
    - **a.** Comfrey and nettles for liquid fertilizers.
    - **b.** Garlic, nettles, lavender, rosemary, and scented geraniums for insect deterrents.
    - **c.** Horsetail as a fungicide.
    - **d.** Rosemary, borage, sweet peas, roses and sunflowers to attract pollinators.
    - **e.** Coriander, nasturtiums and fennel to attract bugs away from vegetables.
    - **f.** Chives, garlic and marigolds as insect repellents.
    - **g.** A pot of basil or rue by the door to repel flies.

ANIMAL AND STINGING INSECTS:
- Locate and destroy the nests of wasps and hornets.
- Spray wasps around the pool with a dilute mix of ecological washing-up liquid and water, using a small sprayer. Also leave bowls of the liquid around when wasps first appear.
- Watch out for scorpions, adders, processionary caterpillars and biting spiders.

CONTROL BONFIRES:
- When clearing out an overgrown garden or doing the annual winter cutback, avoid bonfires by shredding most material for the compost heap, putting in eco bins, selling to a local compost making eco park or as a last resort use a skip.
- If you do have a bonfire, first obtain the necessary local license and follow local safety bylaws.

• Control the size of bonfires by burning in an oil drum or breeze block screen. One often sees the latter being used in the orange groves.

• Don't leave a bonfire unattended. Always have a working hosepipe or buckets of water nearby to get fierce or spreading fires back under control.

• Put out and dampen down any fire before leaving it.

TOOLS AND EQUIPMENT:

• Purchase good tools and keep them clean.

• Repair or replace any loose or broken handles or parts immediately.

• Ensure that guards and safety catches on machines are operable, secure and used.

• Don't leave sharp-edged tools lying around.

• Use safety catches on secateurs.

• Ensure that rungs, legs, rubber feet and catches on ladders and stepladders are safe.

AVOID STRAINS:

• When buying tools, choose ones that are ergonomically designed such as Fiskars.

• Use the right tool for the job, especially when trying to prune thick branches.

• Avoid lifting heavy rocks, sacks, etc., without help.

• Avoid overloading the wheelbarrow or plastic baskets.

• Don't mix too much mortar or concrete at any one time.

• Warm up, especially in cool weather, before doing heavy jobs.

• Don't overdo it by working long hours day after day. We are in Spain to enjoy life! What is an extra month or two if the completion of a DIY project is extended?

7.4 THE HISTORY OF MY SPANISH GARDEN

This chart is included to help you maintain a record of the evolution of your Spanish garden from the day you took over a bare plot or an established garden to the day you achieved your vision of what it should become. Naturally you may achieve this within a year or two through an instant garden planted up with mature plants by an expensive contract with a landscaping company. But the average gardener coming to Spain will take longer whether working solo or with the support of a gardener. We therefore provide space for a record of the first five years of your garden. By then you should be nearing your dream garden as plants mature and blend together in harmony, with only a minimal amount of maintenance required.

Flower garden

Fruits

Vegetables

Geranium window box

No	IMPORTANT EVENTS	20....				20....				20....				20....				20....			
	Record the most important initiatives, projects, events and achievements.	S	S	A	W	S	S	A	W	S	S	A	W	S	S	A	W	S	S	A	W
1																					
2																					
3																					
4																					
5																					
6																					
7																					
8																					
9																					
10																					
11																					
12																					
13																					
14																					
15																					
16																					
17																					
18																					
19																					
20																					
21																					
22																					
23																					
24																					

PART EIGHT

VOCABULARY AND INDEX

The comprehensive gardening English-Spanish vocabulary includes the following sections.

400 Botanical - English – Spanish plant names are included in Part Four.

The General Index commences on page 292.

VOCABULARY

USEFUL WORDS

allotment: huerto
bed, cultivated: bancal
garden: jardín
garden, vegetable: huerto
garden, fruit: jardín frutero
gardener: jardinero
bonfire: hoguera
climate, macro: macroclima
climate, micro: microclima
climate, nano: nanoclima
cloche: campana de cristal/plástico para
    proteger plantas
cloche, tunnel: túnel de plástico
companion plant: planta beneficiosa
    acompañante
composter: compostador
compost heap: montón de abono vegetal,
    pila de compuestos, pila de compostaje
container: contenedor
copse: bosquecillo
diet: dieta
disease: enfermedad
diversity: diversidad
drainage: drenaje
drought: sequía
fence: cerca, vallado
flower bed: cuadro, macizo, lecho de flores
frost, air: escarcha del aire
frost, ground: escarcha
fruit: fruta
fruit tree: árbol frutal
furrow: surco
garden frame: mini invernadero
gardening, vegetables: horticultura
greenhouse: invernadero
grow bag: saco para cultivar
gutter: gotera, canal
hail: granizo
hedge: seto
hole: hoyo
hose: manguera
house: casa
injury: herida
insect: insecto
irrigation system: sistema de riego
ladder, step: escala
lawn: césped
moon/lunar calendar: calendario lunar
mound, earth: montón de tierra
mulch: alcolchado
nature: naturaleza
orchard: huerto de frutales
path: vereda/senda
patio: patio
pergola: pérgola
pest: plaga
plant: planta
plantlet: plántula
plant pot: maceta
pollination: polinización
pond: estanque
property: propiedad
rain: lluvia
rain, to: llover
rainwater: agua de lluvia

raised bed: macizo elevado
ridge: caballón
rockery: jardín de roca
row: hilera
seat: silla
seed bed: semillero
seed box: caja de simientes
shade: sombra
shed, garden: cobertizo
shrubbery: arbustos
slope: cuesta, pendiente
smallholding with house: finca
smallholding without house: parcela
snow: nieve
strip plot: huerto estrecho
sun: sol
terrace (cultivated): terraza, bancal
tub: cubeta
ten-tub vegetable garden: huerta de diez cubetas
tie: atadura
tools, garden: útiles de jardinería
trellis: enrejado
view: vista
water: agua
water butt: tina/barril para agua
waterway, channel: canal, acequia
watering-can: regadera
wall: muro
watering system: sistema de riego
weather: tiempo
wildlife: fauna
windbreak: abrigada, cortavientos
wormery: vermicompostador
worm: lombriz
yard: patio, corral

MATERIALS

bag: saco
basket: capacho, cesta
bottle: botella
box: caja
bucket: cubo
cane: caña
chippings: gravilla suelta
compost: abono vegetal
face mask: mascarilla
fertiliser: abono
fertiliser, foliar: abono foliar
fertiliser, granular: abono granulado
fertiliser, soluble: abono soluble
fleece: malla térmica, fleece
fungicide: fungicida
gloves: guantes
goggles: lentes protectoras
grit: cascajo, grava
handle, spare: manga disponible
herbicide: herbicida
insecticide: insecticida
labels, plastic: etiquetas de plástico
manure: estiércol
mulch: mantillo
netting: red
peat: turba
pesticide: pesticida
Ph meter: contador de Ph
post: poste
rock: roca
sack: saco
sand: arena
sheet plastic (solid): hoja de plástico
sheet plastic (woven): malla de plástico

slab of rock: bloque
soil: suelo, tierra
stake: rodriga, estaca
string: cuerda
thermometer: termómetro
timer: interruptor horario
water: agua
wax: cera
weedkiller: herbicida
wire: alambre
wood: madera
worm, earth: lombriz
worm compost: humus de lombriz

TOOLS
axe: hacha
blower/vacuum cleaner: aspiradora
broom: escoba
bucket: cubo
bucket (basket-like): capacho
cane: caña
chisel: escoplo
dibber: plantador, almocafre
dryer: secadora
duster (see powder blower)
fork: horca
funnel: embudo
grafting tape: cinta de injertar
hammer: mortillo
handle, spare: mango disponible
harrow: grada
hedge trimmer: recortador de setos
hoe: azadón, peta
hose: manguera
knife: cuchillo
mallet: mazo
mattock: azadón, pico
multi-headed tool: herramienta de multi-cabeza
pick axe: pico azado
pipe, plastic: tubo plástico
pliers: alicates
plough: arado
powder blower: espolvoreador
pruners, extendable: tijeras de podar extensibles
rake: rastrillo
ridging rake: bilbadora, rastrillo de caballones
rotavator: moto azada, retovato
saw: sierra
secateurs: tijeras de podar
scissors: tijeras
sharpening stone: piedra de afilar
shovel: pala grande
shredder: trituradora
sieve: criba
sledge hammer: mazo
sock: calcetín
stocking: media
spade: pala
sprayer: pulverizadora
sprinkler: rociadera
step-ladder: escalera de tijera
strimmer: desbrozadora
swoe: azada
tank: cisterna
teaspoon: cucharilla
tool: herramienta
trowel: desplantador, palustre
watering-can: regadera
weeder: escardera
weed extractor: extractor de malas hierbas
wheelbarrow: carretilla

water pump: bomba para agua

PARTS OF PLANTS
bark: corteza
blossom: flores
branch: rama
bud: brote
bud (flower): capullo
bud (leaf): yema
cutting: esqueje
flower: flor
flower head: cabezuela
fruit: fruta
graft: injerto
leaf: hoja
perfume: perfume
plantlet: plántula
pollen: polen
root: raíz
seed: semilla
seed head: cabezuela
seedling: plántula
spray of flowers: ramita
stem: tallo
string of onions/garlic: ristra de cebollas/ ajos
texture: textura
trunk: tronco
twig: ramita

TYPES OF PLANTS
annual: anual
bamboo: bambú
bulb: bulbo
cactus: cactus
climber: trepadora
corm: bulbo
creeper: enredadera
fruit tree: frutal
grass: hierba
ground cover: cubierto por el terreno
house plant: planta de interior
herb: hierba aromática
palm: palma, palmera
perennial: perenne
rambler: enredadera
shrub: arbusto
succulent: suculento
tree: árbol
tree (evergreen): árbol de hoja perenne
tree (deciduous): árbol de hoja caduca
vegetable (green): verdura
vegetable (general): hortaliza
vegetable (pulses): legumbres
variety: variedad
vine, grape: vid
weed: mala hierba

GARDENING VERBS
axe: hachear, dar hachazos
bear fruit: dar fruto, frutar
bloom, flower: florecer
brush up: cepillar
build: construir
burn: quemar
bury: enterrar
buy: comprar
cascade: caer en cascada
change: cambiar
choose: elegir
clean up: limpiar
climb: subir

connect: conectar
cook: cocinar
construct: construir
cover over: cubrir
create: crear
cultivate: cultivar
cut: cortar
cut back: recortar
cut down: talar
dampen: mojar, humedecer
deadhead: descabezar
decide: decidir
design: diseñar
develop: desarrollar
die: morir
dilute: diluir
dig: cavar
dig a hole: excavar
dig in: añadir al suelo
dig over: recavar
dig up: desarraigar
distill: destilar
divide: dividir
do: hacer
drip: gotear
dry: secar
eat: comer
earth up: tomar caballón de tierra
employ: emplear
empty: vaciar
emulsify: emulsionar
enjoy: divertirse
fertilise: fertilizar
fill in: rellenar
flood: inundar
force: forzar
garden (general): trabajar en el jardín
garden (work on vegetable plot): cultivar el huerto
graft: injertar
grow (a fruit): cultivar
grow (process of): crecer
hammer: clavar
harrow: gradar
harvest: recoger
hoe: azadonar
identify: identificar
irrigate: regar, irrigar
label: etiquetar
level: nivelar
line: alinear
kill off: exterminar
maintain: mantener
mark: señalar, marcar
maximise (something): sacar el máximo partido
measure: medir
minimise: minimizar
mix: mezclar
mix in something: añadir algo
mow: cortar
open: abrir
pinch out: quitar con los dedos
plan: planear
plant: plantar
plough: arar
pollinate: polinizar, fecundar
pour: echar
propagate: propagar
protect: proteger
prune: podar
pump: bombear
rain: llover

rake: rastrillar
ridge: caballonar
rotate, crops: cultivar en rotación
rotavate: trabajar con motorcultor, roturar
saw: serrar
select: escoger
separate: apartar
screen: tapar
shade: proteger del sol
shake up: agitar
sharpen: afilar
sieve: cribar
shear: cortar
shred: triturar
shelter: resguardar
snow: nevar
soak: remojar
sort out: clasificar, separar
sow: sembrar
spray: pulverizar, rociar
spread: extender
sprinkle: rociar
stake: rodrigar
start, motor: arrancar
stimulate: estimular
stir: agitar
strim: desbrozar
sweep up: barrer
take out: quitar
thin out: entresacar
tidy up: arreglar
tie up: atar
till: labrar
top up: llenar
train: guiar, dirigir
transplant: trasplantar
trench (to dig): excavar
turn on: abrir
turn off: cerrar
turn over: volver
turn (rotate): girar
use: usar
water: regar
weed: desherbar, escardar, sacar las malas hierbas
weigh: pesar
wet: mojar
wilt: marchitar

MEASUREMENTS

pulgada: inch
pie (.308 metres): foot
metro: metre
area: 100 square metres
hanegada (traditional measurement used in Valencia and other regions): 833.33 square metres
fanega, fanegada (measurements used in Andalusia): 64 areas, 6460 square metres, 1.59 acres
hectare: 10,000 square metres
acre (.405 hectares or 4047 square metres): acre
arroba: 25 pounds
kilo: 2.2 pounds
1000 kilos, tonelada métrica: metric ton
litro: 1.76 pints
cubo lleno: bucketful

INDEX

SOME USEFUL ADDRESSES AND SOURCES OF INFORMATION

Gardens in Spain open for visits — See list in April 2009 archives of
www.gardeninginspain.com.

Ecological insecticides, fungicides and fertilizers — www.seipasa.com and
www.trabe.net.

Ecological snail bait — Ferramol antilimacos – www.neudorff.es and www.seipasa.com.

Neem oil and powder — as above plus Gerald Moser at kontact@niem-handel.de.

Ergonomic garden tools — www.fiskars.com – good for Secateurs extendable pruner
spade and fork.

Soil improver — www.terracottem.com / www.terra-vida.com – can reduce water needs
by 50 to 70%.

Comfrey plants – young plants from consuelda@haciendadelcarrizal.com.

Garden water improver — strengthens plants and reduces watering needs –
www.viaqua.ie.

Seeds for Spanish wild species — www.semillassilvestres.com – several hundred
varieties available.

Plants of Spanish wild species — www.cultidelta.com – several hundred plants and
trees.

Seeds for Tropical/subtropical plants — www.chilternseeds.co.uk,
www.jungleseeds.co.uk.

Rare Bulbs — www.heritagebulbs.com – an easy way of accessing an interesting
collection.

Sacks of dried manure — Try your local Agricultural Cooperatives. If not ask your local
garden centre to order you some sacks of worm compost.

Composting worms — www.wiglywigglers.co.uk and consuelda@haciendadelcarrizal.com.

Inexpensive compost — Eco-parks that compost local garden waste and seaweed –
currently Mijas Pueblo Andalucia, Benissa and La Xara Alicante.

Design and construction of natural pools — two useful books and advice available from
www.ecodesignscapes.co.uk.

Dryer for drying seeds, fruit and vegetables — English data sheet from order@conasi.biz.

Plants for health — www.dulcerevolucion.com – an interesting growing collection of plants.